Marx in Motion

MARX IN MOTION

A New Materialist Marxism

Thomas Nail

OXFORD
UNIVERSITY PRESS

Oxford University Press is a department of the University of Oxford. It furthers
the University's objective of excellence in research, scholarship, and education
by publishing worldwide. Oxford is a registered trade mark of Oxford University
Press in the UK and certain other countries.

Published in the United States of America by Oxford University Press
198 Madison Avenue, New York, NY 10016, United States of America.

Library of Congress Cataloging-in-Publication Data
Names: Nail, Thomas, author. Title: Marx in motion :
A New Materialist Marxism / Thomas Nail.
Description: New York, NY : Oxford University Press, [2020] | Includes index.
Identifiers: LCCN 2020001781 (print) | LCCN 2020001782 (ebook) |
ISBN 9780197526484 (paperback) | ISBN 9780197526477 (hardback) |
ISBN 9780197526507 (epub) | ISBN 9780197526491 (updf) | ISBN 9780197526514 (online)
Subjects: LCSH: Marx, Karl, 1818-1883. | Philosophy, Marxist. | Socialism.
Classification: LCC HX39.5 .N35 2020 (print) | LCC HX39.5 (ebook) | DDC 335.4—dc23
LC record available at https://lccn.loc.gov/2020001781
LC ebook record available at https://lccn.loc.gov/2020001782

To Robert Urquhart

CONTENTS

ILLUSTRATIONS

ACKNOWLEDGMENTS

I am indebted to a number of people for their support and encouragement of this project. Robert Urquhart, my colleague at the University of Denver, has been an incredible inspiration and mentor to me. His influence on this book and on my life has been enormous.

Before this book was in writing it was spoken on long late-night strolls around Harvard Gulch park with Chris Gamble and Josh Hanan.

I am grateful to my research assistants, who helped me with various aspects of the project: Kevin Buskager, Benjamin Fisher, and Adam Loch. In particular, I asked them to keyword search through fifty volumes of the Marx/Engels *Collected Works* and gather quotes on various themes, which took months.

I thank my anonymous peer reviewers for their constructive feedback and everyone I worked with at Oxford University Press for guiding this book to publication. I would also like to thank my editorial assistants, Dan Thomas and Jacob Tucker, for their excellent close corrections and suggestions.

Thanks also to the University of Denver Rosenberry Fund for its financial support.

Finally, I would like to thank my family, and especially my wife, Katie, for her continued support.

ABBREVIATIONS

Works by Marx and Engels

C	*Capital, Volume 1*
C II	*Capital, Volume 2*
C III	*Capital, Volume 3*
DD	*The Difference Between the Democritean and Epicurean Philosophy of Nature*
G	*Grundrisse*
GI	*German Ideology*
MECW	*Marx and Engels Collected Works*
MEGA	*Marx-Engels-Gesamtausgabe*

Introduction

A rebirth of Marxism is occurring today. For many people Marx never faded away, but for the rest of the world Marx made his most recent return to the public eye during the financial collapse of 2008. After the financial meltdown, international book sales of *Capital* exploded for the first time in decades. Marx's face and ideas appeared all over the world, in newspapers, on television, and on the internet. Universities and occupation teach-ins hosted public events in which Marxists were asked, for the first time in a long time, to speak out widely on capitalist crisis and "the idea of communism."[1] Everyone, it seems, was reading *Capital* again.

The reason for the return to Marx is obvious: taxpayer bailouts of banks "too big to fail," government austerity, student-loan debt, millions displaced from their homes by the collapse of subprime mortgages, historically large income inequalities between the 99 percent and the 1 percent, record-breaking migration, and human-induced climate change all appeared to be inextricably connected to global capitalism. As the most historically foundational and systematic critic of capitalism to date, Karl Marx remains our contemporary. "Marxism," as Jean-Paul Sartre once wrote, "remains the philosophy of our time because we have not gone beyond the circumstances which engendered it."[2]

Every era after Marx has reinvented his ideas to fit its needs. The present era, inaugurated by the 2008 financial crisis, is no exception. There is not one Marx forever and for all time, just as there is not one theory of capitalism, materialism, or communism for all time.[3] There are a thousand Marxes. In fact, one of the greatest insights and contributions of Marx's work is that it treats theory itself as a historical practice. Marxism is not

Marx in Motion. Thomas Nail, Oxford University Press (2020). © Oxford University Press.
DOI: 10.1093/oso/9780197526477.001.0001

just an interpretive activity but a creative one. As our historical conditions, including new knowledge in physics, economics, ecology, culture, and so on, change, so do the kinds of questions we pose and the kinds of answers we find. *Marx in Motion* is a contribution to a twenty-first-century return to Marx.

The return found in this book, however, is not a "return to Marxism," which focuses on Marx's historical reception. This book is a return to the writings of Marx read again through the lens of the pressing philosophical and political problems of our time, most notably ecological crisis, gender inequality, colonial appropriation, and global mobility.

The aim of this book is not to "supplement" or "correct" the apparent deficiencies or anachronisms of Marx's writings or even to make his theory "relevant" by "applying" it to contemporary issues. These interventions have their place, but they are not the focus here. Rather, my aim in this book is to return to the writings of Marx himself and to read them again as if they were absolutely contemporary. The outcome is neither an update of an old Marx nor a new application, but a different Marx altogether.

More specifically, this book reads Marx as a philosopher of movement and motion, inspired by his earliest dissertation writings. From this unique perspective, I argue that Marx was not a historical determinist, reductionist materialist, anthropocentric humanist, or structuralist, and he *did not* hold a labor theory of value. These bold claims strike at the heart of well-trod interpretations of Marx and motivate my rereading of him as a process philosopher of motion and a new materialist *avant la lettre*. The aim of this introduction is to contextualize this intervention and introduce the theses, methods, and consequences of this project.

I wrote this book on the 200th anniversary of Marx's birth, but I would like to begin by diagnosing the cause of his apparent "death." For it is only in his death that he can be born again.[4] It is only in the movement of the decline of Marxism that a swerve to a twenty-first-century Marx is possible.

THE DECLINE OF MARXISM

Prior to the 2008 financial crisis, Marxism as a political ideology had been in decline since the 1970s. There are many reasons for this.[5] However, three reasons stand out as major criticisms upon which Marxism declined but now makes its return.[6] These well-established criticisms come not only from outside but also from within Marxism itself.

Historical determinism: The first axis of criticism is that Marxism subscribes to a deterministic theory of history. Various Marxisms endorsed a theory of human history that was not only entirely deterministic but also headed toward a pregiven end: communism, the destiny of humanity. This idea did not work out. We do not need to go back too far in recent history to see that World War II, the unplanned political revolutions of 1968, the threat of global nuclear war, global climate change, and other events do not fit at all into any clear historical pattern of development or liberation. If anything, the opposite is the case. Today, our future seems bleaker than ever.

There is even less evidence that anything like the lockstep necessity of communism, whatever that might look like, is on the immediate horizon. As in all great developmental historical narratives, which not coincidentally tend to be told from the perspective of their present historical "achievement," the future happens. The rise of Soviet socialism came to an end.[7] The predictions of socialist historical determinism did not come to pass, and the ironclad laws of economic necessity, the falling rate of profit, and other factors failed to hold. The supposedly universal laws of historical development and capitalism changed.

Furthermore, the creation of a socialist state, party, and vanguard did not result by historical necessity in revolution or communism. At worst, these entities led to new forms of militarism, patriarchy, imperialism, and authoritarianism. This is not to say the opposite—that such political forms necessarily lead to their worst outcomes—only that the forms of the party and state did not dictate in any deterministic way the results that followed.

Reductionism: The second axis of criticism of Marxism is that it subscribed to a falsely reductionist model defined by strictly economic causal laws. Everything, some argued, can be deduced and explained by the one-directional causal connection of an economic "base" (the forces of production) to the cultural "superstructure" of ideas, feelings, and sensations of the world: ideology, which is the strict product of reducibly economic modes of production. Even social relations such as race, gender, sexuality, animality, and nature are categories *constituted by* the capitalist mode of production, not the other way around. All phenomena are reducible to economic phenomena. This reductionism, however, simply assumes what needs to be explained in the first place—namely, the noneconomic conditions for the emergence of economic conditions themselves.

Although economic relations are undoubtably important aspects of reality, historically they have not always played an strictly determining role in political struggle. For example, many post-1970s liberation movements and twenty-first-century political struggles have been focused on the intersectionality of gender, race, sexuality, animal rights, ecological, indigenous, and decolonial issues.[8] These are certainly related to the capitalist mode of production but are hardly completely determined by it in a any reducible manner. It is not at all clear how or if such disparate movements can be understood by economic analysis alone. This led Marxism to various "supplemented" versions of Marx that "add on" critiques of nature, gender, race, and other factors.[9]

Furthermore, the very possibility of "ideology critique" or "revolution" must also entail the fact there can be no strictly reducible relation between base and superstructure, or else one could never think or do otherwise than what is determined by such a base. In other words, critique would be pointless if determinism were actually true.

Another aspect of the critique of reductionism is leveled against Marx's materialism. Reductionist materialism says that there are reducibly dialectical laws of all matter and nature. Economic laws are only one expression of a larger set of natural laws that matter follows. In this version of dialectical materialism, there is a natural developmental or evolutionary pattern followed by all matter, conceived of as discrete, actual particles. What is reductionist here is not only that everything is made of actual discrete particles, but also that matter itself is reducible to eternal "laws of motion" known and knowable to science.

This classical thesis, however, is no longer a tenable description of matter by the standards of twenty-first-century physics. In quantum theory, matter is not discrete particles, but vibrating fields. Matter is not reducibly empirical or entirely knowable; much less are there any so-called universal mechanical laws of its motion below the Planck scale.[10] Furthermore, the very idea that matter is something knowable *independent of its observation* (not just human observation) is not possible because of quantum entanglement.[11] Where Marxist science has yoked its materialism to a nineteenth- and even twentieth-century idea of mechanistic materialism and so-called universal laws, it encounters the limit of quantum systems.[12]

Anthropocentrism: Insofar as Marxism grants methodological or even ontological privilege to human beings or human social and economic structures above others, it remains incapable of dealing with one of the most important events of the twenty-first century: global climate change, the "Copernican revolution" of our time.[13] Anthropocentrism in all its varieties remains at least partly complicit in the human-centric focus that has led to the current ecological catastrophe. However, there are at least three major variations on the theme of anthropocentrism in the history of Marxism that I should mention here.[14]

The first is the straightforwardly *productivist* version, which emphasizes the human effort to subordinate nature through technological innovation. What it means to be a human being, in this version, is to appropriate as much of nature as possible for the benefit of humanity regardless of the ecological consequences. Supposedly no other animal has this unique ability. Humans are special in their consciousness of their own domination of nature, hence the anthropocentrism of the term "Anthropocene."

The second version is more *humanist* in orientation and defined primarily by the sensuous enjoyment of nature. What it means to be human is to be that animal that knows itself to be experiencing the aesthetic enjoyment of nature. In this version, too, animals do not have this unique capacity, and ecological problems remain fundamentally *human problems* vis-à-vis their limits to the strictly human enjoyment of nature.

The third version is *constructivist.* Constructivism is antihumanist insofar as it rejects the idea of a human essence, in the place of which it puts human *structures.* The human being, for Marxist constructivists, is not a primarily ahistorical essence but rather a historical *product* of social, political, psychological, economic, and linguistic structures. All human knowledge of nature is thus limited strictly by these structures. What nature really is, however, remains ultimately a "thing in itself" beyond the limits of all human structures. Nature and matter are what exceed or are left out of our structures, and this lack or failure is our only, albeit paradoxical, form of knowledge.[15]

* * *

Given the practical and theoretical success of these criticisms of Marxism, it is not surprising that their textual origins, Marx's writings, have suffered the same fate. Considering the volumes of criticism on Marxism, is it still possible to return again to Marx and his work to find new ideas? My argument is that it is not *despite* the success of these criticisms but precisely *because* of their success that the answer today is "yes." The *decline* of Marxism makes possible a *declination* or swerve toward something new. In fact, this has already happened more than once in the history of Marxism: once when the humanist "young Marx" of the 1844 manuscripts was discovered in the 1950s (to swerve away from Stalinism) and again when the "pre-*Capital* Marx" of the *Grundrisse* was discovered in the 1970s (to swerve away from the young humanist Marx of the 1950s and 1960s).

The argument of this book is that it is time for yet another swerve, this time to the least read of all Marx's works: the "first Marx" of his doctoral dissertation (to swerve away from both the humanisms of the 1950s and the constructivisms of the 1970s). Each shift was not exclusive but operated as a lens through which the other works were reread and returned to. One always returns from somewhere, depending on the previous turns.

Through the lens of contemporary physics, ecology, politics, economics, and Marx's doctoral dissertation, it is possible to return to Marx again and find new answers to the questions of our time. If Marxism is going to be responsive to the issues of today, it is going to have to move beyond the three criticisms just discussed. And I think it can.

THE UNDERGROUND CURRENT OF KINETIC MATERIALISM

Marxism is not a static doctrine of theses but a continuously flowing current of theoretical practice. It is something taken up anew and transformed by each generation. Therefore it is crucial to understand Marx today as part of a larger and longer tradition of philosophical materialism, of which Marxism is a subset. By explicitly taking up the tradition of ancient materialism in his doctoral dissertation, Marx saw himself as putting forward a new materialism, irreducible to all previous materialisms both ancient and modern, including their vitalistic and deistic versions.[16]

Marx saw himself as putting forward a contemporary materialism for his time through an original reading of Epicurean atomism. Long before Marx had ever read Hegel, his first and original philosophical engagement was with Epicurus. Before there was the Hegelian Marx, there was the Epicurean Marx. And since a major source for his knowledge of Epicureanism was Lucretius's *De Rerum Natura*, one could say there is a Lucretian Marx as well.

Marx's intervention and contribution to philosophy can be situated within the longer tradition of an underground current, starting with Lucretius. This is the current of "kinetic" or "process" materialism.[17] Lucretius was the first to interpret Epicurus in a completely new way, just as Epicurus had done to Democritus (as Marx was the first to show).[18]

Lucretius's novelty was that he replaced the discreteness of the Greek atom with the continual flow and kinetic flux of matter. This was not an insignificant move. Matter, for Lucretius, was not some *thing* in motion, as it was for modern materialists such as Francis Bacon and even Friederich Engels. Matter, for Lucretius, was not subject to the kind of deterministic laws and empirical reductionism that defined most modernist versions of atomism, including classical physics. Although separated by more than a thousand years, what Marx and Lucretius have in common is that they both read Epicurus in the same unique way, stressing the continually flowing, non-discrete, and kinetic features of matter, as I discuss in chapter 1.

Within this larger tradition of materialism, Marx was the first to herald a "new materialism" that gave historical-ontological primacy to the stochastic motion of matter opposed to its *discrete* interpretation in

Democritus, Newton, and others.[19] One of the arguments of this book is that Marx held a very contemporary theory of matter, on a par with recent new-materialist ones. Unfortunately, most of what is commonly known about Marx comes not from Marx but from what other people have said he said—hence the oft-cited claim by Marx, "What is certain is that I myself am not a Marxist."[20]

It is impossible to give a full history of the diverse reception of Marx in this introduction. However, not to provide at least a brief one would fail to properly contextualize the main interventions of this book. Thus, in the short sections that follow I describe three major revolutions in the interpretation of Marx's work and their connection to the three main criticisms previously described. My intention is to identify where Marxism is today and foreground what problems need to be overcome.

The First Revolution: Soviet Marxism

The first revolution of Marxism occurred during the early twentieth century alongside the rise of Soviet communism. Soviet Marxism drew on the work of Marx and Engels to provide a single set of universal principles or foundations for all future knowledge and social policy. The theory of "dialectical materialism" or *Diamat*, as it was formalized, was drawn from Engels's *Dialectics of Nature* and provided a synthetic and reductionist theory of all matter and nature. The law of a universal dialectic was formalized thus:

1. The law of the unity and conflict of opposites.
2. The law of the passage of quantitative changes into qualitative changes.
3. The law of the negation of the negation.

The metaphysical view of nature was interpreted from Engels's *Anti-Duhring* thus:[21]

1. The unity of the world consists in its materiality.
2. Never and nowhere has there existed, or can there exist, matter without motion.

In short, the aim of Soviet Marxism was to produce universal philosophical doctrines for Marxism that secured it as a fixed theoretical document and a doctrine of state governance.[22] In doing so, however, Soviet Marxism fell prey to all three of the criticisms described previously.[23] The Soviets interpreted Engels's theory in *Dialectics of Nature* as universal laws of historical evolution and social development. They saw Soviet socialism as the final stage of world-historical development. They reduced the historical philosophy of nature to metaphysical propositions about the being of nature forever and all time. In doing so they reduced the activity and creativity of matter to a passive servant of metaphysical laws. Above all, they followed an aggressively productivist anthropocentrism, especially under Stalin. Nature was industrialized and treated as a mere storehouse of raw materials.[24]

The Second Revolution: Humanist Marxism

The second revolution of Marxism occurred during the early twentieth century as a response to the Soviet appropriation of Marxism for deterministic and reductionist ends. For many years Marx had been criticized in France because of his association with Soviet authoritarianism. However, in the 1930s Marxism began to return again under the aegis of the recently published *Economic and Philosophic Manuscripts of 1844*, written by the young Marx. This occurred alongside the rise of French Hegelianism championed by Alexandre Kojève and Jean Hyppolite. Students of this return, such as Henri Lefebvre, Lucien Goldmann, Jean-Paul Sartre, and Maurice Merleau-Ponty, found in the young Marx none of the rhetoric of economic determinism and historical reductionism. Instead, they found a new discussion of "human being" and "social alienation" uncontaminated by economic formulas, historical doctrines, and Stalinist political terror.

The more humanist and anti-Soviet writings of György Lukács, Karl Korsch, and Herbert Marcuse circulated widely. The new existential and phenomenological traditions in France and Germany from the 1930s to the 1960s were increasingly combined with Hegelian Marxism in the works of Theodor Adorno, Max Horkheimer, Erich Fromm, Walter Benjamin, and others associated with the Frankfurt Institute for Social Research. However, the Frankfurt school differed from the existential and phenomenological interpretations and took up a position against any kind of bourgeois or socialist "human essence," historical "universalism," and unilateral relation between the base and superstructure.[25]

This second revolution, although split between widely differing interpretations, decidedly rejected the deterministic and metaphysical Marxism of Engels and the Soviets in favor of an approach grounded in sensuous human practice. The nature of human existence was to be free from any deterministic laws of nature, history, or matter. Although, human existence also tended to find itself everywhere constrained by social structures that alienated it from itself.

In this way, humanist Marxism overcame the problem of determinism. However, although it rejected economic reductionism, it still held onto an existential and psychoanalytic reductionism in which the relation between base and superstructure was merely reconfigured around human-centric social psychology. Even if they differed on the question of humanism, phenomenological and Frankfurt school style Marxism both made little attempt to conceal their overt anthropocentrism.[26]

The Third Revolution: Post-Structuralist Marxism

The third revolution of Marxism occurred during the 1960s and 1970s as a response to the humanist neglect of the larger structural conditions of capitalism and the hierarchical centralization of the communist party itself. In Italy, for example, the autonomist Marxists emphasized the idea of "living labor" as the heart of political and social (not just economic) life. Living labor has the power not only to work but to play, to live and self-organize outside the structure of the factory, union, and party. Autonomism created social movements distinct from and in contrast to political parties. Their revolts were against authoritarian socialism as well as contemporary representative democracy.

The 1970s also saw the rise of third world Marxisms, in which the division between colonizers and colonized became the main axis of struggle and analysis. Class division was not fundamental but derived from colonial relationships first and foremost. At the end of *Capital* Marx suggested that one should expect to see in the projects of colonization the geographical rebirth of primitive accumulation and the historical techniques of capitalism again and again. Third world Marxism takes this seriously as the starting point of critique and resistance and not class antagonism.

Feminist Marxism during this time rejected the male-worker-centric interpretation of *Capital* by emphasizing the assumption that only waged male workers were laborers. In fact, Women's cheap or free work is fundamental to the capitalist mode of production and thus cuts to the heart of where value comes from.

In French Marxism, Louis Althusser initiated a new "return to Marx" and began to reread the later Marx of *Capital*. His reading focused on the "relations and forces of production," against the young Marx of the manuscripts, which focused on human essence and alienation.[27] Althusser, Étienne Balibar, Roger Establet, Jacques Rancière, and Pierre Macherey copublished

Reading Capital in 1965, which emphasized the nondeterministic and nonreductionist nature of the structure of capitalism but also the way in which capital itself shapes and produces the human subject.

Most famously, Althusser argued that there was an "epistemological break" between Marx's earlier work, influenced by German idealism and classical political economy, and his later work, which introduced an entirely new philosophical system centered around the production of knowledge. Knowledge, Althusser argued, was produced through "problematic" or "conjunctural" historical sites, entirely independent from the ideological superstructure. Althusser definitively broke with the deterministic and reductionist Marx as well as the humanist Marx. Later, post-structuralist Marxists such as Gilles Deleuze, Jacques Derrida, Francois Lyotard, Alain Badiou, and Michel Foucault were all influenced by Althusser but also diverged from him in significant ways that I cannot address here.[28]

With respect to the major axes of criticism described here, however, the important commonality was that Althusser, the post-structuralist Marxists, autonomists, postcolonial Marxists, and feminists all largely returned to a definitively new Marx without historical determinism, economic or materialist reductionism, or humanism. The human subject was something that was completely dissolved into the various social, linguistic, unconscious, historical, political, geographical, gendered, and economic structures. The human became simply the site or terminal of an intersection of one or more interlocking social, gendered, or geographical structures.

However, and importantly, all these *social structures* (gender, race, politics, etc.)—or "assemblages," "apparatuses," "relations of forces," and so on—are *human structures*, outside of which nothing can be said or thought.[29] In the post-structuralist treatments of Marx, then, Marx remained an anthropocentric social constructivist of one variety or another.[30]

MARX AND THE PHILOSOPHY OF MOTION

Each of these revolutions overcame a problem posed by the previous interpretations, but only by introducing another problem. The aim of this book therefore is to provide a reading of Marx that tries to overcome all three of the problems previously described without having to go outside Marx's own writings. In particular, the charge of anthropocentrism has proven to be the most entrenched in all three major interpretive revolutions. It has thus become the focus of much recent criticism from such new-materialist philosophers as Jane Bennett, Bruno Latour, Manuel DeLanda, and Rosi Braidotti. New materialists even interpret post-structuralist Marxism as hopelessly "old-materialist" and anthropocentric, alongside the three criticisms already discussed.[31]

However, Marxists have also been quick, and right, to point out the political limitations of any sort of "new materialism" that would leave Marx and political economy behind altogether.[32] Despite their apparent incompatibility, I think these two traditions have much to gain from each other. This book is the first attempt to bring Marxism and new materialism together in the hope of revitalizing Marxism for the twenty-first century.[33]

Efforts have already been made in this direction.[34] To my knowledge, however, this is the first book-length work on this topic. At the same time, this book is also meant to make an important contribution to the broader return of Marx to the popular political imagination. In short, I hope to make the case for a new materialist Marxism—nondeterministic, nonreductionist, and nonanthropocentric.

In particular, what this book adds to the long tradition of underground kinetic materialism in general and to the recent interest in Marx and new materialism in particular is a reinterpretation of Marx as a philosopher of motion. If taken seriously, this simple, and for some intuitive or naive, approach is the methodological key to overcoming the three criticisms of Marxism previously listed. For some, Marx's interest in motion might even appear to be so obvious that it is not worth saying much more about, but that is precisely the problem. It is *all too well-known* that Marx "is always talking about movement and motion,"[35] and that dialectics is the "science of movement."[36] However, what is not so well-known (or at least not agreed upon) is exactly *what* Marx meant by motion and *why* it was the key to his new materialism.

At the core of all three axes of interpretive criticism discussed previously is a particularly problematic interpretation of motion that I argue does not accurately reflect Marx's own theory of kinetic materialism. Accordingly—and this is the most ambitious claim of this book—each interpretive revolution has fallen prey to the historical criticisms mentioned, in part because it has not sufficiently theorized the nature and primacy of motion in Marx's work.

When I first began researching this topic, I was shocked to discover an almost complete lack of scholarship on the topic of movement, motion, and mobility in Marx. Why had an almost ubiquitous theme in Marx's work, such as movement, not been the primary object of at least a few studies? I think there are at least three major reasons for this lacuna, which I address in this book.

Engels: First of all, Marx's theory of motion has been neglected because of its historical association with the more metaphysical and scientific theory of matter-in-motion associated with Engels's *Anti-Duhring* and *Dialectics of Nature.* Unlike Marx, Engels adopted a specific historical theory of matter-in-motion along the lines of nineteenth-century classical physics, which was committed to a mechanistic theory of discrete, particle-like bits of empirical matter. There has thus been a tendency in at least recent scholarship to avoid this topic in favor of less metaphysically burdened ones.[37]

The Soviets: Second, and relatedly, Marx's theory of motion has been neglected because of its doctrinal appropriation by Soviet Marxists. The Soviets, perhaps more than anyone else, were responsible for adopting Engels's theory of matter-in-motion and insisting it was also Marx's when it was not. In principle, this is only a theoretical error, but practically and historically Stalin tied this interpretation directly to his practice of terror and authoritarianism. After this, no humanist or post-structuralist Marxist wanted anything to do with such metaphysical and Soviet-tainted theories of motion and matter.

The doctoral dissertation: Third, Marx's theory of motion has been neglected because hardly anyone reads or writes about Marx's doctoral dissertation and his notebooks on Epicurean philosophy. However, they provide the single most-concentrated theory of matter and motion in his oeuvre.[38] Unfortunately, Marx's doctoral dissertation and Epicurean notebooks remain among the least-read and most marginalized of all his works for several reasons. The dissertation was unpublished during Marx's lifetime, was missing its last two chapters, was only published in German as recently as 1927, and was only published in a complete English translation in the collected works as late as 1975.[39] Only recently, in 2004, was an *abridged* English translation made available at an affordable price. Therefore, the neglect of Marx's theory of motion is in part a result of the late arrival and inaccessibility of its primary source material.

However, even after the doctoral dissertation and Epicurean notebooks were published, there was a lack of interest in them and even an active burying of anything in Marx's oeuvre that smacked of metaphysical materialism, German *Naturphilosophie*, Soviet-style doctrines of nature, and so on.

Furthermore, lack of interest in the doctoral dissertation might also be attributable to the fact that it is so different from Marx's other writings that it is not obvious at all how it has any connection to the privileged early manuscripts and mature *Capital* that dominate the humanist and post-structuralist traditions, respectively. The technical details of Greek and Latin classical philology hardly seem relevant to the imperatives of the class struggle, ecological collapse, colonialism, or anything else.

Even when Marxists have returned to Marx's theory of nature, matter, and motion, they have tended to either avoid the doctoral dissertation, as the Frankfurt humanist Alfred Schmitt does in *The Concept of Nature in Marx* (1962), or reject Marx's conclusions altogether, like post-structuralist Gilles Deleuze. For example, Deleuze explicitly subordinates matter and motion to *force* in his book on Nietzsche, contrasting himself and Nietzsche with Lucretius's and Marx's kinetic materialisms.[40]

THE THESIS OF THIS BOOK

The thesis of this book is that Marx's theory of kinetic materialism is the key to overcoming the three major problems of Marxism previously identified. This is a bold claim that will require the length of the book to demonstrate, but in place of a full defense of my interpretation, I give the reader here the short version of three core contentions to be proven.

Kinetic dialectics: Marx's theory of motion rejects deterministic theories of nature and society. Matter does not follow mechanistic, vitalistic, classical, or any other deterministic laws of motion. History is not predetermined, linearly developmental, progressive, or teleological. Furthermore, there is no historical necessity for party, state, or vanguard politics nor any necessity for their absence for revolutionary praxis. In contrast to deterministic or law-governed motion, Marx proposes, first in his doctoral dissertation and then throughout his work, a pedetic or stochastic theory of what I call "kinetic dialectics." Pedesis is a kind of physical motion that is neither strictly necessary nor strictly random. Each new motion is directly related to the previous one but is not determined by the history of motions leading up to it or even strictly by the motion immediately prior. Pedetic motion has no teleological end goal. For Marx, there are no universal laws of nature that matter passively follows. Matter itself is active and creative. Laws are emergent tendencies in nature.

Historical materialism: Marx's theory of motion also rejects the economically reductionist division between "base" and "superstructure." Not only is there no merely causal relationship between the two, but there is also no "interaction" between them. There is, strictly speaking, no material division between them at all. The transformations and co-productions of the two domains are collectively self-caused or self-moved. There is only a kinetic transformation and redistribution of the whole historical situation.

Furthermore, Marx's theory of motion is in conflict with any reductionist theory of matter. Marx's theory of motion in his doctoral dissertation and Epicurean notebooks provides a rejection of all atomistic theories of matter. There are no discrete particles following universal natural laws. Marx's theory of motion completely conflicts with both crude mechanistic and strictly empirical theories of matter as well as contemplative or speculative metaphysical theories. Marx has no metaphysics of matter or motion. Unlike typical interpretations of Greek atomism, Marx was the first modern thinker to reject the discrete interpretation of matter in favor of continual and pedetic flows. Unlike other modern interpretations of atomism that treated atoms as eternal and unchanging (Bacon) and reintroduced God (Gassendi) or vitalism (Cavendish), Marx was the only one who dared to treat matter as a *kinetic process* and thus reject any reductionist or substance-based theory of what matter "is."

Marx thus provides a decidedly anticlassical theory of matter much closer to contemporary quantum theories than most Marxists have hitherto considered. Matter, for Marx, is not reducible to actual, observable, empirical matter, not because it is speculative or ideal (as in Democritus) but precisely because matter is in motion and flux. Matter is not reducible to sensuous things or substances because it is the condition for sensation itself *as a process*. The irreducible primacy of motion at the heart of matter persists throughout Marx's work and resists all forms of reductionism.

Historical ontology: Marx's theory of motion is not an ontology of matter or of motion; it is a historical ontology. Marx grounds his kinetic materialism neither in a metaphysical theory of matter "in itself" nor in a strictly anthropocentric or social practice of how matter is "for us." For Marx, there is no ontological division between nature and society. Marx's theory of matter instead is strictly grounded in praxis, but praxis is *not* something only humans do. Human theoretical practices of describing nature are always embodied and historically situated. Philosophy relies on the material conditions of its inscription. But so do nonhuman practices.

In other words, this position is distinct from two common positions in contemporary Marxism. On one side, it is distinct from anthropocentric constructivism or "social monisms," which argue that human descriptions of matter are antirealist and can say nothing about matter or nature "in itself" outside capitalism. On the other side, it is distinct from metaphysical theories of how nature or matter is "in itself" forever and all time. Between anthropic constructivism and naive realism, this book argues that Marx was a nonanthropocentric realist.

Human descriptions of nature *are nature* describing and changing itself in one way or another. But other natural beings are also entangled with one another in a transformative way. Nature *really constructs* itself. Marx's ontology is thus historical in the sense that it is a real description/transformation of nature from a certain region of nature. In the future, matter will change, and new positions will open new regions of nature. Marx provides us with an ontology that is entirely regional and yet also realist at the same time. For Marx, there is no ontological dualism or interaction between humans and nature; nor is there a simple monism, either. Rather, there is a multiplicity of folds or knots.

Marx does not give us a "flat ontology" in which the agency of matter is equally distributed horizontally, like the fraternal relations of bourgeois liberalism and various new materialism political theories. Rather, he gives us a twisted ontology in which different regions of matter are unevenly developed and circulated. This book therefore presents neither a humanist Marx nor an antihumanist Marx but rather a new-materialist Marx of uneven material agencies: an entangled and kinetic Marxism.

These are some of the main claims this book aims to prove in its return to Marx. I do not expect that the reader will find these theses to be immediately obvious. If they were, there would be no need to write this book. However, since it is my aim to refrain from merely supplementing Marx's work with other theorists, I ask for the reader's patience and goodwill until I can demonstrate whether these theses sink or swim through a close reading of the texts themselves. Especially if the reader is not well-versed in Marx's doctoral dissertation, I think some very surprising discoveries and unexpected connections to Marx's later work await them. I am not arguing that Marx's dissertation is the key to the "true Marx," only that it is an important missing piece of his philosophy that may help us resolve some contemporary difficulties in Marxist theory more generally.

METHOD

This book is structured along four methodological lines.

Close Reading

First and foremost, this book is structured by a close reading of volume 1, chapter one of *Capital*, in which Marx puts forward his intended and fully edited core theory of value, upon which his whole theory of the capitalist mode of production rests. However, in preparation for this close reading, I first look at his theoretical framework of motion and kinetic materialism, initially put forward in his doctoral dissertation and Epicurean notebooks. Once I have identified this guiding methodological thread throughout several of Marx's books, I use this method to read a number of key concepts in *Capital* from this new perspective. In other words, motion is not a local dispute or something that hinges on a line or two in one of his books. I am arguing that it is something completely integral to the entire core of Marx's thought and touches upon every aspect of it. It is what makes Marx's work and methodology so absolutely original and heretical in the history of Western philosophy.

The aim of my close reading is not to pick and choose quotes favorable to the arguments of this book but to confront difficult and contrary passages head on. My aim is also not to provide a creative reinterpretation that merely floats above Marx's text but to go line by line and show the nuance and consistency of my interpretation in chapter one of *Capital*. These aims are achieved by staying as close to the core text as possible and supporting it with relevant material from his collected works.

Translation

This leads to my second methodological line: translation. This book offers not only a fresh interpretation of Marx but also a few novel interventions regarding the English translation of the German text. In general, I have tried to pay special attention to the kinetic valences of Marx's vocabulary, especially where the English translation does not show this plainly enough. Since I cannot comment on all these interventions here, I simply draw the reader's attention to a few of the most important and interrelated German words that guide my translation and interpretation.

The first translation intervention is that I have highlighted a kinetic and conceptual connection between three important and interrelated German words in Marx's vocabulary: *zusammenhängen*, *wechsel*, and *verkehr*. Marx uses these three words extensively throughout his works to describe the continual process of kinetic entanglement among different matters. *Zusammenhängen* literally means "to hang together" in mutual and interrelational support but is unfortunately translated as "connection" or "conglomerate," which covers over the idea of mutual intra-action. *Wechsel* means "to continuously change or fold" and is used to describe the "continuous flux or fold of matter" or *Stoffwechsel*, which is often translated as the more technical scientific term "metabolism." Marx also uses the word *wechsel* to emphasize when actions or effects (*Wirkungen*) fold back into each other in a kind of immanent feedback loop or continual transformation of the whole (*Wechselwirkung*). Finally, the term *Verkehr* is an "interchange or intercourse," and Marx uses it in such a wide variety of contexts (economic, military, semantic, and sexual) that it seems to be connected to the "process of mutual transformation" previously mentioned. Throughout this book I have tried to show how these three words and their important kinetic meanings function as a guiding preoccupation in Marx's work from the doctoral dissertation to *Capital*.

My second translation intervention is that I have tried to develop all the interpretive valences included in the rich German verb *tragen*. Although typically translated as "to bear," *tragen* also means to support, maintain, carry, give birth, bear fruit, wear clothing, take, and drag. This is an important set of meanings because Marx places them at the heart of his theory of value. "In the form of society to be considered here, they [use-values] are also the material bearers [*Träger*] of exchange-value" (C, 126). Marx says that before the creation of value, there must be use-values that support and maintain the material conditions of value. In other words, the material bearer (*Träger*) supports and maintains (*tragen*) value. Bearing is not only an active and kinetic term (indicating the birth origins of value-in-movement) but also refers directly to the constitutive labor of nature, women, animals, and slaves. This is the supportive activity that is *appropriated* by capitalism. This idea is crucial for reinterpreting Marx's theory of value as continuous with his theory of primitive accumulation.

Argumentation

There is also an argumentative method followed by this book. Marx did not follow Engels's approach to the dialectics of nature but had his own materialist dialectics. Marx's dialectics was quite different and based on an original philosophy of motion. After Lucretius's reading of Epicurus, Marx was the first to give the movement of matter historical-ontological primacy, untethered by the static constraints of the typical interpretations of Greek atomism. Such a controversial thesis, I admit, is not immediately transparent and will entail more than a few battles with prevailing paradigms of contemporary Marxism. This book therefore contains a number of argumentative lines of reasoning alongside its more close readings and translation interventions, not from a love of polemic but to show at each step the novelty and force of the readings and translations that support the larger theses of this book.

However, there is a limit to this method of tying close reading with argumentation. The core theses of this book remain tied strictly to the close readings. In other words, this book does not attempt to extend its arguments beyond the texts considered, although I believe it is possible to do so, just not in a single book.

My reading will not and cannot be extended here because of the length and depth necessary to textually support arguments of this kind. How far it can be extended must remain an open question for future work. The arguments presented here are therefore not universal or synthetic arguments that speak for the whole of Marx's corpus or aim to reinterpret or defend everything Marx has ever written. With the exception of identifying a movement-oriented methodology through his works, the scope of most of the arguments of this book pertains, at least for the moment, exclusively to chapter one of *Capital*, although I have also drawn in support from the rest of the collected works to show that such an argument could in principle be extended and elaborated more broadly.

History

The fourth and final methodical line of this book is historical. My argumentative thesis allows me to demonstrate a new historical resonance that has recently emerged between Marx and the present. Every new epoch changes the conditions in which the past is understood. New lines and legacies are drawn up constantly. In particular, the current historical conjuncture at the turn of the twenty-first century (postcolonial global migration, ecological collapse, global feminism) makes a new reading of Marx both possible and urgent.

Marx is not a relic of history. All that was solid has now fully melted into air, just as Marx had anticipated. The world is more mobile today than ever before and more than Marx could have imagined. Thus Marx continues to speak to us as a contemporary of a world in motion. It is now time to return his work to the surface of our world and allow the underground current of materialism to erupt once again.

CHAPTER 1

Marx and Motion

We live in an age of movement. More than at any other time in history, people and things move over longer distances, more frequently, and faster. All that was solid melted into air long ago and is now in full circulation around the world, like dandelion seeds adrift on turbulent winds. We find ourselves, in the early twenty-first century, in a world where every major domain of human activity is increasingly defined by motion.[1] Marx was the first modern philosopher to anticipate this. If it is possible to return to Marx today, it is because Marx's philosophical insight into the primacy of motion is more relevant than ever before. This is nowhere more clear than in Marx's very first writings on ancient materialism.

It is often thought, in part because of Marx's writings on capitalism, that the methodological primacy of motion is strictly identical with the historical dominance of capitalism.[2] Since capitalism, according to Marx, is defined by the primacy of motion, some argue that any philosophy that chooses the same method is identical to capitalism. This is false, but there is a grain of truth to it.

Marx began his philosophy under historical and material conditions dominated by the capitalist mode of production, the Industrial Revolution, colonialism, slavery, patriarchy, and so on, in which the whole world was being "thrown into circulation" (C, 216). From this situated position, Marx set out to develop a historical ontology of his kinetic conditions. He set out to write a regional ontology for his time, a historical ontology of motion. However, conditions are never identical to that which they condition, or critique would be mere tautology.

Marx in Motion. Thomas Nail, Oxford University Press (2020). © Oxford University Press.
DOI: 10.1093/oso/9780197526477.001.0001

For Marx, everything is in motion, not just capitalism. Capitalism, like all modes of production, produces a specific regime or pattern of motion.[3] The issue for Marx is not between capitalist movement and revolutionary stasis. The question, as is especially clear in volumes 2 and 3 of *Capital*, is how a specifically capitalist pattern of circulation works. Based on this form of motion, we can see more clearly what it would mean to genuinely move differently and why we would want to do so. Marx's great discovery was precisely that capitalism is not a natural or universal structure, as the classical political economists thought. Capitalism is something that emerged historically under specific conditions of great violence, dispossession, and expulsion. It emerged because it was able to create a new pattern of motion based on its capacity to expand and contract "elastically" (C, 579) and quantify all motions with discrete and exchangeable units of "time."[4]

The point is this: capitalism is only one of many historical social patterns of motion. Motion is not reducible to capitalist motion. Capitalism gets its power from the historical mobility of matter, not the other way around. If "capital can only be understood as motion, not as a thing at rest" (MECW 36: 110–111), that is because capitalism feeds on increasing circulation and requires a constant input of more and more kinetic activity and energy. Therefore, while the historical starting point of Marx's critique is nineteenth-century capitalism, the aim of his critique is not merely to provide a historical description but to show the material conditions for the emergence of this starting point itself.

Since capitalism appears explicitly as a type of motion, Marx needs a movement-oriented philosophical method in order to understand the emergence of capital's unique pattern of motion. The movement of capital comes from somewhere, and it can go elsewhere because it is movement that is primary, not capitalism. This is what Marx discovers early on in his work. His philosophy of motion is the philosophical groundwork for the critique of political economy.

Before moving on to Marx's critical historical method at work in *Capital* volume 1, I first turn to the development of what I call Marx's "philosophy of motion," which runs continuously and consistently through his works up to *Capital*.

ON THE DIFFERENCE BETWEEN DEMOCRITEAN AND EPICUREAN PHYSICS (1841)

Marx's theory of motion is nowhere more evident and focused than in the earliest writings of his doctoral dissertation and Epicurean notebooks. Long before Marx had read Hegel, he had already been working out a critique of religion and a new theory of materialism through ancient atomism. After his exposure to Hegel, Marx used his dissertation to simultaneously critique the reactionary modernist and enlightenment interpretations of ancient atomism, materialism, idealist theories of freedom, religion, and the Hegelian philosophy of nature. Thus, the theory of motion and materialism put forward in Marx's dissertation is not just a Hegelian residue; it is his first effort to develop a materialist and kinetic theory of dialectics.

Marx made at least three original, but underrecognized, contributions in his dissertation. First, he showed that Epicurus and Lucretius, contrary to Democritus, rejected the theory of mechanistic and deterministic materialism. Since atomism, mechanism, and determinism were largely synonymous in modern theories of materialism, this is a major contribution.[5]

Second, he showed that Epicurus and Lucretius, contrary to Cicero and modern interpreters, rejected any spiritual, vital, or external causal force as an explanation for the motion or swerve of matter. Since vitalism was the other major component of modern materialist theories, this was, again, a major shift.

Third, and perhaps most originally, Marx was the first since Lucretius to reinterpret Epicurus's atoms not as discrete particles but as continual flows of matter. Together, these three innovations allowed Marx to overcome the deterministic, reductionistic, and anthropocentric problems with previous materialisms and the Hegelian philosophy of nature. But before showing this in detail, it is worth seeing precisely how he did this. The following threefold conceptual moves return again and again throughout Marx's work and allow him to keep overcoming these same problems all the way through his mature philosophy.

Dialectics: The Threefold Motion of Matter

Marx's first theory of a material-kinetic dialectics is derived partially from Hegel's philosophy of nature but more importantly from the three interrelated motions of matter in Epicurean and Lucretian philosophy:

> Epicurus assumes a *threefold* motion [*dreifache Bewegung*] of the atoms in the void. One motion is the *fall in a straight line*, the second originates in the *deviation* of the atom *from the straight line*, and the third is established through the *repulsion of the many atoms*. Both Democritus and Epicurus accept the first and the third motion. The *declination of the atom* from the straight line differentiates the one from the other. (MECW 1: 46)

Marx's truly brilliant move here is to treat all three motions as a single threefold motion (*dreifache Bewegung*) (MEGA 1: 33). The traditional and almost universal interpretation has been, and still is, to treat each of these motions as distinct and even chronological events. First there are atoms falling straight down in a void, and then at some indeterminate point one of them swerves and knocks into all the others, creating a cascade of composite reality.

However, Marx says, when all three motions are treated "disconnectedly" (MECW 1: 48) or sequentially, then the whole description appears absurd. This is why, Marx notes, commenters such as Cicero and Plutarch mocked Epicurus and Lucretius. They demanded the addition of some vital "soul atom" or deity to secure causality. By rejecting the discontinuity of the motions and treating them instead as a simultaneous threefold, Marx abandons not only determinism but also the metaphysics of causality altogether. Marx concludes, by following Lucretius, who he says is "the only one in general of all the ancients who has understood Epicurean physics," that nature is immanently caused (MECW 1: 48). In other words, if everything is matter and matter is "the cause of everything, [then matter is] without cause itself," or it is imminently self-caused (MECW 1: 50). "In the void the differentiation of weight disappears—that is, it is no external condition of motion, but being-for-self, immanent, absolute movement itself" (MECW 1: 474).

There is not first a fall and then a swerve and then a collision. Each occurs simultaneously and immanently, just as Lucretius describes in Book II of *De Rerum Natura* (2.221–4):

> *quod nisi declinare solerent, omnia deorsum*
> *imbris uti guttae caderent per inane profundum*
> *nec foret o ensus natus nec plaga creata*
> *principiis; ita nihil umquam natura creasset.*

> Because unless they were accustomed to swerving, all would fall downwards like drops of rain through the deep void,
> nor would a collision occur, nor would a blow be produced
> by the first beginnings.

If and only if [*nisi*] (2.221) matter were not already in the habit [*solerent*] (2.221) of curving or bending [*declinare*] (2.221) would it fall downward without collision, like rain [*caderent*] (2.222). The straight fall of matter is therefore a *counterfactual* and not a speculative point in time that ever existed. The swerve existed already before space and time, or at least coexistent with their emergence. There was never a time when there was only the *caderent* without collision (*plaga*) (2.223). Fall, swerve, and collision must have always already been doing so together simultaneously, or nothing would result. If there were such a time when there was only one or two of these, nothing would be, which is obviously not the case.

The movement of declination: The movement of declination itself is also composed of a threefold movement of matter. This is one of the most important passages in the whole dissertation and thus worth quoting at length:

> Just as the point is negated [*aufgehoben*] in the line, so is every falling body negated in the straight line it describes. Its specific quality does not matter here at all. A falling apple describes a perpendicular line just as a piece of iron does. Every body, insofar as we are concerned with the motion of falling, is therefore nothing but a moving point, and indeed a point without independence, which in a certain mode of being—the straight line which it describes—surrenders its individuality [*Einzelheit*]. . . . The consequence of this for the monads as well as for the atoms would therefore be—since they are in constant motion—that neither monads nor atoms exist but rather disappear in the straight line; for the solidity of the atom does not even enter into the picture, insofar as it is only considered as something falling in a straight line. To begin with, if the void is imagined as spatial void, then the *atom* is the *immediate negation of abstract space*, hence *a spatial point*. The solidity, the intensity, which maintains itself in itself against [*behauptet*] the incohesion of space, can only be added by virtue of a principle which negates space in its entire domain, a principle such as time is in real nature. (MECW 1: 48)

The German word *aufgehoben* is crucial to understanding the kinetics at work in this core passage of the doctoral dissertation. The English translation "negation" typically refers to logical negation and strict opposition, which in turn assumes the discrete identity of the original term being negated. This cannot possibly be what Marx had in mind, precisely because there can never be a discrete separation of the threefold motions to begin with. The German word *aufgehoben*, borrowed from Hegel, is by contrast an explicitly kinetic term describing three moments of a single process: a raising up from the ground that both leaves the ground behind and retains a relation to it. It is a process of unfolding.

Now let us look at the three material moments of what Marx calls Epicurus's "immanent dialectics" of motion (MECW 1: 413).

First movement: Up from and out of the creative void rise various distinct regions, or *atoms-of-the-void*. The atoms are not radically other than, but entirely immanent to, the void itself. "The void, the negation, is not the negative of matter itself" (MECW 1: 441). The void, like the similarly used Greek word *chora* and Latin word *locus*, used by Lucretius, *is made through motion*.[6] The Greek and early Latin meaning of space is not empty Cartesian space, as is frequently projected anachronistically onto it, but an active movement of generation and production. The void is thus what is made through the process of materialization itself, as we will see in the third movement. Marx interprets the traditional atomist dualism instead as a continual dialectical process of folding and unfolding. The atoms emerge or unfold out of the ground or void as an immanent region that also "holds its ground" (*behauptet*) as it unfolds out of the ground (MEGA 1: 35). In short, the void is already folded-up matter now regionally unfolded as particle.

Second movement: But in the unfolding movement of the void out of itself into various regions, the atom is thrown into motion. "Just as the point is unfolded [*aufgehoben*] in the line, so every falling body is unfolded [*aufgehoben*] in the straight line it describes." The atom in motion thus raises up and out of its folded region or "self-holding" (*behauptet*) while still continually connected to it. As a "constant motion" the discreteness and "solidity of the atom does not even enter into the picture." One can hardly imagine a more radical departure from the atomist tradition than to say, as Marx does here, that qua motion, "atoms do not exist!" In other words, there is no discrete or ontologically different substance called an eternal atom. The atom is only one kinetic moment in a continual threefold unfolding of matter in which it appears relatively discrete. In absolutely immanent motion, which all matter is in, there is no individual or discrete atom separate from any other.

The rectilinear flow of matter itself also unfolds or moves away from itself, thus producing a curvature or "declination from the straight line" (MECW 1: 49). The movement of declination for Epicurus and Marx is neither deterministic nor random but pedetic. That is, declination does not move in a random motion but in a motion related to its previous motion. However, this relation does not completely determine its future motions. This is not a random universe but a dialectical one, in which motions move beyond and yet always in relation to their previous motions. This pedetic dialectics has nothing to do with logical negation, identity, or difference but rather with an *indeterminate* relational process.

Declination is a movement of matter away from itself but still within itself. It is an indeterminate process of continual differentiation. It makes possible the return of matter back to itself in the sensuous form of the fold: "*The being to which it relates itself is none other than itself*" (MECW 1: 51; emphasis in original). Through a continual unfolding of matter from itself,

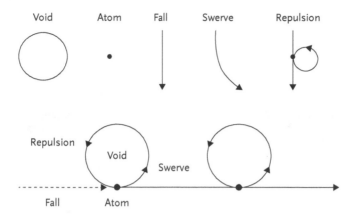

Figure 1.1 Kinetic dialectics

it refolds back over itself in a new fold. This new fold, in turn, makes a new void or space of motion from which the dialectical process begins again, iteratively without original beginning, final synthesis, telos, or closure (MECW 1: 440).

The curvature of the flow of matter is crucial for the repulsion of matter against itself. Repulsion makes possible what Marx calls the self-sensuous and self-aware (*Bewußtsein*) "form determination" (*Formbestimmung*) of matter itself (MEGA 1: 36). "*Repulsion is the first form of self-consciousness*" (MECW 1: 52; emphasis in original). That is, when the flow of matter folds back over itself through declination, it produces a "sensuous form" (MECW 1: 53): material qualities. Repulsion unites matter and form into "sensuous form" kinetically or "kinomorphically," where "Democritus only knew its material existence" (MECW 1: 53).

In other words, the sensuous qualities of matter do not preexist their material-kinetic and historical emergence. Qualities occur when matter folds back over and senses itself. Matter is both sensation and sensed (see figure 1.2).

It is the repulsion or intra-action of matter with itself that generates qualities in what Marx calls a "dialectic of sensuous certitude," in which "the whole of sensuous certainty will be considered as this fluctuating process" (MECW 1: 458). "It is from repulsion and the ensuing conglomerations [*zusammenhängenden Conglomerationen*] of the qualified atoms that the world of appearance [*erscheinende*] now emerges" (MEGA 1: 47/MECW 1:61). The German word Marx uses here to describe the intra-action and coproduction (*zusammenhängenden*) of matter is crucially *missing* from the English translation, as if it were merely redundant

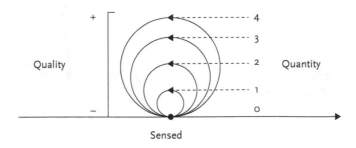

Quality and quantity

Figure 1.2 Quality and quantity

with the German word *Conglomerationen*. However, this concept of *zusammenhängen* is not only absolutely central to Marx's initial theory of material-kinetic dialectics but also runs through all his major works, weaving them together around this core idea of "hanging [*hängenden*] together [*zusammen*]." With respect to the doctoral dissertation, this word, left out of the English translation, is *precisely* what defines Marx's original interpretation of Epicurus. Cicero, Bayle, and others have all interpreted the void, atom, fall, swerve, and repulsion as discrete, "disconnected" (*zusammenhängslos*) aspects of the same threefold dialectical process (MEGA 1: 35/MECW 1: 48).

Zusammenhängen, however, is poorly translated by the English words "connection" or "coherence" or even "dialogue" (as it is translated in the manuscripts), which are closer in meaning to the German words *Verbindung* and *Dialog*, respectively. Connection and dialogue are something that occur between discrete things. *Zusammenhängen*, however, is not a dialogue, interaction, connection, or composite between separate parts, particles, or atoms. To interpret it as such is to misunderstand the entire thesis and novelty of Marx's intervention into ancient materialism and his materialist dialectics. The verb *zusammenhängen* means to hang together in collective mutual support and non-self-sufficiency. To hang together is to have one's conditions in others, who in turn have their conditions and support in you. To hang is precisely not to be self-sufficient but to be suspended by others precariously, tentatively, at the risk of falling. The threads of a spiderweb or a woven tapestry hang together not because they interact as separate, self-sufficient entities or as parts of a larger entity that contains them but as intra-active or mutually co-constituted threads immanent to and entangled, enmeshed, with one another in a kind of knot work.

This is not a minor concept in Marx's work or an eccentricity of his academic thesis but the central idea he continues to use to describe the enmeshed character of nature, humanity, and society. As early as his legal writings on wood theft, Marx already used this term to describe the material co-production of humans and wood. By transforming the woods into private property, "The natural connection [*natürlichen zusammenhängenden*] with property has been replaced by an artificial one [*künstliche zusammenhäng*]. Therefore, anyone who takes away felled wood takes away property" (MEGA 1: 202/MECW 1: 226–227). The distinction is important—*zusammenhängen* can be both natural and artificial. There is no ontological dualism between nature and society. All matter hangs together.

However, it also hangs together in different and important ways. It can hang together in a "natural" or "organic" way (*organischen zusammenhängen*) such that the lives of the peasants who produce, consume, and reproduce the forest hang together with it (MEGA 1: 208). Matter can also hang together in an artificial way when the "metabolic" intra-action of peasants and wood, for example, is redistributed elsewhere as private property. As property, the wood is turned into a commodity and the peasant into waged labor that can (or cannot!) buy the wood in the city. Whether they are private property or not, the peasants and the wood still hang together (*zusammenhängen*) because they depend on each other.

All three movements of the kinetic dialectic are threefold movements of the same continual movement. For Marx, there is no ontological division between void, atom, fall, swerve, and repulsion. Marx's move here is radical. He rejects almost every major traditional interpretive category of ancient atomism. The void is not empty, the atoms are not discrete, the swerve is not causal, and repulsion is not secondary. All three movements are only regional and interdependent moments of a continual and indeterminate movement of matter.

* * *

At this point, I hope it is clear how Marx's theory of motion in his doctoral dissertation overcomes the criticisms of determinism and reductionism, since he clearly describes the motion of matter as pedetic and the substance of matter as an indeterminate *process* of dialectical and kinetic determination. It should also be clear that this account is far from anthropocentric, since humans are not the only or ontologically privileged site of self-sensation or awareness. Matter, just as in Epicurus and Lucretius, is already active and self-sensitive before humans are even on the scene.

However, the reader also might be concerned that this interpretation of Marx overcomes these major criticisms only by falling back into a metaphysical or speculative materialism. In fact, most Marxists have typically read the doctoral dissertation as the early metaphysical speculations of an immature philosophical Marx trying to make claims about the being of nature and matter in itself, independent of human praxis.[7] Critics of the doctoral dissertation even argue that this book is only an early dialectical materialism, taken up poorly by Engels and eventually corrected in Marx's mature work.[8] I disagree.[9]

For Marx, theoretical practice, "practical motion," always begins from the point of sensation (MECW 1: 438). For Marx, humans, as the preceding account shows, are not the only beings capable of sensation. Insofar as matter senses itself through motion, it is already actively aware of itself *to some degree and in some capacity*. In fact, if it were not aware or sensitive to some degree, then humans would not be either, since humans are also matter. Marx, like Epicurus, "proceeds from the sphere of the sensuous" (MECW 1: 471) but discovers *through sensation* that the material condition of this very human sensation is the sensation of matter by itself—which is not always, totally, or necessarily directly sensible by humans. Therefore, although Marx does not dispute that human theoretical practice always begins from human sensation, his "critical" methodology is also interested in the material conditions of sensation more broadly in nature. This raises questions about the sensuous nature that we are. Here Marx gets his critical method directly from Epicurus and Lucretius, who also both begin from human sensation in order to discover the historical and material conditions of this very sensation. Or, to put this more formally, (a) if human theoretical inquiry begins in practice, for example, in sensation, (b) and if humans are natural material bodies produced historically, (c) then matter must be capable of sensing itself.

However, since matter is always *in motion* or *in process*, this philosophical conclusion, by definition, cannot be a metaphysical or ontological one. Metaphysics makes universal claims about "everything, everywhere, forever and all time." Because Epicurus, Lucretius, and Marx all restrict their inquiries to the historical and regional conditions of sensation, their conclusions can pertain only to the *historical ontological* conditions of present sensation. In other words, their question is not, "What is the nature of being forever and all time?" but "What are the material and historical conditions that must be the case for the present to be what it is?"

Just because there are *real conditions* for the present inquiry does not mean that they are the only conditions for the present, are the conditions for all beings, or will continue forever to be the conditions in the future. As such, this disqualifies such conditions from being purely ontological and foundational. Nonetheless, such conditions can be real (albeit regional) conditions. Marx, quoting Epicurus, writes, "All senses are heralds of the true" (MECW 1: 39), suggesting that it is not only human sensation that has access to the real but sensation more broadly that is real. Therefore philosophy, for Marx, is not naively or metaphysically realist but rather "critically or historically realist."[10]

This is an incredibly important, although perhaps subtle, distinction, passed over by the few readers of Marx's dissertation who have had only the traditional philosophical divisions in mind: "metaphysical realist" or "anthropic constructivist." A major novelty of Marx's thesis, therefore, is that it puts forward a third category of "historical" or "regional" realism, taken explicitly from Epicurus and Lucretius.[11] This is a clear precursor to certain contemporary "critical realisms"[12] and "new materialisms"[13] that support a kind of regional onto-epistemological realism. This third position allows Marx, as he says, to overcome the skeptical positions of Democritus and Kant and the metaphysical positions of Plato, Aristotle, and Hegel (MECW 1: 436).[14] "With Plato [and Hegel] motion becomes ideal" (MECW 1: 439) and therefore "lacks motion" (MECW 1: 440).

All versions of anthropocentrism, including post-structuralist ones, necessarily assume a division between the *for itself* and the *in itself*, which limits what we can know about nature in itself. For Marx, however, there is no such ontological division. Nature *really constructs* itself *through* humans and vice versa.[15] To say that the "critical" method is therefore limited strictly to the *anthropic* material conditions of practice (society, power, language, culture, the unconscious, and so on) is an arbitrary limitation that assumes an untenable ontological division between humans and nature.

The kinetic (and indeterminate) continuum between nature, humans, and society is a point to which Marx returns repeatedly.

ECONOMIC AND PHILOSOPHICAL MANUSCRIPTS (1844)

Three years later Marx began to specify more concretely the details of a historically situated theory of motion. The doctoral dissertation does not give us an incorrect metaphysical starting point to be overcome later but only a very minimal materialist and dialectical starting point from which to *build upon*. I argue in this next section that the manuscripts should be read not as a "break" from the dissertation but as *building on* its material-kinetic framework.

For example, instead of starting from human sensuous practice generally, the manuscripts further specify the kind of historically unique sensuous practice that humans begin from "now." This allows Marx to move beyond the more general material conditions of matter and motion and gain more specific knowledge of the historical patterns of motion that condition human practice and contemporary practice in particular. Given the contemporary existence and dominance of such patterns or sensuous forms, Marx then can ask the same critical ontological question Epicurus and Lucretius posed: "Given the present historical existence of existing sensuous forms, what are the material conditions for the emergence of these forms?" Again, this is an entirely regional ontological question.

The core method of inquiry does not change from the doctoral dissertation to the manuscripts. Marx remains committed to a nondeterministic, nonreductionist, and nonanthropocentric framework.[16] In the *Manuscripts*, however, the scope of his original framework is narrowed to account for the regional conditions of his starting point and its form of motion: waged labor. He does this in three main ways: first through a kinetic theory of the human, second through a kinetic theory of the object, and finally through a kinetic theory of private property.

Kinetic Theory of the Human

Following his original kinetic framework, Marx's theory of the human in the manuscripts cannot by definition be essentialist.[17] For example, based on the definition of a material-kinetic essence in his dissertation, Marx cannot possibly mean by "essence" an "eternal unchanging a priori quality or form." Essences, "form-determinations," or qualities, for Epicurus, Lucretius, and Marx, emerge only through the immanent process of material-kinetic folding. An essence or quality of matter is something that is *produced historically* and, like everything else, dissolves historically:

> Through the qualities the atom acquires an existence which contradicts its concept; it is assumed as an externalized being different from its essence. It is this contradiction which mainly interests Epicurus. Hence, as soon as he posits a property and thus draws the consequence of the material nature of the atom, he counter-posits at the same time determinations which again destroy this property in its own sphere and validate instead the concept of the atom. He

therefore determines all properties in such a way that they contradict themselves. (MECW 1:54)

Epicurus says both that matter has no qualities and that through motion
it acquires qualities and then loses them again. In other words, there are
not such thing as a priori eternal essences, only kinetic existences. Or, al-
ternately and more paradoxically, the essence of matter is to flow and continually change its qualities, that is, not to have an eternal essence at all.

This Epicurean theory has its direct expression in Marx's theory of the
human when he writes in the *Manuscripts*:

> Both the material of labour and man as the subject, are the point of departure
> as well as the result of the movement. . . . Thus the *social* character is the general
> character of the whole movement: *just as* society itself produces *man as man*, so
> is society *produced* by him. Activity and enjoyment, both in their content and in
> their *mode of existence*, are *social*: *social* activity and *social* enjoyment. The human
> aspect of nature exists only for social man; for only then does nature exist for
> him as a *bond* with *man*—as his existence for the other and the other's existence
> for him—and as the life-element of human reality. Only then does nature exist
> as the *foundation* of his own *human* existence. Only here has what is to him his
> *natural* existence become his *human* existence, and nature become man for him.
> Thus *society* is the complete unity of man with nature—the true resurrection of
> nature—the accomplished naturalism of man and the accomplished humanism
> of nature. (MECW 3: 298)

This is an extremely strange definition of "human essence," since the essence of the human being is something apparently produced through
movement, by humans, as nature. Humans, just like the sensuous form
determinations of the Epicurean materialism, both are the product of composite sensuous qualities and in turn recompose and dissolve themselves
through motion. Just like the kinetic process of material declination and
repulsion, the human being and other matters are the point of departure
and the result of the movement of matter.

Matter becomes human through sensuous, form-generating movement.
As Marx writes quite explicitly, "*[S]ensuous* form [thus reveals] the extent
to which the human essence has become nature to man, or to which nature to him has become the human essence of man" (MECW 3: 296). Marx
refines his general materialist theory of motion into a theory of human
activity—in particular, human social activity.

The material condition of human practice is first of all the sensuous activity and productive power of matter in motion. Within this movement,

humans emerge as social or collective animals capable of reproducing themselves in nature as nature, that is, as social nature. "History itself is a *real* part of *natural history* and of nature's becoming man" (MECW 3: 303–304). Through this natural social activity, humans participate in the production of themselves as nature and thus *as humans*. This is not an activity unique to humans, nor does it give them any ontological or sensuous primacy. Human constructivism is a natural, material, and real constructivism. What we do and know has a genuine reality to it because we are sensuous folds in the real itself. Essence and existence become two aspects of the same metastable and pedetic flow of matter. This is precisely why

> communism, as fully developed naturalism, equals humanism, and as fully developed humanism equals naturalism; it is the genuine resolution of the conflict between man and nature and between man and man—the true resolution of the strife between existence and essence, between objectification and self-confirmation, between freedom and necessity, between the individual and the species. (MECW 3: 296)

Marx repeats this kind of unity between naturalism and humanism so many times in the manuscripts because one of his main goals is to show the complete continuity between his kinetic theory of matter (naturalism) in the doctoral dissertation and his more restricted inquiry into social patterns of motion (humanism) (see figure 1.3).

Marx continues to follow the Epicurean and Lucretian rejection of speculative metaphysics. "Who begot the first man and nature as a whole? I can only answer you: Your question is itself a product of abstraction. Ask yourself how you arrived at that question" (MECW 3: 305). In his doctoral dissertation and manuscripts, Marx rejects any attempt to provide first principles of humanity or nature because critical philosophy begins from

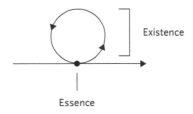

Figure 1.3 Existence and essence

the sensuous existence of matter and humans and looks to their regional conditions, not their origins or a priori essences.

Kinetic Theory of the Object

The second way Marx focuses the theoretical scope of his materialism from the doctoral dissertation in the manuscripts is by introducing a kinetic theory of the object. In the doctoral dissertation, Marx contrasts Epicurus's theory of "objective appearance" with the "subjective semblance" (*Schein*) of Democritus (MECW 1: 40). Sensuous objects of appearance emerge through the threefold movement of the kinetic dialectic. The object, in Marx's interpretation of Epicurus, emerges when matter swerves and folds back over itself, generating a sensuous form or quality. However, since matter has no fixed form or quality, the contradiction is objectified in the atom (MECW 1: 58). "The nature of appearance is justly posited as objective—sensation is justly made the real criterion of concrete nature" (MECW 1: 64). The sensuous object is the kinetic fold between an active flow of matter and a metastable fold reproduced by the movement of matter. Marx writes:

> These forms of the things stream constantly forth from them and penetrate into the senses and in precisely this way allow the objects to appear. Thus in hearing nature hears itself, in smelling it smells itself, in seeing it sees itself. Human sensuousness is therefore the medium in which natural processes are reflected as in a focus and ignited into the light of appearance. (MECW 1: 65)

Nature actively objectifies itself into sensuous qualities and then senses itself. The natural object is both sensed and sensing. The human qua nature is also sensible and sensed as well. The sensuous object is therefore the material-kinetic basis of the human.

This kinetic theory of the object is carried over and further developed in the manuscripts, where Marx writes:

> *Man* is directly *a natural being.* . . . On the one hand . . .—he is an active natural being. These forces exist in him as tendencies and abilities—as instincts. On the other hand, as a natural, corporeal, sensuous, objective being he is a suffering. . . . *To be* objective, natural and sensuous, and at the same time to have object, nature and sense outside oneself, or oneself to be object, nature and sense for a third party, is one and the same thing. . . . The sun is the *object* of the plant—an indispensable object to it, confirming its life—just as the plant

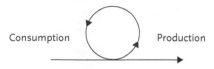

Figure 1.4 The kinetic object

is an object of the sun, being an *expression* of the life-awakening power of the sun, of the sun's *objective* essential power. A non-objective being is a non-being. (MECW 3: 336–337)

For Marx, all beings are sensuous objects. This does not mean that everything is made of static blocks of atomistic, discrete stuff following mechanistic laws—as we know from the doctoral dissertation. Objects are continually produced because matter flows. These flows then constantly fold over themselves again and again to produce and reproduce stable cycles of sensation. Objects are not merely passive, suffering things. Again, for Marx, objects are both active and passive, both producing and consuming at the same time. They objectify the contradiction between essence and existence through continual modulation. The material-kinetic object is a continual "movement of production and consumption" (MECW 3: 297) (see figure 1.4).

Humans are not exceptional in this respect. The plant is an object for sun, and the sun is an object for the plant. The plant is folded-up sunlight, and sunlight is unfolded in the plant. Each affects and is affected by other objects, and all objects are folded and unfolded following the kinetic dialectics of matter described in the doctoral dissertation. Thus when objects produce and consume one another, they express their active power and confirm their receptive power at the same time. This is what Marx calls their "objective essential power" (MECW 3: 337).

The Movement of Private Property

To the kinetic theory of the human and object Marx adds an important new concept: "the movement of private property" (MECW 3: 290). Here Marx's theory of motion becomes even more refined with respect to the material-sensuous conditions of practice. Contemporary practice takes place under the condition of the capitalist mode of production.

Private property is an object like all objects insofar as it is produced by a flow and fold of matter (including human matters). That is, contrary to political economy, which has "looked upon private property as a mere *condition* external to man," private property is above all "a product of the real *energy* and the real *movement* of private property" (MECW 3: 290). Private property is an object, like other objects, produced by a more primary flow and folding of matter (both human and nonhuman). Without this material-kinetic understanding of the object, "political economy does not grasp the way the movement is connected [*zusammenhäng der Bewegung*] to the object" (MEGA 2: 235/MECW 3: 271). Economists are "fetishists" who worship discrete objects independent from the material-kinetic conditions of their production. This is precisely the same criticism Marx leveled at the "disconnected" or discrete (*zusammenhangslos*) atomist interpretations of Cicero and Bayles and the treatment of peasant forests as private property. Private property still involves, like all matters, a kinetic hanging together of movement, even if it alters the intra-actions in a way that kills the peasants and the forests. The stupidity of political economy is that it fails to grasp the unique ways that the metabolic movements of "definite modes of life" hang together.

However, private property is also different than other objects because the real material movements and energies that produce private property (both human and nonhuman) undergo, unlike other object relations, a threefold kinetic separation (*entfremden/Entäußerung*) from the whole process.[18] Following the framework of the doctoral dissertation, Marx does not have in mind an ontological separation but a strictly material-kinetic separation that entails only a local externalization and *redistribution* of matters, as the frequently interchangeable use of the German words (*entfremden/Entäußerung*) suggests.[19] Since the real flow of matter is not discrete, the "separation" here is more like a bifurcation, redirection, or shift, not an absolute "cut."[20]

Separation from the object: The first separation is the separation of production from the object it produces. The process of kinetic production realizes itself in objectification, but the process is itself also composed of other objects, both human and nonhuman. As Marx reminds us, "The worker can create nothing without *nature,* without the *sensuous external world.* It is the material on which his labour is realized, in which it is active, from which and by means of which it produces" (MECW 3: 273). The three-fold materialist dialectic from the doctoral dissertation returns here in the material-kinetic theory of production. "Material production in general" as Marx will write later in the *Grundrisse,* occurs *from* matter (fall), *through* matter (declination), and *on* matter (repulsion). As shown in the doctoral dissertation, there is nothing uniquely human in the material process of production in general or in the local separation of the parts of a production process from one another. However, the human worker does experience this local separation in her own way, with respect to the kind of being that she is. The human is only one instance of a larger process of separation or redistribution.

In the case of the production of private property, the object of production is not returned to the production process. Because the capitalist owns the product, it does not return back to the productive process, and the process thus becomes locally separated from the material means of reproducing its own production (the exhaustion of the soil, the starvation of the worker, the robbery of domestic labor, and the devastation of colonial dispossession). The process becomes the apparent servant of the final object *as if* the object had a discreteness and independence from the material conditions that produced it—even though the object is only a moment of the process. While there is a threefold material continuity, private property acts *as if* the parts were discrete, just as Cicero did with atomism.

Separation from the activity: The second separation is the separation of production from its own activity. When the productive activity of matter is "forced" into rote mechanical motion, it "does not develop freely [its] physical and mental energy but mortifies [its] body and ruins [its] mind" (MECW 3: 274). Since the produced object does not correspond directly to the creative activity of the production itself, it does not "belong" to the activity properly. In other words, insofar as the pedetic movement of matter is forced into merely mechanical activity, its creative activity is separated from the nature of its movement (which is pedetic) (MECW 3: 321). Production is forced into "self-sacrifice" and "mortification" when it becomes an "activity directed against" its "own spontaneous activity" (MECW 3: 274–275). Again, there is no ontological separation here but rather a kind of forced mechanical repetition of an otherwise freely generative movement that pertains to the soil as much as to the human organism.

Separation from being: The third separation is the separation of production from its being (*Wesen*). All beings are produced and reproduced by material "inorganic nature" in different arrangements that define the type (*Gattung*) of being (*Wesen*) that they are. Again, these are not immutable essences but produced and productive historical and material "types of beings" (*Gattungswesen*). "Plants, animals, stones, air, light, etc." and all of nature have their own *Gattungswesen*.[21] Living types (*Gattungsleben*) of beings (*Wesen*) "both man and animals . . . live from inorganic nature" and are simply parts of "nature's *inorganic body*" (MEGA 2: 239–240/MECW 3: 275–276). All living beings maintain (*bleiben*) themselves as constant (*beständig*), continual processes (*Prozeß*) of intra-action (*zusammenhängen*) with this inorganic body of nature (MEGA 2: 240). All beings thus "hang" (*hängen*) "together" (*zusammen*) in relations of mutual interdependence and coproduction *though* inorganic material process. "That man's physical and spiritual life is intra-active [*zusammenhängen*] with nature means simply that nature is intra-active [*zusammenhängen*] with itself, for man is a part of nature" (MECW 3: 276).[22]

The English translation of *zusammenhängen* in this passage as "linked" or "interchange" makes it sound like humans and nature are independent, self-sufficient, discrete links that interact with one another or connect together into a chain. Such an interpretation is especially absurd in the case of the phrase "nature is *linked* [*zusammenhängen*] with itself." Here again is a version of an "atomist" translation/interpretation in which matter/nature is composed of discrete bits of stuff that link together into larger composites and so on. Marx's doctoral dissertation and earliest writings show conclusively, however, that *zusammenhängen* cannot possibly mean the linkage of discrete bits. Nature hangs together with itself in continually moving and folding patterns of co-production, mutual support, and precarity. Nature "hangs together as a whole" (*zusammenhäng des Ganzen*) (MEGA 2: 314). Nature intra-acts with itself through folding, thus producing sensation, qualities, and sensuous forms. Humans are one of those sensuous forms—a fold in a kinetic web of flows.

However, through the production of private property, beings are separated from doing many kinds of things they can do. They are forced into mechanical patterns of motion, and their products are not returned to them (*künstliche zusammenhängen*). For example, in factory farms, animals are forced into confined feeding operations that treat their bodies as machines for meat extraction (*Entäußerung*). Women's bodies are turned into factories for the extraction of new workers and domestic labor. Plants are genetically modified not to reproduce. Rivers are dammed up to extract energy. Entire populations are transformed into colonies for raw material extraction (slaves, timber, sugar, gold, and so on).

In doing so, private property separates these beings from their historical capacities for action and thus from the types of beings (*Gattungswesen*) that they are. This produces four interrelated separations of their being: (a) beings are relatively separated from their specific process of intra-action (*zusammenhängen Prozeß*) with nature, (b) they are separated from themselves and their own capacities for action, (c) they are separated from their collective ecological conditions and treated only as individual instruments, and (d) they are separated from their fellows.

All three separations occur as three aspects of the same process of separation. Marx is quite clear that this is not an ontological separation but a historically regional and relative separation of *specific beings* from their *specific* inorganic process of intra-active production and reproduction. Separation is not something static, preaccomplished, or existential. It is a material-kinetic process that itself *both produces and is reproduced by* "the movement of private property." "Only at the culmination of the development of private property does this, its secret, appear again, namely, that on the one hand it is the *product* of separated [*entäusserten*] labour, and that on the other it is the *means* by which labour separates [*entäusserten*] itself, the realization of this separation [*entäusserten*]" (MECW 3: 279–280). There is no dualism here. Matter is both the production and product of local separations and redistributions. Furthermore, this important quote explicitly prefigures the "theory of the secret" developed later in *Capital*, that is, the constitutive role played by theft, appropriation, and primitive accumulation in the production of value. All this brings us to the dramatic conclusion of the kinetic analysis of private property:

> This *material*, immediately *perceptible* private property is the material perceptible expression of *separated human life*. Its movement—production and consumption—is the *perceptible* revelation of the movement of all production until now, i.e., the realisation or the reality of man. Religion, family, state, law, morality, science, art, etc., are only *particular* modes of production, and fall under its general law. (MECW 3: 297)

In other words, while Marx's analysis begins with the sensible material conditions of the contemporary world of private property and its threefold separation, his conclusion is to have discovered the historical, material, and kinetic conditions of all production until now: the hanging together of all material production more generally. Marx's kinetic theory of material production is therefore not just an economic theory of capitalism but a historical ontology of all intra-active material production from the contemporary standpoint. Marx thus discovers what must have been the material-kinetic conditions of production in general such that the capitalist mode of production in particular could have emerged today.

In the series of books leading up to the *Capital* volumes, Marx uses this kinetic theory of material production as a critique against other materialist philosophers before returning with renewed intensity and confidence in his method to the focused study of the capitalist mode of production.

THE HOLY FAMILY (1845)

In *The Holy Family*, Marx and Engels wrote a sustained critique of previous theories of materialism. They did not, however, provide a detailed theory of their own materialism in this text. In part, this is because Marx had already worked out his theory of materialism in his dissertation.

The Holy Family, however, makes it quite explicit what Marx's new materialism *is not* and how others failed to interpret ancient materialism properly. In other words, Marx's new materialism is not mechanism, deism, vitalism, or contemplative materialism, but kinetic. "French and English materialism was always closely related to Democritus and Epicurus," Marx says, but both traditions failed to develop a new theory of materialism out of these ancient thinkers (MECW 4: 126).

English materialism: Marx argues that Francis Bacon was materialism's "first creator." Bacon lionized "Democritus and his atoms" and privileged "sensation as the source of knowledge." He even made motion fundamental to matter. However, Bacon also treated the movement of matter as mechanical, mathematical, and caused by vital spirits:

> Among the qualities inherent in matter, motion is the first and foremost, not only in the form of mechanical and mathematical motion, but chiefly in the form of an impulse, a vital spirit, a tension—or a "Qual," to use a term of Jakob Böhme's—of matter. The primary forms of matter are the living, individualizing forces of being inherent in it and producing the distinctions between the species. (MECW 4: 128)

Bacon thus crushed the dialectical creativity of matter by making it discrete, law-abiding, causally directed, and driven by vital forces "imported from theology."

Hobbes systematized Bacon's materialism but did so by making motion purely mechanical and mathematical and extracting it from sensation. With Hobbes, "materialism has to chastise its own flesh and turn *ascetic*" (MECW 4: 128). Hobbes's materialism turned back against its foundations in human sensation and became "misanthropic" because Hobbes did not start with human sensation but rather with geometrical forms.

French materialism: The two trends of French materialism can be traced back to two origins: Descartes and Locke. "Descartes, in his physics, endowed matter with self-creative power and conceived mechanical motion as the manifestation of its life" (MECW 4: 125). Le Roy, La Mettrie, Cabanis, Newton, Bayle, and others all affirmed Descartes's mechanism against his metaphysics.

Locke, however, recovered the primacy of human sensation in his materialism from the mechanistic and geometrical materialism of Descartes and Hobbes. "Locke's *immediate* pupil, *Condillac*, who translated him into French, at once applied Locke's sensualism against seventeenth-century *metaphysics*" (MECW 4: 128). This provided Helvétius with the basis from which to develop a more social theory of sensation. Later French materialism emerged out of English materialism and gave it a less mechanistic and more social style.

German materialism: Ultimately, Marx and Engels expose the critical target of the book, the nineteenth-century German philosopher Bruno Bauer. Bauer, they write, completely misread the history of French materialism and put forward an idealist theory of matter. Marx paraphrases Bauer's reading of the French materialists in order to show precisely how idealist Bauer's reading really was:

> The French materialists did, of course, conceive the movements of matter as movements involving spirit, but they were not yet able to see that they are not *material,* but *ideal* movements, movements of self-consciousness, consequently pure movements of thought. They were not yet able to see that the real movement of the universe became true and real only as the *ideal* movement of self-consciousness free and freed from *matter,* that is, from *reality;* in other words, that a *material* movement distinct from ideal brain movement exists only in *appearance.* (MECW 4: 140)

For Marx, by contrast, the movement of matter is a real sensuous material movement, not a movement of self-consciousness. Matter moves not mechanistically nor by vital forces, nor by God nor by the contemplation of thought, but immanently *on its own.* Human thought is the material-kinetic product of this motion, not the origin and sole moment of it.

THESES ON FEUERBACH (1845) AND THE GERMAN IDEOLOGY (1846)

In *The German Ideology,* Marx and Engels, among many other things, extend similar criticisms against other German idealist philosophies of matter and history, including Bruno Bauer, Ludwig Feuerbach, and Max Stirner. *The German Ideology* continues to deploy the operative kinetic concepts of "moveable private property" (MECW 5: 68), the practical primacy of "material relations" (MECW 5: 59), and the continual and intra-active process or "intercourse" (*Verkehr*) of collective production of "even the objects of the simplest 'sensuous certainty'" (MECW 5: 39). Since these have already been discussed, I do not repeat the kinetic interpretation of them here.[23]

The *Theses on Feuerbach*, however, offer a strikingly clear continuation of the theoretical primacy of sensuous material practice originally put forward in the doctoral dissertation. This is in contrast to previous versions of merely objective (mechanistic) or idealist (contemplative) theories of materialism:

> The chief defect of all previous materialism (that of Feuerbach included) is that things [*Gegenstand*], reality, sensuousness are conceived only in the form of the object, or of contemplation, but not as sensuous human activity, practice, not subjectively. Hence, in contradistinction to materialism, the active side was set forth abstractly by idealism—which, of course, does not know real, sensuous activity as such. (MECW 5: 3)

Marx thus rejects both the mechanistic movement of matter as merely passive objects caused by an external force and the idealist contemplation of matter from a purely active and abstract side independent from the matter that it contemplated. This was also Democritus's antinomy. Democritus reduced the movement of matter to the deterministic and mechanical laws of discrete fundamental and insensible atoms, or objects. In doing so, his theory of knowledge also reduced knowledge to "abstract individuals" and objects to purely *ideal* objects-of-contemplation (MECW 1: 39, 50). In this way, Democritus became a skeptic of the sensual world because the fundamental objects of matter "atoms" could not be sensed. Here "the concept of the atom and sensuous perception face each other as enemies. Thus Democritus does not escape the antinomy" (MECW 1: 39).

Following Epicurus and Lucretius, Marx escapes the Democritean/German idealist antinomy by beginning from the sensuous form of practical activity itself. Humans do not describe independent objects from bodies independent of objects. In the manuscripts, it is clear that the human itself is made of sensuous objects, as is all of nature. Therefore practical philosophical description begins from some region of nature and not others. Only insofar as one begins as already entangled and hanging together (*zusammenhängen*) with nature does it make any sense to give a practical description of one's material conditions and entangled relations.

Since the human body really is a sensuous body of nature, (1) nature must really have sensuous objects and (2) the practice of description is not representational but above all really practical and transformative as an *act of description*. In other words, philosophy is not a representation of reality; it is reality itself really doing something. It is matter moving itself in certain patterns. This is the sense in which Marx's materialism is also and must be a kinetic realism:

> The question whether objective truth can be attributed to human thinking is not a question of theory but is a *practical* question. Man must prove the truth, i.e., the reality and power, the this-worldliness of his thinking in practice. The dispute over the reality or nonreality of thinking which is isolated from practice is a purely *scholastic* question. (MECW 5: 3)

The question is not a scholastic question of what theory "represents" about reality but a practical question of what theory (as reality) *does as a performative transformation of reality itself*. In other words, if "nature hangs together with itself," then human practice qua nature is nature intra-acting with itself—constructing itself. The kinetic and performative act of philosophical inscription is a material act that is *both* constructive and hung together in nature.[24] Theory, like all matter in motion, is nature folding over itself in sensuous practice. Thus the material reality of philosophy is not an isolated epistemological or social constructivism but a real region of nature that really constructs and transforms nature into various patterns of motion. It proves itself practically. Marx writes:

> The coincidence of the changing of circumstances and of human activity or self-change can be conceived and rationally understood only as *revolutionary practice*. (MECW 5: 4)

Changes in theoretical practice and historical circumstances are not representational or even mechanically causal but rather collectively or immanently self-causal. Nature "hangs together as a whole movement," not as separate interacting objects linked to one another. Therefore,

> all social life is essentially *practical*. All mysteries which lead theory to mysticism find their rational solution in human practice and in the comprehension of this practice. (MECW 5: 5)

All matter is essentially *practical*. If theory is treated as a representation of reality, and not as a region *of material reality itself*, it will lead to mysticism and the Democritean antinomy. However, if our starting point, as humans, is to treat the human body as a sensuous object of nature, then there is no initial split between the for-itself and the in-itself. There is only a continual modulation, a real practical construction, of nature as a natural process. Furthermore, since it is our sensuous practice as humans that makes theory possible, other sensuous objects of nature also intra-act and construct nature as well—since they are nature, too. In fact, these are the very material conditions that make narrowly human theoretical practice possible to begin with.

Nature hangs together and *really* constructs itself. The central question of theoretical practice should be changed from one of *interpretation* (as representations of reality) to one of *transformation* (as real practical constructions of reality). "The philosophers have only *interpreted* the world in various ways; the point is to *change* it" (MECW 5: 5).

THE POVERTY OF PHILOSOPHY (1847)

Here I look at one final text with respect to the development of Marx's kinetic materialism before moving on to *Capital*—*The Poverty of Philosophy*. In this book Marx makes extremely clear that we are not to interpret his kinetic theory of political economy as beginning with a metaphysics of movement *in general*, following Hegel and Proudhon. The kinetic theory of matter is not an abstract theory of "all that exists," *in general* (MECW 6: 163) but rather a practical theory that begins from the perspective of a strictly historical region of sensuous movement: the present. This does not mean that Marx cannot draw any historical ontological conclusions beyond the present but simply that the present must be the practical point from which to discover the material and historical conditions of that present itself.

It is true that Marx does offer at times, as in the doctoral dissertation, a very broad description of matter and motion. However, he does so strictly insofar as these are the real material conditions for his own theoretical and sensuous practice itself—and not as an empty ahistorical category or a view from nowhere.

In fact, taking the *Theses on Feuerbach* seriously, Marx's kinetic materialism is not a theory "of" anything at all but is itself a practical and performative act that transforms matter kinetically. Theoretical practice is not and cannot be independent from the world it describes, because this is precisely how it really accesses and constructs a real description of the world. The greatest danger of the philosophy of movement is that it can easily be made into an abstract and contemplative method, which Marx rightfully wants to distance himself from:

One has only to make an abstraction of every characteristic distinctive of different movements to attain movement in its abstract condition—purely formal movement, the purely logical formula of movement. If one finds in logical categories the substance of all things, one imagines one has found in the logical formula of movement the *absolute method*, which not only explains all things, but also implies the movement of things. (MECW 6: 164)

Marx here accuses Proudhon of reducing political economy to applied Hegelian metaphysics. Proudhon and Hegel treat the movement of all things as a purely logical category: the movement of matter *in general*. This is something Engels and Soviet Marxism would also be guilty of later on—a metaphysics of nature and movement in general:

All things being reduced to a logical category, and every movement, every act of production, to method, it follows naturally that every aggregate of products and production, of objects and of movement, can be reduced to applied metaphysics. (MECW 6: 164)

Marx directly equates the "act of production" with movement and the product of that production with an "object-in-motion." Hegel and Proudhon make a similar observation but then err by going on to theorize the "movement of the production of objects" from the perspective of a universal and ahistorical general method in which all motion is generalized and abstracted into a single method or logical category of thought.

The problem with such a method is that it treats all movement as if it were the same forever and for all time and as if theoretical practice were not itself a region of this movement as well. Movement becomes "absolute," "abstract," "logical," and "a movement of pure reason" (MECW 6: 164). This is what happens when one abstracts the kinetics out of the kinetic materialism: One is left with a purely abstract metaphysics of motion on the one hand and a strictly contemplative object of matter on the other. Movement becomes pure thought, and matter becomes the object of thought's contemplative dialectical movements: "thesis, antithesis, synthesis" "affirming itself, negating itself and negating its negation." The movement of this kind of thought is, for Marx, *not real movement at all*.

By contrast, as previously discussed, real movement is not metaphysical or universal but material and historical. Matter is not something thought simply thinks but something thought *does*, practically and materially. Matter practically affects itself through thinking bodies. Theoretical practice is part of matter, and thus its acts are not representational, categorial, or absolute, but rather affective, sensuous, regional, historical, and transformative.

CONCLUSION

What I have tried to prove in this chapter is that Marx's dissertation is not a marginal or anomalous text in his corpus, as it has often been treated. Rather, the doctoral dissertation provides a foundational philosophical perspective that continues through all the major theoretical moves of his subsequent works up to the *Capital* writings.

Together, these pre-*Capital* works develop what I call a "material-kinetic dialectics." Historically, this was a truly unique and powerful idea. Marx's kinetic materialism is neither deterministic, reductionist, nor anthropocentric. Marx explicitly rejects all forms of mechanism, determinism, vitalism, deism, and contemplative materialism, and all metaphysics of motion.

With this philosophical method in place, I return again to Marx's most systematic, focused, and sustained philosophical project: *Capital*. By starting the reading from the darkest and most obscure corner of Marx's work (the doctoral dissertation), we are in a new and interesting position to reread *Capital* again, differently. This way of proceeding makes possible a number of surprising discoveries in Marx's work as well as some startlingly contemporary conclusions regarding the theories of value and primitive accumulation.

CHAPTER 2

Method and Critique

The return to Marx in this book is a return to the most maligned idea of Western philosophy: movement.[1] Marxism, the second major philosophical current of *kinetic materialism* after ancient atomism, has too often succumbed to deterministic, reductionistic, and anthropocentric interpretations of Marx that have subordinated the movement of matter to something else: laws of history, forces of nature, discrete particles, human constructivisms both social and contemplative, and so on. So, by beginning again with Marx's doctoral dissertation, this book offers a rereading of Marx that aims to restore the philosophical primacy of movement to Marx's work and overcome the three axes of critique that have defined its decline.

The remainder of this book is dedicated to a close reading of chapter one of volume 1 of *Capital*. This is the most notoriously difficult and abstract chapter of *Capital* but also the most important and theoretically crucial to the philosophical foundations of the book as a whole. I think this is an extremely fertile place to begin another return to Marx, because getting a different foothold on chapter one has transformative consequences for rereading the rest of Marx.

The aim of this book is to develop a reading of Marx from the perspective of what I call his kinetic materialism, introduced in the previous chapter. The aim of the present chapter in particular is to show the previously unacknowledged continuity between Marx's earlier method of kinetic materialism with the methodology he lays out at the beginning of *Capital*. Furthermore, and more generally, I show that Marx's critical method in *Capital* has nothing to do with any sort of determinism, reductionism, or anthropocentrism.

Marx in Motion. Thomas Nail, Oxford University Press (2020). © Oxford University Press.
DOI: 10.1093/oso/9780197526477.001.0001

METHOD

Marx begins *Capital* with a methodological statement about the nature of how the book will proceed. The first two sentences of the book are extremely dense and important:

> The wealth of societies in which the capitalist mode of production prevails appears [*erscheint*] as an "immense collection of commodities"; the individual [*Einzelne*] commodity being [*seine*] its elementary form. Our investigation therefore begins with the analysis of the commodity. (C, 125)

Appearance

Marx begins *Capital* just as Epicurus and Lucretius began their materialist philosophy: with sensuous appearance. All theoretical practice begins with the sensation of matter, but for Marx, humans, as the previous chapter showed, are not the only beings with sensation. Sensuous appearance always has a double genitive character; sensation is both the active *sensation of* matter and the receptive sensation *of matter*. Sensuous appearance is thus both active (subject) and receptive (object) at the same time and with respect to both sensing and sensed objects.

For example, the philosophical starting point of *Capital* for Marx is an explicitly sensous action in which "we *take* the individual product *in our hand* and analyze the formal determinants that it contains as a commodity and which *stamp* it as a commodity" (C, 1059).[2] Sensuous appearance is both an active taking or grasping of something as well as a receptive being taken or stamped by something. Furthermore, the being doing the taking is also already a sensuous object. For the object to make itself appear to someone it must actively make itself appear as an object for others. In short, in order for a human being to take a commodity in hand, there must already be a fourfold relation of activity and receptivity. Sensuous appearance requires that each object in the sensing/sensed relation be itself both self-sensing and self-sensed.

Therefore, first philosophy for Marx does not begin with being or nature *in general*, as it does in Hegel's logic; this is pure abstraction. Nor does philosophy begin with first ideas or concepts of doubt, being, thought, and so on. For Marx, philosophy begins in praxis, in the material-kinetic act of sensuous appearance. Marx's use of the German word *erscheinen* indicates precisely this. Appearance is something that actively shines (*erscheint*)

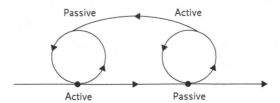

Passive   Active

Active   Passive

Figure 2.1 *Zusammenhängt*

forth (*er*) *and* is received by something else that in turn itself shines forth. Appearance thus entails a double genitive and mutual shining-forth in which each object mutually illuminates the other. Appearance, as shown in chapter one of this book, is something that hangs together (*zusammenhängen*) in co-constitution (see figure 2.1).

Marx uses the word *erscheinen* as distinct from the word *scheinen*, which indicates only a one-sided, abstract, and thus false shining in which things merely "seem" to be the case. *Scheinen* is a shining without a shining-forth to something else outside it. "Seeming" here indicates a falseness, a one-sided objectivity that does not occur in nature. Matter is always active and receptive. If it were not, sensation and appearance would not be possible. Thus, to read "appearance" here as "semblance" or "seeming" would be to fundamentally misunderstand the fundamental starting point and philosophical foundation of Marx's methodology.

The Individual

What appears in this moment of kinetic praxis—picking up an object— is that society shines forth as a "wealth" composed of a large "collection" (*Sammlung*) of "individual" (*Einzelne*) commodities. This appearance is not a semblance or something false, as it was for Democritus. It is a real, sensuous appearance of reality, as it was for Epicurus and Lucretius. "All senses," as Marx quotes Epicurus, "are heralds of the true" (MECW 1: 39). Such a statement is impossible to reconcile with any form of antirealism or humanist constructivism. For Marx and Epicurus, all sensuous appearance is *real* sensuous appearance. Semblance is not wrong because it has made a representational error of reference but because the observer has accepted the idea of representation in the first place. Objects really appear as commodities because the relations that produce such appearance themselves are real ones. The commodity is not the whole of appearance, nor is it an objective representation of all appearance. The commodity is a real relational appearance of a certain region of entangled sensuous objects.

The contemporary appearance of reality and "wealth" is as a collection of discrete and individual objects that are exchanged. Wealth appears as a collection of apparently discrete quantified objects of exchange. The discreteness of individual objects is not strictly false, but such individual objects do not come from nowhere. Their individualness is only a regional appearance of larger continual processes that produce them. Wealth appears as a static product, but this product is the product of a more primary process of "production . . . in the movement of becoming" (G, 488). Individual objects that define the appearance of wealth are only relatively or regionally discrete, like a chain of volcanic islands on a vast ocean. Below the reflective, shining surface of the water are the continual material and volcanic process from which these relatively discrete islands emerge. Commodities are not false images or ideological representations of reality; they have their own sensuous reality in the more primary process of production.

Atomic Commodities

Interestingly, Marx begins *Capital* with the same problem as in his doctoral dissertation: the problem of the appearance of discrete matter or atoms. Marx says the commodity is the economic atom or "cell-form" of political economy (C, 90). The original contribution of the dissertation and *Capital* is that the supposed discreteness of matter is not strictly false but only the tip of an iceberg of deeper material and kinetic process. The starting points are different in his dissertation and *Capital*, but the method and solution are the same. Marx shows the material and kinetic conditions by which the sensuously apparent object of atomic and economic wealth comes to be in the first place. However, since the condition does not resemble the conditioned, Marx ultimately shows us the nonatomic origins of the atom and the noneconomic origins of the economy.

For Marx, the primary methodological starting point of *appearance* is the key to undermining both atomic and economic discourses of discontinuity and discreteness. In their place we find an alternative kinetic dialectics of materialization or process materialism. In atomism, for example, Marx shows that the idea of a discrete atom is contradictory precisely because theoretical practice itself begins under the general condition of material sensation more broadly. The discreteness of the atom is impossible because of the threefold conditions of its material and kinetic emergence in appearance. If matter appears at all, the following three conditions must be met.

Flows: First of all, the atom must move. If the atom does not move, then it does not appear. The universe would be static. Appearance assumes motion. However, if all matter is in continual motion, then there can be no such thing as a discrete atom. The discreteness of the atom "disappears in the fall." The atom is not distinct or separable from its continual flow, fall, or movement.

Folds: Second, the flow of matter must decline or swerve pedetically, not mechanically or deterministically. If the flow of matter only moved in a straight line, there would be no composition or repulsion and thus no sensation or appearance. Appearance assumes affection, and for something to have affection it must also be sensible to something else. Declination must occur entirely immanently to matter such that it can sense itself as a fold or pleat in itself. Matter's relation to itself Marx calls a "sensuous object" or "form determination."

Fields: Third, the flows and folds of matter must also be able to circulate among one another in relations of mutual transformation and co-production. For objects to appear to other objects (including human and nonhuman objects), they must be able to practically affect one another, not just themselves. Appearance thus assumes the collective self-transformation of the whole of matters.

The goal of Marx's intervention is to draw conclusions about the broader material conditions of appearance, beginning from the specific sensations of theoretical practice. In doing so, Marx shows precisely the problem with all ideas of "abstract individuality and self-sufficiency" (MECW 1: 50), of which the "individual commodity" is one.

The very fact that the commodity appears at all already assumes, as is clear from the doctoral dissertation, a similar threefold material-kinetic condition. Appearance, unlike abstract individuality, is a fundamentally relational process. For the commodity to appear, it must flow, fold, and circulate across a field of co-producing relations. The appearance of discreteness is only a region, an island, a shining surface or glimmer. Wealth appears as a glimmer of shining fragments like the white foam on the crests of ocean waves. As the French poet Paul Valéry writes, "Events are the foam of things; it is the sea that interests me."[3]

In other words, the philosophical and methodological question remains the same from the doctoral dissertation to *Capital:* "Given the present region of sensation, what are the minimal conditions that must hold for this sensation to be?" What conditions must be and have been historically such that the apparent discreteness of wealth as a collection of individual commodities is what we see and feel when we take the object in our hands?

This leads us into the analysis of the "birth of value" in the next chapter. However, before moving on, there is one more crucial point to make regarding Marx's method and the nature of his sensuous "critique" of political economy.

CRITIQUE

Marx's definition and method of critique come directly from his materialist theory of appearance, described in the previous chapter. This same method guides the opening of *Capital*. The method of beginning theoretical practice with the sensuous appearance of the practical body means that the method of presentation of the theory will be the inverse of its practical inquiry. Practice precedes theory, but then theory describes practice, and so on in dialectical procession.

Marx's method is in contrast to almost every other philosopher in the Western tradition, who begins with concepts and ideas and then uses them to explain or redescribe the world. Marx completely inverts this method. From the doctoral dissertation up to *Capital*, Marx names his inverted method "critique,"[4] which always begins somewhere practically and then aims to discover the immanent conditions of emergence for that practice. Its aims are not universal or transcendent "conditions for all being forever and all time" but are strictly regional and immanent. The very performance of the critique is also transformative, to some degree, of what it describes. This is because the critique is immanent to what it is critiquing, as is plain in the *Theses on Feuerbach*.

The Ends of Capital

Theoretical practice therefore begins at the end of a long process of natural and historical materialization, composition, and recomposition. Afterward, from the relative end of this material practice and production in the present, it becomes possible to inquire into some of the conditions and processes that have made our present what it is. Like the owl of Minerva, theoretical practice flies at dusk after the day has ended and looks back on its immanent conditions, but also *alters them*.

Once it has seen the practical and historical conditions of its own sensation and appearance, theoretical practice can then describe them. It does so not from nowhere but precisely from the very point where it is. Theoretical description is thus always backward looking, like the twentieth-century

German Marxist Walter Benjamin's reading of Paul Klee's *Angelus Novus* (1920) as an angel of history (see figure 2.2). The angel of history theoretically faces the past but is continually and practically propelled blind into the future.

Marx therefore writes in the postface to the second edition of *Capital*:

Of course the method of presentation must differ in form from that of inquiry. The latter has to appropriate the material in detail, to analyze its different forms of development and to track down their inner connection. Only after this work

Figure 2.2 Paul Klee, *Angelus Novus* (1920). Image by Author

has been done can the real movement be appropriately presented. If this is done successfully, if the life of the subject-matter is now reflected back in the ideas, then it may appear as if we have before us an a priori construction. (C, 102)

Marx holds the commodity sensuously in his hand and then begins an inquiry into the historical and material conditions under which such sensuous appearance could occur. He begins by looking at the "gray, meticulous, and patiently documentary"[5] details of the material process involved in the long history leading up to the present.

In other words, the emergence of political economy begins where *Capital*, the book, ends: with the advent and process of primitive accumulation and colonialism. Before capitalism and even before economy more broadly, there is a noneconomic process of appropriation. Appropriation simply steals or takes all kinds of matters without counting them as economic value (the appropriation of women's labor, ecological systems, colonial peoples, and so on). Once an initial mass of materials is appropriated, the question becomes how to accumulate more, pay less for it, and get more for what is paid (surplus value). In other words, practically and historically speaking, *Capital* should be read *backward* with respect to its mode of inquiry *and forward* with respect to its mode of presentation.

Once the historical inquiry (from primitive accumulation to value) is completed, Marx is then able to look back upon this history and see how things hang together transhistorically through all the materials covered (from value to primitive accumulation). In other words, only on the condition of the historical inquiry beginning with primitive accumulation do we then reach the book's "conclusion." Marx then can put forward the general conceptual features of value in chapter one. Therefore, what *appear* as a priori concepts in the first chapter of the book are only immanently extracted from the historico-empirical details themselves and not impressed upon them. Although the method of presentation reads as if Marx had just invented conceptual first principles and applied them to the empirical datum of capitalism, it would be a mistake to read it this way. All the core concepts of chapter one—use-value, exchange-value, and value—are immanent to the historical conditions of the inquiry itself.

One of the methodological features of *Marx in Motion* is that it takes this inverted methodology quite seriously and "reads *Capital* backward." This means, among other things, beginning with the "end" in two senses. First, I begin with the *end of the inquiry* by starting with the theoretical apparatus in chapter one. However, I also do so by weaving it together with the *end of the presentation*: the process of primitive accumulation found in part VIII. In other words, I am proposing here a kind of "bookended" or "double-ended" reading of *Capital* in which the historical primacy of primitive accumulation at one "end" is read back into the theory of value at the other "end." That is, I aim to locate a *theory* of primitive accumulation in chapter one that will allow a simultaneous rereading of the "the double ends" of *Capital* all the way back through the whole book.

The conceptual apparatus of *Capital* reaches its apparent limit in part VIII on primitive accumulation, where the concepts of value, surplus, and accumulation have not yet emerged. Yet this limit is only apparent, since it is actually primitive accumulation that is the secret constitutive *becoming of value* from the beginning of chapter one, or so I argue. In other words, in true dialectical fashion, we only realize at the end of the logic of value that the end was already contained logically in the beginning as the dialectical process of becoming itself. Primitive accumulation is therefore the dialectical becoming of all value and of the whole capitalist mode of production.

Dialectical and Historical Materialism

In the opening lines of *Capital*, Marx proposes a complete inversion of traditional philosophical methods and begins not with a priori concepts or ideas but, like Epicurus and Lucretius, with an immanent critique of sensuous appearance:[6]

> My dialectical method is, in its foundations, not only different from the Hegelian, but exactly opposite to it. For Hegel, the process of thinking, which he even transforms into an independent subject, under the name of "the Idea," is the creator of the real world, and the real world is only the external appearance of the idea. With me the reverse is true: the ideal is nothing but the material world reflected in the mind of man, and translated into forms of thought. (C, 102)

Contra Hegel, Marx's dialectical method is a strictly material one in which matter intra-acts with itself *through the human*. Humans and societies are nothing other than "nature hanging together with itself." Nature is not a product of dialectical logic, but dialectical logic emerges immanently within nature. Nature, for Marx, is not the "dead husk" of spirit, as Hegel wrote.[7] The starting points of Hegel and Marx could not be more different. Marx, following Epicurus, begins with sensuous appearance of moving matters, while Hegel begins with the presupposition-less thought of being in itself. It is the history of matter in motion that makes possible theoretical practice, not the other way around.

However, Marx's inversion of Hegel's dialectical method should not be understood as a "mere inversion," as I have shown in detail. Marx is not just giving us a Hegelian dialectic with matter instead of mind; the inversion changes the dialectic. Instead of deterministic laws of motion, Marx offers *pedetic flows*. Instead of logically opposing moments, Marx offers *kinetic folds*. Instead of logical synthesis, Marx offers an open-ended process of circulation. Marx's dialectic is therefore historical as well insofar as it looks to the generative movement of matter itself as the origin, process, and product of the conditions of theoretical inquiry. The "rational" or material-kinetic form of the dialectic therefore has dramatically different consequences:

> In its mystified form, the dialectic became the fashion in Germany, because it seemed to transfigure and glorify what exists. In its rational form, it is a scandal and an abomination to the bourgeoisie and its doctrinaire spokesmen because it includes in its positive understanding of what exists a simultaneous recognition of its negation, its inevitable destruction; because it regards every historically developed form as being in a fluid state, in motion, [*Flusse der Bewegung*] and therefore grasps its transient aspect as well; and because it does not let itself be impressed by anything, being in its very essence critical and revolutionary. (C, 103)

Hegel's mystified idealist dialectic appears to show the glory of the mind and all that has come to be as the end, product, or goal of historical progress: the end of history. The rational or materialist dialectic for Marx, however, as pedetic, folded, and open-ended, shows precisely the opposite: that the current state of affairs is only a metastable product of a more primary kinetic and fluid process. Capitalism is not the end of history. Every historical form is in a state of fluid motion.

It is precisely the movement and motion of the materialist dialectic that gives it its properly critical and revolutionary character. The dialectic is "critical" insofar as matter is in motion, and this motion resists any attempt to impress or stamp a form upon it once and for all. This does not mean that matter is formless or that revolution is formless or any such metaphysical statement. Rather, through motion, matter gives itself its own "form determinations," as shown in the previous chapter, but none is permanent, and all are open to further transformation.

Critique is the continual change and mutation of reality through practice. Again, critique is not just theoretical criticism but actually and practically does something transformative. Thus the commodity appears as produced by "formal determinants that it contains as a commodity and which stamp it as a commodity" (C, 1059). The commodity in this light is just one stamp or impression of a continually changing and self-forming process of material kinetic formalization. However, the very essence of critique is to show its kinetically open and pedetic character.

Transcendental Materialism

Critique, for Marx, is not and cannot be merely a historical study or an empirical or deterministic material chronology of previous "facts" leading up to the present objectively. A description of what happened will not yield the conditions of its emergence. Furthermore, critique cannot be merely conceptual or based on a priori notions applied to history. A conceptual historical method sees only the subjective side of its own ideas reflected back.

For Marx, historical method is "transcendentally material" insofar as it reveals the real and material patterns or processes that must have occurred historically such that theoretical practice itself would have been capable of locating such patterns in the first place. In other words, there are transcendental conditions for Marx, but they are not ideal, as they are in Kant, or universal as they are in Hegel. Rather, Marx begins with the reality of practice and then aims to discover the real material conditions for that practice.

Dialectical and historical materialism, then, is not about identifying universal and deterministic laws of motion but rather regional patterns of motion that already are immanent features of the present that they condition. Every historical formation is not determined by ironclad laws of Democritean or Hegelian necessity but rather by a constant fluid state of motion. Marx calls this the *Flusse der Bewegung*, that resists every attempt to impress a permanent form upon it. The passage quoted above from the postface to *Capital* is impossible to reconcile with any so-called deterministic theory of history in Marx. Marx is extremely clear here: history throws off every attempt to formalize it once and for all. Revolutionary critique alone realizes the creative and pedetic nature of matter to move and transform itself further.

Historical analysis, then, is not the study of the development of forms toward a final end. Marx is explicit about this in the *Grundrisse*. For Marx, we can only do a history of political economy and maintain a kinetic materialism because of the regional- or historical-ontological nature of the inquiry. The conditions for the present have not disappeared, but the present appears as a rich and hybrid composition of other forms previously and elsewhere. As Marx writes:

The concrete is concrete because it is the concentration of many determinations, hence unity of the diverse. It appears in the process of thinking, therefore, as a process of concentration, as a result, not as a point of departure, even though it is the point of departure in reality and hence also the point of departure for observation [*Anschauung*] and conception. (G, 101)

The appearance of a concrete commodity in one's hand is concrete precisely because of all the numerous other form determinations and processes that bring it about. It does not stand on its own, nor do our ideas about it, whose views (*Anschauung*) are entangled relationally with the sensuous appearance of the commodity. We can inquire into the real historical conditions of the object are precisely because the object is already a manifold concentration of numerous processes that have existed and continue to persist in the production of the object.

Conceptually, chapter one of *Capital* is possible only because of the rich material and historical conditions from which it was abstracted: "As a rule, the most general abstractions arise only in the midst of the richest possible concrete development, where one thing appears as common to many, to all" (G, 104). The general character of a concept such as "production" is possible not as an abstract or universal idea but only insofar as it refers transhistorically and immanently to the history of its emergence:

Bourgeois society is the most developed and the most complex historic organization of production. The categories which express its relations, the comprehension of its structure, thereby also allows insights into the structure and the relations of production of all the vanished social formations out of whose ruins and elements it built itself up, whose partly still unconquered remnants are carried along within it, whose mere nuances have developed explicit significance within it, etc. Human anatomy contains a key to the anatomy of the ape. (G, 105).

Only because contemporary bourgeois society still carries within it the remnants and ruins of previous historical processes can we perform a historical ontology of the conditions of our contemporary being. Given that contemporary being is a complex and hybrid mixture of numerous previous patterns, we cannot provide an abstract theory of the present without reference to all these prior patterns from which it emerged. One historical formation does not develop teleologically from the other, but all of them mix together relationally at each state. The present, simply by virtue of being the present, happens to be the most complex mixture and thus provides us the vantage (*Anschauung*) from which to get at the hidden conditions just below the shimmering (*erscheinen*) surface of the commodity.

These conditions are not the "true" below the "false" but rather the real itself folded up over itself in sensuous appearance. Historical ontology, then, is more like unfolding origami than it is like looking behind a mask of semblance to find reality. History is less a series of discrete masks, as Nietzsche writes, than like the unraveling of a single folded and knotted string.[8] The present is the past folded up into a knotted and unevenly distributed surface. Every unfolding is not simply the revelation of more previous truth, but rather, as Marx says, a practical and transformative activity. It is something that changes the whole. Historical ontology is not merely interpretation but also transformation at the same time. Unfolding changes the shining surface. The revolutionary power of critique is not to unmask but to transform, unfold, and redistribute things. Production and product are completely woven into each other.

Human anatomy contains a key to the anatomy of the ape, as Marx says, not because we project human anatomy onto the ape (humanism) but because the human carries within it the "still-unconquered remnants" of the ape. Historical ontology is not an anthropocentric constructivist projection of the present back onto the past but rather the discovery of the living past within the present itself. It is the material and sensuous nonhuman body of the ape within us that allows us to discover the real, material, and historical conditions under which our sensuous materiality came to be. The ape does not exist because of false or antirealist anthropocentric constructions we project onto the ape, but the complete opposite. We exist only because the ape already existed and exists in us still, providing the very real material conditions by which a theoretical practice of anatomy can inquire into the anatomy of the ape in the first place.

CONCLUSION

The opening two lines of *Capital* are indeed dense but worth unpacking. From them we can see the primary orientation of the methodological problem with political economy: the appearance of discrete individual atomic commodities. In order to unravel this shining appearance, Marx provides neither a merely empirical history nor a metaphysics of value but a historical and critical ontology of the present. Dialectical critique exposes the material-kinetic conditions immanent to sensuous appearance.

The first major subject of this method is to show the kinetic process by which the commodity is produced. This will be discussed in the next chapter.

CHAPTER 3

The Birth of Value

The commodity first appears as a simple individual unit, but it is vastly more complex than this. The first complexity, Marx notes, is its twofold aspect as use-value and value. This twofold nature of the commodity derives from the commodity's existence as a *thing* with both quality and quantity.

The goal of this chapter is to show the material conditions for the idea of use-value through a close reading of the first two pages of *Capital*. I begin from Marx's theory of *things*, of which commodities are particular types. I also look at his theory of *material production*, within which human labor is one particular type. Chapters 1 and 2 have laid some of this groundwork. This chapter aims to remedy one of the shortfalls of previous interpretations of *Capital*: that they have tended to begin and end the analysis of the commodity and of labor strictly at the level of the *human*. In this chapter I look more closely at the material and nonhuman basis of the commodity.

When scholars have looked at Marx's things, objects, appearances, qualities, and quantities, they have typically returned to Hegel for their theoretical context. This makes perfect sense, but it makes just as much sense to return to Epicurus and Lucretius, who also held robust theories of things, objects, qualities, quantities, and appearance. In fact, I argue, it actually makes more sense to return to Epicurus and Lucretius, given their explicit materialism and Marx's clear repudiation of Hegel in both his dissertation and *Capital*. Unfortunately, this line of research has not been pursued, for the reasons I mentioned in the introduction. So the aim of this chapter is to reinterpret Marx's theory of "objects" in *Capital* based on his theory of kinetic materialism from his dissertation.

Marx in Motion. Thomas Nail, Oxford University Press (2020). © Oxford University Press.
DOI: 10.1093/oso/9780197526477.001.0001

This may sound like a minor gesture, but it is exciting to see what new meanings can be uncovered in such a well-read text as *Capital* by looking at it from a different perspective. Marx's dissertation and *Capital* are typically treated as having almost nothing in common with each other. However, I hope to show in this book, among other things, that a number of important terms and ideas connect the two works and make possible a new way of reading *Capital*.

In particular, this chapter argues that it is not human use-value alone that provides the basis of value (abstract labor time) but also, and more important, *extra-human* and other *nonvalued* material processes. In other words, this chapter also aims to set the stage for a material-kinetic theory of value to be developed in future chapters.

THEORY OF THE OBJECT

Marx begins his theory of the commodity with the theory of the object. Unfortunately, as with many terms in chapter one of *Capital*, Marx simply uses this term without explaining or referring directly to his previous writings on this subject. Therefore, to understand the passage cited here will require a bit of background and context to situate the commodity first and foremost as an *object* and *thing*.[1] Interestingly, in earlier drafts of *Capital*, Marx did not begin with the commodity at all but with production. As we will see, however, Marx's theory of the object already contains in it a theory of material production and consumption:

> The commodity is, first of all, an external [*äußerer*] object [*Gegenstand*], a thing [*Ding*] which through [*durch*] its qualities [*Eigenschaften*] satisfies human needs [*Bedürfnisse*] of whatever kind. The needs, whether they arise; for example, from the stomach, or the imagination, makes no difference. Nor does it matter here how the thing satisfies man's need, whether directly as a means of subsistence, i.e. an object of consumption, or indirectly as a means of production. (C, 125)

Since the commodity is first of all an external object or thing, let us begin our analysis with Marx's theory of the object, first developed in his dissertation and manuscripts. The commodity is a specific kind of thing. Therefore, I begin with the broader context or conceptual category of which the commodity is only one instance.

The German word *Gegenstand* (object) gives us an initial sense of what an object is for Marx. An object is something that "moves against" (*gegen*) itself such that it stays or stands (*stehen*) where it is. The object continually stays where it is by throwing itself back against itself. The Latin origins of the English word "object" indicate a similar kinetic structure: *ob-* ("against") + *iaciō* ("I throw"). The object is thus a fundamentally kinetic process: a flow of matter folded and thrown against itself or looped back around itself. It is like an eddy in a river current. It returns to itself again and again and in doing so stays (*stehen*). But its staying or standing is something that occurs only through its moving against or back onto itself continually.

The Thing

This kinetic description of the object helps make sense of the twofold character of the thing. A thing, according to Marx, has both an extensive or objective aspect (*äußerer*) and an intensive or qualitative aspect (*Eigenschaften*). Here I examine each in turn to understand the twofold nature of the thing, of which the commodity is a particular type.

Extensive: The thing is first of all an *external or extensive object*. In his manuscripts, Marx writes that

> *to be* objective, natural and sensuous, and at the same time to have object nature and sense outside oneself, or oneself to be object nature and sense for a third party, is one and the same thing. . . . Hunger is an acknowledged need of my body for an *object* existing outside it indispensable to its integration and to the expression of its essential being. The sun is the *object* of the plant—an indispensable object to it confirming its life—just as the plant is an object of the sun, being an *expression* of the life-awakening power of the sun, of the sun's *objective* essential power. A being which does not have its nature outside itself is not a *natural* being, and plays no part in the system of nature. A being which has no object outside itself is not an objective being. A being which is not itself an object for some third being has no being for its *object*; i.e., it is not objectively related. Its being is not objective. A non-objective being is a *non-being*. (MECW 3: 336–337, emphases in original)

To be is to be an object. To be an object is to have an externality or an extension and thus to relate externally to other objects that are also mutually external to one another. The sun is an object for the plant, and the plant is an object for the sun. External object relations are not anthropocentric or even reducible to biocentric criteria of "living labor." Objects are always objects of production (the sun's objective production for photons) and consumption or reproduction (the plant's consumption of photons and its production of chlorophyll). As a natural being, the human being is just one kind of collection of objects that is also both productive and reproductive.

The first feature of the thing is that it has an objective or extensive character that puts it into relation with the rest of external nature.

Intensive: The second feature of the thing is that it has an *internal* or *intensive* aspect. The German word *Eigen* used here means "internal," "own," "quality," or "proprietary." So the thing has both an objective aspect defined by its externality and a subjective or qualitative aspect (*Eigenschaften*) defined by its internality. The twofold aspects (*Faktor*) of the thing are absolutely inseparable. All things have this dual character, each necessarily entailed in the other. Immediately following the theory of the external object, Marx describes its immanent continuity with qualitative and sensuous aspects of the thing:

> But a *non-objective* being is an unreal, non-sensuous thing—a product of mere thought (i.e., of mere imagination)—an abstraction. To be *sensuous*, that is, to be really existing, means to be an object of sense, to be a *sensuous* object and thus to have sensuous objects outside oneself—objects of one's sensuousness. To be sensuous is to *suffer*. (MECW 3: 337, emphases in original)

An object without any qualities is a pure mental abstraction. This follows from the definition of the object as external. If objects have an externality, they must have this externality with respect to other external objects that sense others outside themselves and are in turn sensed by those others. There are only "sensuous objects," as Marx stresses continually in the manuscripts. Objects are always sensuous (sensing and sensible), and sensations are always objective (mutually external).

In other words, the whole world of objects co-constitute one another through the co-production and consumption of their mutual sensation and collective self-transformation. The human is a natural object like the others, and so "neither nature objectively nor nature subjectively is directly given in a form adequate to the *human* being. And as everything natural has to *come into being, man* too has his act of origin—*history*" (MECW 3: 337, emphases in original). Since every object is located in and continually transformed by history, there is no such thing as a purely objective or purely subjective access to nature as a whole. All things practically produce and consume; all things sense and are sensed, in a continually transforming network of historical material relations. This is precisely why Marx begins *Capital* methodologically with the sensuous *appearance* of the commodity.

Marx first put this twofold theory of the thing in his doctoral dissertation. The twofold problem with Democritus's atomism was that he provided a theory of the thing as a passive, quality-less, material-external object following mechanistic and deterministic laws: the atom. In doing so, however, he also had to introduce a purely subjective theory of knowledge in which the being of the atom is something that can only be thought ideally. All the qualities that appear in the world, for Democritus, are mere semblances of the purely objective, quality-less atoms, known only to our skeptical minds. Epicurus, according to Marx, solved this problem by defining the atoms as *flows of matter* whose self-affection, produced through kinetic acts of folding, continually generate new qualities and dissolve them. In this interpretation, subject and object, form and matter, become two aspects of the same *process of kinetic folding*:

> The contradiction between existence and essence, between matter and form, which is inherent in the concept of the atom, emerges in the individual atom itself once it is endowed with qualities. It is from repulsion and the ensuing conglomerations of the qualified atoms that the world of appearance now emerges (DD, 130).

Extended and existing material objects can only appear sensuously. Intensive and essential formal sensations can only appear objectively. The two always occur together.

The Fold

This leads us directly to a kinetic solution of the apparent contradiction between externality (objectivity) and internality (sensuousness) in the sensuous object. In his doctoral dissertation, Marx, through Epicurus and Lucretius, resolves the Democritean antinomy of subject and object by theorizing the thing as a *kinetic fold*:

> If Epicurus therefore represents the materiality of the atom in terms of its motion along a straight line, he has given reality to its form-determination in the declination from the straight line, and these opposed determinations are represented as directly opposed motions. (DD, 112)

The kinetic flow of matter curves and returns to itself and others in sensation and affection. It is precisely the curvature of the flow of matter that gives it its shape or "form-determination." Form is the kinetic curvature of matter. But again, Marx is clear that this is not a chronological description in which first there are straight flows, then there are spontaneous swerves, and so on. There is only the threefold kinetic dialectic.

In the fold, "their materiality, which was posited in the fall in a straight line, and the form-determination, which was established in the declination, are united synthetically" (DD, 117). Matter and form are united kinetically as a process of motion and pedetic curvature. "Motion is established as self-determination" and produces a "sensuous form" (DD, 118). The atom "objectifies the contradiction" between matter and form. The atom or thing thus has both a subjective aspect in its kinetic formation and an objective aspect in its kinetic materialization. As Marx says, "Epicurus makes the contradiction between matter and form the characteristic of the nature of appearance" (DD, 133).

The pedetic movement of matter becomes "the reflection of appearance in itself, the nature of appearance is justly posited as objective, sensation is justly made the real criterion of concrete nature" (DD, 134). The reflection or intra-action of matter with itself occurs in the kinetic self-affection of the fold. Since "sensuous perception reflected in itself" occurs kinetically through the declination, this produces a fold. Nature senses itself through the kinetic curvature and reflection of matter back onto itself.

The point is this: what is absolutely clear in Marx's theory of the sensuous object from his earlier works is that objects and things, including the commodity, cannot be thought of as merely passive, individual, inert units of discrete matter for subjective sensation or consumption by humans. Human objects and commodity objects are both active and passive groups of sensuous objects. Together they form a nonanthropocentric assemblage of objects with their own collective agency.

THE COMMODITY

The commodity is first and foremost a sensuous object. But it is also a specific type of sensuous object that "satisfies human needs [Bedürfnisse] of whatever kind" (C, 125). As previously discussed, all kinds of objects are sensing and satisfying one another's desires, like the sun and the plant. However, the commodity is a specific kind of object that, among other things, satisfies the desires of the *human*.

The human, however, is also nothing but a specific composition of sensuous objects desiring one another. Marx is also clear that the "earth, [is] the 'universal object,'"[2] of which the human is merely one desiring region. Human desire only occurs through nature "by means of which and in which man's labour can be embodied."[3] It follows, then, that humans are not the origin of desire but simply a *region of it*, as Marx says. "Human sensuous-ness is the existing reflection of the sensuous world in itself" (DD, 134). "These forms of the things stream constantly forth from them and pene-trate into the senses and in precisely this way allow the objects to appear. Thus in hearing, nature hears itself, in smelling it smells itself, in seeing, it sees itself. Human sensuousness is therefore the medium in which natural processes are reflected as in a focus and ignited into the light of appear-ance" (DD, 135).

The human sensuous object is one focus or medium in which nature is reflected in itself and should not be thought of as the only kind of object that desires or senses other objects. Human sensation and desire get this capacity from nature, not the other way around. The human is just one region or focus where nature has folded itself up into a highly complex knot. From this knot of object relations, a fire is lit that reflects its own shining (*erscheinen*) light back out (*erscheinen*) onto the world of appear-ance (*erscheinen*).

Desire

The commodity is a thing with qualities that satisfy human desires. First of all, Marx's theory of desire does not consider the origin of that desire, that is, from the stomach, the imagination, and so on. This is because the origin of desire is a metaphysical question that would only lead us to ahistorical speculation. There is no single source or end of desire, no beginning and no end, just as Lucretius sings.[4]

Second, Marx says it "does not matter how the thing satisfies man's need, whether directly as a means of subsistence, i.e. an object of consump-tion or indirectly as a means of production" (C, 125). This is the case prima-rily because desire *as sensation* is both productive and consumptive at the same time. The twofold nature of production and consumption follows the twofold nature of all things. For example, the plant *consumes* sunlight and reproduces itself at the same time that it *produces* oxygen and other quali-ties as well. The sun consumes helium and hydrogen and produces photons at the same time. It does not matter which side we look at—we still see the sensuous object acting and interacting with other sensuous objects.

Production and consumption: Desire (production) and satisfaction (consumption) are the two sides of the externality of objects: the flow of matter and the fold of form. Production flows, and consumption folds, con-tinually consuming what it produces and producing or transforming what it consumes.

Desire, for Marx, according to his definition of sensuous objects, cannot be a reductively anthropic or purely subjective desire for a passive object. Nature and its qualities are not "just there" passively awaiting consumption. Nature produces qualities that "use" (desire and satisfy) one another. Again, humans are just tiny regions within a much larger material-kinetic process of production. Therefore, any theory of human use and desire must be understood in the larger context of what Marx calls "material production" within which such desire/usage occurs.

The doctoral dissertation explicitly provides the philosophical context for this material-kinetic production of "sensuous objects" or "sensuous forms." Qualities are products produced by, in, and through nature. As Marx writes throughout his economic works, sensuous objects are "products of the earth" (MECW 19: 333) because "the earth [is] the source of all production and all life" (MECW 18: 43, 416). He writes that "the earth is the reservoir, from whose BOWELS the use values are to be torn" (MECW 31: 465). Human production is only a region of this expanded definition of what I hereafter refer to as the "material production" of sensuous nature more broadly.

Marx is quite explicit in his attribution of all material production to the earth: "Bourgeois industry and commerce create these material conditions of a new world in the same way as geological revolutions have created the surface of the earth" (MECW 12: 222). Quite literally, bourgeois industry is a geological force that moves minerals in the form of coal, cotton, and human migrant bodies. Geological production changes the distribution of the earth, and so does human society, precisely because both are processes of material production.

"The fact that man is a corporeal, living, real, sensuous, objective being and a force of nature, means that he has real, sensuous objects as the object of his being and the expression of his life, or that he can only express his life through real, sensuous objects."[5] Just as humans produce products, so "'a natural thing' [is the] power or produce of the earth" (MECW 31: 469). Human production and consumption is accordingly merely "the material of nature transferred into the human organism."[6]

There is first and foremost a primary process of sensuous material production within which humans emerge and begin to desire in specific ways. Human production and the commodity in particular are like islands in a vast ocean of material production.

Desire is first a kind of sensation and is something active or materially productive, in the sense that it goes outside itself and sensuously uses the qualities of objects. Whether it uses them directly in consumption or indirectly to produce something else does not matter, because both require an active or productive movement outside itself. Second, consumption is not achieved without the production of consumption, that is, without the performative act of shaping its appropriation by an external quality. Consumption is a practice and must be actively produced by the real qualities of the thing itself.

For Marx there is no ontological division between production and consumption; both are aspects of the same material process of desire. Desire is not merely subjective (lacking its object) or objective (contained or made entirely by the object itself); it is the material dialectic between production and consumption, sense and sensation. There is nothing uniquely human about sensuous desire, even if there is something unique about the desire of specific humans or types of animals. Every object, as a kinetic flow of matter, continually reproduces (consumes) itself and produces or shapes the way that external objects can consume it. In this sense, to desire or "use" something means that the object is both active and passive. This is the sense in which the object can never be a "mere [passive] natural object" but is already an active sensuous natural object that produces or shapes the subject that consumes it.

Consumption is thus always an active production of consumption (G, 91–93). Consumption also assumes that the object being used is active in reproducing itself and passive insofar as it can be appropriated by something else. As Marx says in the *Grundrisse*:

> Production, then, is also immediately consumption—consumption is also immediately production. Each is mediately its opposite. But at the same time a mediating movement takes place between the two. Production mediates consumption; it creates the latter's material; without it consumption would lack an object. But consumption also mediates production, in that it alone creates for the products the subject for whom they are products. (G, 91)

Production and consumption occur simultaneously as the two aspects of the same kinetic process or "movement" of sensation: "as moments of one process" (G, 94). But again, subjective production and objective consumption are *not just something humans do*. To restrict sensation to humans would deny the dialectical nature of all other sensuous matters and to posit some things as one-sidedly passive and without agency—a typical bourgeois move. All things must be both subjective and objective to some degree. This is what Marx's doctoral dissertation, Epicurus, and Lucretius all teach us.

Quality and Quantity

The commodity is a thing, but it is a thing that is desired (produced and consumed) or "used" by humans. Like all things, it is defined extensively and intensively or quantitatively and qualitatively:

> Every useful [*nützliche*] thing, for example, iron, paper, etc., may be looked at from the two points of view [*doppeltem*] of quality and quantity. (C, 125)

The useful thing is twofold (*doppeltem*) or (*zweifach*), as we have seen. The twofold nature of the thing, however, is not a *logical* feature of the thing as it is in Hegel but a material-kinetic feature produced by the tendency of matter to move and fold over itself and produce sensation, as it is in Epicurus and Lucretius. A quality is matter's sensation of itself, as Marx describes in the doctoral dissertation. The exterior is produced by the fold of the interior, and the interior is produced by the fold of the exterior at the same time. Interior and exterior are the twofolds of the continual flow of matter.

THE MULTIPLICITY OF QUALITIES

Every thing (*Ding*) contains a multiplicity of qualities, which come into being through the movement of folding. Therefore, matter can always fold and unfold itself in new ways. Again, this is the brilliant insight of Epicurus against Democritus. For Democritus, matter has no qualities at all, and the qualities that do appear are merely semblances. For Epicurus, on the other hand, matter is always and continually *becoming sensuous*. Its sensuousness changes and mutates kinetically in its real appearance. Marx writes:

> Every such [*solches*] thing is a whole [*Ganzes*] composed of many [*vieler*] qualities [*Eigenschaften*]; it can therefore be useful [*nützlich*] in various ways. The discovery [*entdecken*] of these ways and hence of the manifold [*mannigfachen*] uses of things is the work of history. (C, 125)

Every thing as a whole or singular quantity has an indefinitely great many qualities, which are the condition for the use or desire between things. This is an absolutely crucial material condition for both the unlimited possibility of desire and the limitless expansion of capitalist value creation. If qualities were fixed, then desires between qualities would be fixed, history would be fixed, and capitalist value creation would be absolutely limited to the appropriation of these qualities. History would have a necessary and pregiven limit, as it does in Hegel.

However, for Marx and Epicurus, the fact that qualities emerge and dissolve through the movement of folding means that the process of qualification is open, as are history, desire, and capitalist value creation. In fact, precisely because desire is itself a performative act that is both productive and consumptive, it acts on and transforms the qualities being produced and consumed. This means that desire and use should be understood as entirely immanent to the continual kinetic transformation of the qualities themselves. Consumption is not just destruction. When the plant consumes photons, it transforms them into energy, motion, cells, and so on. Consumption is the productive creation of new qualities and thus new desires.

Things therefore are not discrete units with fixed qualities or essences. Rather, matter folds up into things with this twofold character of being both productive of new qualities and consumptive of them. Desire, for Marx, by his definitions previously discussed, cannot be immaterial, vital, subjective, or strictly human. Rather, desire is nothing more than the immanent transformation of matter-forms or sensuous objects. Desire is the endless multiplication or many-folding of qualities.

History

History is the name of the process by which matter is folded and unfolded, produced and consumed into these various sides of quality and quantity, through desire. History makes possible the manifold (*mannigfachen*) existence of qualities and the manifold desire of those qualities at the same time.

History folds and unfolds the many different sides (*Seiten*) of things, and from this springs the manifold usages of things. "The discovery [*entdecken*] of these ways and hence of the manifold [*mannigfachen*] uses of things is the work of history" (C, 125). History is the kinetic process by which matter folds and produces qualities that can be desired. It is an endless proliferation of qualities and an endless invention of new desires.

Discovery (*entdecken*) here does not mean, for Marx, finding something already there; *entdecken* literally means the act of "un-covering" as itself a *productive act* in which something closed is opened up and unfolded through the act of the uncovering itself. Unfolding *changes* what was folded. Through production and consumption, new qualities are generated and transformed. "Consumption creates the need for new production" (G, 91). Consumption is not merely a passive process of "physical" objects "out there." Rather, discovery and consumption are active processes of production that transform qualities and produce new ones at the same time.

Production is immediately consumption, and both are immediately a material transformation.

Measurement

The historical ontological primacy of sensuously produced and consumed qualities also means that any subsequent attempt to measure these qualities must also assume the prior historical process of their generation, transformation, and decay. Just as qualities are processes of emergence and multiplicity, so are the techniques for measuring these qualities by some standard of measurement:

> So also is the invention of socially recognized standards of measurement for the quantities of these useful objects. The diversity of the measures for commodities [*Waarenmaße*] arises in part from the diverse nature of the objects to be measured [*messenden Gegenstände*], and in part from convention. (C, 125–126)

Measurement is not simply quantification but assumes prior qualities and quantities in things such that two or more things can be compared or coordinated with one another. Quantity alone is just the "oneness" or unity of the object. Measurement, however, links one thing (a quantity with qualities) to another thing (quantity with qualities). The invention of standardized weights and measures in ancient Mesopotamia, for example, selected some things (a bar of silver with a fixed quality and quantity) and used them to compare things with one another through measure. This practice of comparing two or more things through a third thing is already the basis of exchange-value, as discussed in the next chapter.

Two key points follow from the usage of this third thing. First, the practice of measurement and exchange-value cannot be absolutely arbitrary or purely socially constructed acts. They have their material conditions in the specific qualities produced by natural things. Human measurement must respond to existing qualities, which it can change and which change it dialectically. This is what Marx means when he says that measurement, of which exchange-value is one type, is defined in part by the natural qualities of sensuous objects but also in part by social convention. The importance of this point is crucial for understanding exchange-value more broadly in the next chapter.

Marx is not a constructivist. Like the history of measurement, sensuous desire and "use-values" are not something humans just arbitrarily make up, either subjectively or socially. Use-value really and materially occurs in the kinetic production and consumption of the real bodies and their real qualities. Again, humans are not the sole producers of nature and matter. Their activity, like the rest of nature's activity, is simply the formation and reformation of matters, which are neither created ex nihilo nor destroyed. Marx writes:

> The usefulness of a thing makes it a use-value. But this usefulness does not dangle in midair. It is conditioned [*bedingt*] by [*durch*] the qualities [*Eigenschaften*] of the commodity-body [*Waarenkörpers*], and has no existence apart from the latter; It is therefore the commodity-body [*Waarenkörpers*] itself, for instance iron, corn, a diamond, which is the use-value or useful thing [*Gut*]. The being [*sein*] of this quality does not hang [*hängt*] on whether a great deal of appropriation [*Aneignung*] was required by humans to obtain these useful qualities or how little the labor cost [*kostet*]. (C, 126)

The usefulness of a thing is really and concretely tied to the real qualities of the thing, because the qualities are really in the sensuous body (*Körper*) of the thing. The desire between qualities is conditioned on the real externality of those qualities from one another and their sensuous relation. The English translation of *Waarenkörpers* as "physical properties" unfortunately makes it sound like these are universal, ahistorical, and unrelationally constituted aspects of the object. But for Marx, the sensuous object is never only "in itself." Sensuous objects, according to Epicurus and Marx, have no fixed unchanging "properties" but are the qualities they are only in their kinetic process of folding and unfolding. All qualities are real, sensuous qualities and not primary or secondary properties. The qualities of things are not semblances or absolute physical properties. Qualities change one another through their relation. Iron and corn are both continually transformed by nature and by human social relations. To talk of fixed physical properties here is misleading.

Hence the "body" of the commodity is the sensuous body full of kinetic qualities through which desire itself is conditioned but which desire also conditions dialectically. As we have seen, just as there is a mutual coconditioning or co-production between production and consumption in desire or use, so there is also a mutual conditioning of qualities as they are being used or desired by one another. Desire or use is nothing other than the process by which qualities fold and unfold with one another.

Plants, for example, do not have "properties" independent from the sun and their relation to the atmosphere that provides their carbon dioxide and water. Changes in the use-ratios of these qualities to one another actually change the kinds of qualities that can emerge in the first place. Use-value is therefore a kind of feedback system. But it is a real feedback, not a purely human or social construction.

The being of a quality does not hang (*hängt*) by itself, Marx says, floating (*schwebt*) as an abstract individual. Qualities always hang together (*zusammenhängen*) in relations of mutual co-production, as Marx stresses throughout his work. Furthermore, the being of qualities does not hang (*hängt*) solely on the act of appropriation (*Aneignung*). Qualities are not determined unilaterally by subjective desire. Rather, qualities both produce the desire for their consumption and are produced or changed by the desire for them. "Thus production produces consumption (1) by creating the material for it; (2) by determining the manner of consumption; and (3) by creating the products, initially posited by it objects" (G, 92). It is therefore only through the immanent *process or movement of desire itself* (production and consumption) that qualities are co-produced. How qualities are appropriated and the cost of labor to appropriate them are factors in the transformation of their usage, but these methods also depend on the real qualities themselves.

THE BEARERS OF VALUE

The multiplicity of qualities and the body of the commodity are absolutely crucial aspects to Marx's material-kinetic theory of value because they are the "material bearers of value":

> When examining use-values, we always assume we are dealing with definite quantities, such as dozens of watches, yards of linen, or tons of iron. The use-values of commodities provide the material for a special branch of knowledge, namely the commercial knowledge of commodities. Use-values are only realized [*verwirklicht*] in use or in consumption. They constitute [*bildenden*] the material content [*stofflichen*] of wealth, whatever its form may be, in the form of society to be considered here they are also the material bearers [*Träger*] of . . . exchange-value. (C, 126)

As previously discussed, use-value is realized only through an immanent process of production and consumption. There is no production without some kind of consumption. There is no consumption without some kind of production. A use-value is a quality-in-motion. It is a quality whose being is dialectally transformed through a series of production-consumption circuits. Just as measurement, appropriation, and labor cost all depend on the prior material production of qualities, so all wealth, of whatever historical form, depends on qualities-in-motion as its material bearers. Matter is in continual movement as its form is iteratively determined. However, the process of materialization or folding bears or supports all other forms that come to stamp it.

In other words, the process of kinetic materialization is immanent to its own form determination. This also produces sensuous qualities. The process and its qualities are the material basis and content of what gets formed historically. All accumulation or appropriation therefore relies on a previous or primitive accumulation of material production. The value-form is limited selection of the kinetic process of materialization, which supports or bears value. Value is something that is born(e).

Marx's language in the previously cited passage is highly kinetic. The process of using or desiring qualities (use-value) makes a path or passage (*bildenden*) that constitutes the materiality of all forms of wealth. The material process of qualification is the carrier, support, or holder (*Träger*) of all value. This is the first time of many that Marx will use the German word *Träger* in *Capital*, but it is not the first time he has used it in his work. Marx first used this word, unsurprisingly, in his doctoral dissertation, where he describes the atoms as the material bearers of their forms. "Insofar as [the atom] proceeds to reality, it sinks down to the material basis which, as the bearer [*Träger*] of a world of manifold relations, never exists but in forms which are indifferent and external to it" (DD, 130). This passage parallels the one in *Capital* almost exactly. Use-values and atoms are only "realized or proceed to reality" through their "formation or consumption" and thus "bear their manifold forms" as formation's material kinetic or processual support.

The flow of material qualities is only realized or materialized in their formal consumption or folds. Without the process of folding or relation, there are no real material qualities to kinetically bear, carry, and maintain their forms. Another key insight contained in this concept of the bearer or maintainer (*Träger*) is that forms are not static or fixed but are kinetically maintained through cycles of reproduction (production-consumption). There are no fixed Platonic forms or Aristotelian teleological purposes fixed in things from the beginning. Forms and purposes emerge through the interchange or material kinetic maintenance and reproduction (*tragen*) of those forms and purposes. Form is kinomorphic and purpose is kinotelic, because both must be borne or birthed.

The Birth of Value

Sensuous qualities are the material-kinetic bearers in several senses contained in the meaning of the German verb *tragen*. *Tragen* does not mean just to support, maintain, or carry but also to *give birth* to, as in to "bear" a child or in the sense in which the earth "bears" a crop or a tree "bears" fruit. Clothing too is "borne" or carried, in German. *Tragen* is also "to take." For Marx, sensuous material qualities are thus linked to the entire sphere of historically appropriated production: women's activity, the earth's products, and the material conditions, such as clothing, that are the material support of human bodies. The origins and source of social value come from the birth and bearing activity of women, nature, and the body.

These bearers, for Marx, are the vast "reservoir" for the primitive accumulation of sensuous objects. *Tragen* is not some activity "just there" off to the side of value. *Tragen* is immanent to value as its hidden, or what Marx will call its "secret," support. It is the material-kinetic condition for the emergence of the value-form (the commodity) itself. *Tragen* also contains the ambiguity that it is both the productive bearing of creation and also the "taking" of such creation. Sensuous qualities or things are continually produced and consumed without necessarily being mediated by any particular value-form like the commodity. The birth and bearing of qualities, as well as the taking of them, are the dual conditions for the emergence of the value-form as such. Humans are born by women, food is born by the earth, and clothing is born by the body—but all these are also "taken" as so many "free gifts of nature" and used as material support for the invention of the capitalist value-form.[7]

This is an absolutely essential point, which this book develops: the value-form is not separate from the qualities that immanently support and maintain it. Value is born by the direct appropriation of use-values of all kinds. However, only a small portion of this productive activity is valued as waged labor time. In other words, that which bears (*Träger*) is simply *taken* and used to support and carry the value-form.

The term "value," as used by Marx, explicitly refers to a *historical* mode of production invented by capitalism. There are no *ontological* dualisms in nature, for Marx, as we saw in the dissertation. The capitalist mode of production *acts as if* there were a dualism between use-value and exchange value. Marx's critique, though, is that this is a *historical* division that we should abolish. It is the historical division and contradiction at the heart of capitalism's violence against people and the planet. It allows capitalism to *act as if* it can abstract parts of metabolic processes from other parts. The result is the destruction and d(rift) of the metabolic processes that previously hung together, as we will see in chapter five.[8]

Marx's point was not that we need to include more natural use-values (nature, women, and slaves) into the value calculations of capitalist production.[9] Marx wanted "the abolition of value as the social form of wealth."[10] He wanted the abolition of the whole dualism at the heart of modern economics. I note the importance of primitive accumulation in Marx's theory of value throughout this book not to suggest that we should pay rocks, water, or air for their labor. I do it to show that even if we tried to offset ecological destruction through restoration or monetization, the entire capitalist economy would collapse. Capitalism cannot grant value to everything that constitutes that value. Hence, its irredeemable structural failure as a social system. Emphasizing the process of primitive accumulation makes explicit the impossible integration of non-value into value.

So, my position is neither dualist or monist. We need to take seriously the *historical* dualism between use-value and value created by capitalism and abolish it. However, this does not lead me to an *ontological* monism in which we should pay everything a wage. Instead, following Lucretius and Marx's dissertation, I imagine my position as a *kinetic* one where nature flows continually but also folds into knotted metastable regions where one can imagine (wrongly, of course) that the value-fold is separate from the flows that support it. In chapters seven and eight, I try to account for the *historical* emergence of this dualism between use-value and value through the kinetic process of folding.

The great revolutionary novelty of capitalism, according to Marx, was that capitalism used human labor time as the primary measure of social wealth. This did not mean, however, that all human labor was valued by wages. Women, slaves, and others were still unpaid. Capitalism simply stole massive sources of activity and reproductive labor and compensated or valued only a small fraction of it. The name Marx gives to this small portion of compensation is "value" or "socially necessary abstract labor time." The value of this labor is compensated in the capitalist mode of production in the form of wages for "free men"—that is, largely peasants forcibly removed from their land.

***Tragen*form:** There is a more general philosophical point to be made about the conditions of emergence of the capitalist value-form. The German verb *tragen* comes from the Proto-Indo-European root **dreg,* meaning "to draw, pull, or drag." The process of material production is thus a fundamentally kinetic process. The birth of value is not a static relation between two discrete things. It is not merely a distinct one-time, or even ongoing, event of primitive accumulation. Material production is an ongoing reproductive relation immanent to but uncounted or not valued by the value-form. Appropriation is the becoming of value and not an event separable from it.

Material production is a shifting and transformative movement or motion that carries or draws sensuous forms as it flows. *Tragen* makes forms by moving or drawing them out but also continues to support and maintain them by reproducing the formal patterns being drawn. The bearers bear the conditions of their own appropriation. But nothing is drawn once and for all. Value is continually drawn out and drawn up.[11] The entire idea of forms, including value-forms, as immutable essences therefore must be understood as kinetic patterns, forms-in-motion, drawn out and reproduced through the movement of matter.

Tragen is therefore a holding up of something or supporting of something from below. The reflexive use of the word means that something "supports itself." This collective self-supporting of matter and form is precisely what Marx calls the *zusammenhängen* of entangled matters. Material qualities do not hang by themselves in midair; they are knotted and folded with one another such that they support (*tragen*) themselves. The movement of tangled matters thus supports itself and immanently supports the birth of the value-form.

CONCLUSION

This chapter began with the most general *material conditions* for the emergence of the commodity. It moved from the appearance of the individual discrete commodity to the undivided continuum of material production that supports it and gives birth to it. I thus conclude that the value-form is not something fixed or premade but something made and *born,* something *birthed.* Value therefore only emerges on the material condition and support of sensuous material qualities *in motion.* With this conclusion I turn in the next chapter to the question of precisely *how* the value-form emerges and yet remains immanent to this qualitative material support.

CHAPTER 4

Devalorization

The aim of this chapter is to show that the process of primitive accumulation or direct appropriation is and *must be* internal to Marx's theory of value. This is the case for precisely the methodological reasons Marx describes in his postface to the second edition of *Capital*.

The core concepts in the "mode of presentation" (use-value, exchange-value, and value) describe the strictly immanent conditions or "core logic of capitalism" but are also derived from the historical "mode of inquiry." Since primitive accumulation is part of the historical mode of inquiry, there must be a conceptual place for primitive accumulation in the mode of presentation itself. If not, then the mode of presentation is strictly speaking *inadequate to the mode of inquiry*—something that any dialectician, and Marx himself, must reject.[1]

Just as Marx writes in the *Grundrisse* that the historical present contains all the unconquered fragments of the past, so the theoretical mode of presentation of that present also must contain all the fragments of its past:

> In order to develop the laws of bourgeois economy . . . it is not necessary to write the real history of the relations of production. But the correct observation and deduction of these laws . . . always leads to primary equations . . . which point toward a past lying behind the system. These indications . . . then offer the key to understanding the past—a work in its own right. (G, 460–461)

Chapter one of *Capital* is much more than a theory of capitalist economics; it is a theoretical description of the *conditions for* capitalist economics.

Marx in Motion. Thomas Nail, Oxford University Press (2020). © Oxford University Press.
DOI: 10.1093/oso/9780197526477.001.0001

This distinction is crucial and rarely attended to. Critique, for Marx, is the description of the material conditions for the real historical present. The conditions, however, do not resemble what they condition. This was Kant's critical error. Kant made his transcendental conditions resemble what they conditioned: the subject. So his method of inquiry never left its starting point in subjective experience. For Marx, however, we begin with sensuous experience but then actually get to the material conditions of production more broadly. This is precisely what makes possible Marx's conceptual account of the precapitalist logic of primitive accumulation presupposed in the emergence of value.

For Marx, the conditions of value do not resemble what they condition: value itself. If they did, we would have explained nothing. We would have a mere tautology, found in many "labor theories of value."[2] In other words, the conditions for the capitalist mode of production are not and cannot resemble capitalism itself or even the merely social relations between humans.[3] This is why there is no rational or formulaic proportion between labor (which has no value) and value.

This is also why Marx's historical mode of inquiry *begins* with colonialism and primitive accumulation *in the first place*—something value theorists often leave out.[4] Capitalism emerges from the historical conditions of the noncapitalist process of direct appropriation, murder, theft, colonialism, demineralization, and so on: "Capital comes dripping from head to toe, from every pore, with blood and dirt" (C, 926). Capitalist value is dripping with the blood of all the indigenous people it killed and with all the minerals it stole from their land.

Following the language of birth and bearing (*tragen*), Marx writes that "the capitalist economy emerged from the *womb* of the feudal economic system. It therefore describes the historical process by which *divorcing* workers from their means of production converts them into wage workers."[5] Capitalist value is born from something that bears, supports, and maintains it. It comes from the literal wombs of unpaid women and removes workers from their previous cycles of production and consumption. Minerals are pulled from the "bowels of the earth" that bear and support value but themselves have no value:

> The discovery of gold and silver in America, the extirpation, enslavement and entombment in mines of the indigenous population of that continent, the beginnings of the conquest and plunder of India, and the conversion of Africa into a preserve for the commercial hunting of blackskins are all things which characterize the dawn of the era of capitalist production. These idyllic proceedings are the chief moments of primitive accumulation. (C, 915)

The removal of matters both human and extra-human from their previous relations of production and reproduction and their forced migration is the origin of capitalist value. But there is also a twofold process at work in such expansion by expulsion.[6] The emergence of value requires that it immediately distinguish itself from nonvalue. This differentiation is not a passive or neutral process. Value is only value because it "is not" nonvalue, or at least this is what capitalists try to convince us of.

The entire distinction between value and nonvalue is predicated on specific historical practices of simultaneous devalorizations of nature,[7] women, and colonial populations, and the creation of value from white men's paid labor. By "devalorization," I mean the process of distinguishing value from nonvalue. There is thus a complete continuity between what I am calling devalorization and value creation, just as there is a continuity between the twofold sides of use-value and value. For Marx, they are two sides of the same process and mutually define each other, not by logical exclusion but by kinetic circulation.

The details of this process are, of course, historical and specific. Marx therefore limits himself to only the immediate preconditions of capitalism. We should not generalize that all such acts of primitive accumulation always *result in capitalism*. Marx is well aware that primitive accumulation (colonialism, demineralization, extraction, slavery, and so on) is not unique to capitalism. Only in the historical case of England that he describes does primitive accumulation *result* in capitalism.

But if contained in capitalism are all the fragments of the past, then contained in precapitalist primitive accumulation are all the fragments of previous primitive accumulations. Furthermore, if primitive accumulation is the historical condition of capitalism, then the concepts extracted from this history also must bear their own traces of primitive accumulation. This is what this chapter hopes to show.

THE FORM OF APPEARANCE OF VALUE

Marx begins his theory of value in precisely the methodological place we would expect: in the sensuous appearance of value, which appears first and foremost when two sensuous matters kinetically trade places or are exchanged with each other. This material-kinetic process appears as the "exchange-value" of the "commodity-body" (*Waarenkörper*):

> Exchange-value appears [*erscheint*] first of all as the quantitative relation, the
> proportion, in which use-values of one kind exchange for use-values of another

kind. This relation changes constantly with time and place. Hence exchange-value seems [*scheint*] to be something accidental and purely relative, and consequently an intrinsic value, i.e. an exchange-value that is inseparably connected with the commodity, inherent in it, seems a contradiction in terms. Let us consider the matter more closely. (C, 126)

The movement of use-values in exchange appears (*erscheint*) first of all to correspond to a certain proportion or quantity of what is being moved. The logic of proportions, furthermore, seems (*scheint*) to be random, since it seems to vary historically and geographically. It *seems* that if the logic of motion were tied to the qualitative bodies of the objects, then we would be able to recognize a clear and sensuously visible logic with our eyes. But this is not the case. Use-values appear to follow some invisible logic that has to do with their quantity, not their quality.

This is odd because, as we have seen, sensuous material production is the bearer of all value. How is it possible for something that is the material condition and bearer of value to be subject to a logic that is not its own? This is the central question of Marx's value theory and leads directly to considering the process of devalorization in more depth. Political economists, Marx says, are fond of attributing the strange laws of motion of commodities to the "vagaries of supply and demand." In other words, the traditional rationale for explaining the diversity of exchange ratios is purely subjective. Some people want some things sometimes and somewhere and others elsewhere and at other times. For Marx, however, this only "seems" to be the case, because of the idealist and anthropocentric prejudice of political economy.

On the other hand, however, some Marxist value theorists want to locate a specific equation or formal ratio between the duration of labor and the magnitude of value. I argue, however, a third position: that the relation between labor and value is neither random nor mathematically determined but is related to the process of *appropriation and theft*.

The movement of use-values back and forth is tied neither strictly to their qualities nor to the accidental subjective preferences for their qualities or quantities but rather to a foundational theft. The measurement of this theft as "abstract labor time" is neither merely objective in the appropriated qualities or quantities (which have no value) nor purely subjective in the desires of humans but related to a number of concrete historical conditions of what can be appropriated and how easily. Marx focuses first on demonstrating the nonrandom character of exchange.

For example, "a given commodity, a quarter of wheat, for example, is exchanged for x boot-polish, y silk or z gold, etc. . . . But x boot-polish, y silk or z gold, etc., each represent the exchange-value of one quarter of wheat. Therefore x boot-polish, y silk, z gold, etc., must, as exchange-values, be mutually replaceable or of identical magnitude. It follows from this that, firstly, the valid exchange-values of a particular commodity express something equal, and secondly, exchange-value cannot be anything other than the mode of expression, the 'form of appearance', [*Erscheinungsform*] of a content distinguishable from it" (C, 127).

If we look only at the wheat, its relations to other commodities look random. However, if we see that x, y, and z are also made equal with one another through their equality with the wheat, then such relations *can hardly be accidental (merely objective or merely subjective)*. If x boot-polish is equal to a quarter of wheat and y silk is too, then it must follow by necessity that x and y are equal. Marx locates a whole new form of circulation at work beyond the demonstrably visible pattern of movement between qualities and quantities: the *circulation of value*. Value takes the objective qualities and subjective desires and brings them into a dialectic of circulation, in which various patterns of motion are determined not by accident but by their kinetic relation to one another in a field of value. Things now can be moved back and forth in a strict logic of proportion, based on a total field containing discrete units of value. However, the details of this logic must be examined more closely (see figure 4.1).

Exchange value is only the form of appearance (*Erscheinungsform*) of this pattern of circulation. Two qualities, corn and iron, for example, can be exchanged with each other only on the condition that they move in the same field of circulation or that they assume a common denominator or unit of measure. Qualitatively, they have nothing in common. Quantitatively, their amounts are different and vary. However, if both are measured according "to something else," then they can be compared based on "how much" of this "something else" they have.

For example, two surface areas can be measured and compared by the total areas of the number of triangles they can contain. So three things must take place in order for this act of measurement to occur. First, the

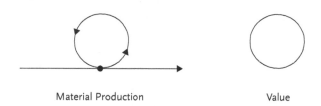

Material Production   Value

Figure 4.1 Fluxions of exchange

continual flow of sensuous material production must be moved or treated *as if* it had no qualities but only a quantity. Recall that Marx is quite clear that an object without sensation, or sensuous externality, does not and cannot exist. Such a thing has "no being." Since sensuous qualities are the bearers and maintainers of value, matter must be supporting quantity. However, it is also possible to treat such qualities *as if* they did not matter or determine the movement of the object. All units of measurement (time, space, money, and so on) have sensuous qualities (clocks, cubits, and coins). However, it is also possible to treat them *as if* those qualities did not matter, even if this results in terrible oversights like approximations and counterfeits. Second, this object (treated as if it had no qualities) then can be used as a measure of other such objects, as if they were defined by a similar unit of this original measure. Third, the different objects now compared can be evaluated and equated with respect to the original unit of measure, no matter what it is.

The form of value begins sensuously in appearance (*Erscheinungsform*) but is then treated as just a form, as if it had no appearance at all. Marx does not go into the origins of this practice, but I have shown elsewhere in some detail that this practice is at least as old as 3500 B.C.E. in Mesopotamia.[8] This general technique emerged alongside the invention of cardinal numbers, written language, and a system of weights and measures. All three inventions relied on this same basic logic. Each treated a given sensuous object *as if* it actually had no qualities of its own when coordinated as the measure of others. Cardinality, for example, is possible only if quantities are additive and exchangeable with one another, as if 1 were contained or identically duplicated in 2. This is certainly not an invention of capitalism, but it is not an ahistorical fact, either. It was invented in a place at a time. Before this, humans used only ordinal counting, in which quantities could be only before or after one another and were not equal or exchangeable at all.

The point is this: the very act of treating a thing as if it had no qualities, which is assumed in the existence of a "measure," relies on a more originary act of appropriation, which cannot be explained internal to the logic of exchange previously described. What are the origins of this measure or common element?

Identity

The invention of this "common element" (*gemeinsame*) has several kinetic features. For Marx, sensuous objects are produced through a process of continual folding or self-affection. Sensation or affection occurs when matter touches itself. Objects are produced at the same time as the extended pattern that matter makes when it folds or swerves. How, then, does a *gemeinsame*, or self-same identical thing, emerge from a continually differentiated material flow of motion?

First of all, it does not. This is because identity is produced or born by the continual flux and flow of matter, as shown in Marx's reading of Epicurus. What happens is that the continual folding of matter produces a metastability like the eddy of a river or the eye of a storm. The invention of something that is the same as itself is possible only by ignoring or devalorizing the rest of the flow that supports this metastability. It would be like watching a bubble at the center of a river eddy and thinking the bubble existed on its own without the rest of the river. Such is the delusion of treating things as if they were discrete and dangled unsupported in midair. Instead of a continual flow folding itself up into a thing, it is as if one sees, as Hegel tends to, circles. The idea of the circle is one of self-unity abstracted from the flows that supported it:

> This common element cannot be a geometrical, physical, chemical or other natural property [*Eigenschaft*] of commodities. Such bodily qualities [*körperlichen Eigenschaften*] come into consideration only to the extent that they make the commodities useful, i.e. turn them into use-values. But clearly, the exchange relation of commodities is characterized precisely by its abstraction from their use-values. (C, 127)

The *gemeinsame* cannot have any qualities for Marx, not even geometrical ones. Even the example of the bubble in the river is only part of the story. The next step in the production of a *gemeinsame* is that the quantity *of something* is considered only as a pure self-identical quantity *in itself*, like the contradictory rational atomism of Democritus. Pure matter in itself and pure idea in itself coincide as two aspects of the same contradiction of abstraction.

Marx then immediately describes this kind of abstraction as containing not an "atom of use-value." In the vernacular, of course, "atom" here can be read as "some small amount." But Marx does not say "some small amount"; he says "atom." It is unlikely that Marx, who cites both Epicurus and Lucretius in *Capital*, does not also have in mind the Democritean contradictory reduction of things (use-values) to atoms of pure matter and thus also to pure ideas of atoms (values). As we know, this is Marx's problem with atomism *and* capitalism.

By contrast, for Epicurus and Lucretius, the two are always mixed in sensuous matter as qualified quantities or sensuous forms. Value is revealed for what it is: a pure religious abstraction, the worst intellectual mistake in world history. The postulated existence of value out of nothing contradicts the well-known Lucretian maxim that *nullam rem ex nihilo* (nothing comes from nothing). Marx even cites this Lucretian maxim in *Capital* on exactly this same question of the posited origin of value out of nothing. "Creation of value," Marx writes "is the transposition of labour-power into labour. Labour-power itself is, above all else, the material of nature transposed into a human organism" (C, 323). Marx could not be clearer here with this obvious (to him) connection to his dissertation and the theory of value in *Capital*.

Value posits an ex nihilo creation of itself just as religion does and just as Democritus's atom does. Just as religion is an immediate devalorization of the nature that gave birth to and bears it, so value entails an immediate devalorization of the very materiality of nature that composes both human productivity and the delusion of a restricted domain of discrete value.[9] Human labor is, for Marx, *above all else* material nature transposed into the human organism. The bearing origins of value are thus thoroughly material and continuous with nature. Value is the deluded, but no less real, human practice of *acting as if* there is something that floats independently and discretely above sensuous nature. There is a genuine continuity between Marx's philosophy of nature in his dissertation and his philosophy of nature as it is transformed into capital. This observation leads to a new appreciation and way of reading *Capital*.

VALUE AND DEVALORIZATION

Value, for Marx, is not just something that emerges ex nihilo as in Adam Smith's mythical narrative about primitive accumulation. For Smith, Marx writes, "This primitive accumulation plays approximately the same role in political economy as original sin does in theology. Adam bit the apple, and thereupon sin fell on the human race" (C, 873). Both work as assumed and unexplained primal conditions that retroactively legitimate a founding violence. These mythical origins supposedly happened so long ago that they must be universal and ahistorical aspects of nature.

For Marx, the origins of the creation of value, just like the origins of the emergence of the capitalist mode of production, are not universal but practical and historical. The logic of the former is contained in the history of the latter. Just as historical primitive accumulation is not the mere discovery of wealth just lying around as a free gift from nature but in fact an extremely violent and ongoing robbery and butchery of women, nature, and colonies, so the logic of primitive accumulation is not just the mental attribution of value waiting to be set in motion. Value is simultaneously devalorization.

Just as slavery relied on racism to devalorize certain human bodies, so value itself relies on the devalorization of material production to define its own form of discrete value. It is not the case that material production is first nonvalue and then value is born, but rather the birth of value itself retroactively devalorizes its material conditions of production only after its birth. As Althusser writes, "The invisible is defined by the visible as its invisible, its forbidden vision: the invisible is not therefore simply what is outside the visible (to return to the spatial metaphor), the outer darkness of exclusion—but the inner darkness of exclusion, inside the visible itself."[10]

Similarly, the myth of original sin devalorizes the body (and especially women's bodies) only *after* the invention of a sky god to justify his role as the redeemer of the very sin it invented in the first place:

> If then we disregard the use-value of commodity-bodies [*Waarenkörper*], only one quality [*Eigenschaft*] remains, that of being products of labour [*Arbeitsprodukten*]. But even the product of labour has already been transformed in our hands. If we make abstraction [*Abstrahir*] from its use-value, we abstract also from the material constituents and forms [*körperlichen Bestandtheilen und Formen*] which make it a use-value. (C, 128)

If we disregard the sensuous qualities of a body, this does not mean that the sensuous body has no qualities; it means that we have actively done something *as if* the body had no qualities. It is possible for men to treat animals and women as if they do not have agency, but this does not mean that they actually lack agency. Just by virtue of holding a product of labor in our hands we have already had to remove this commodity-body from its relational and material context and treat it as if it were something discrete and separate from the material conditions and process that formed it into an object of desire.

Again, the important point to be made here is that the production of value is not just an intellectual exercise in which we contemplate a purely abstract aspect of a body; it is something practical that is and must be continually performed or made (*machen*) with our hands.

Abstraction, like all processes, is a fundamentally kinetic and performative act. It is not an essence or immaterial idea; it is a real historical process. By making an abstraction, we are not just making value, we are devalorizing the material constituents and forms that bear this value. The German word *abstrahir* literally means to "move or pull away from." Abstraction is itself a kinetic and material process in which some part is removed or separated from some others and treated *as if* it came out of nowhere and had no prior relations or qualities of its own. Abstraction is not an ontological separation between things; it is a particular redistribution of things *as if* they were discrete fragments and not iteratively woven sensuous matters.

The material practice of such a relative removal is what the abstraction of value really *does*. Value practically devalorizes something socially by removing a part of a body and treating it as if it were the only thing of value compared to the nonvalued. If this abstraction is practical and historical, then it must be continual and habitual. It is never done once and for all; the conditions for such abstraction, just like those of primitive accumulation, have to persist as well, as we will see.

For example, one can treat a tree or fruit born from the soil as if it came for free from nowhere and had no particular sensuous relation with anything else. This is not an ontological rupture in nature but has historically resulted in the exhaustion of the original soil.

Concrete and Abstract Labor

Here the theme of "separation" against the "hanging together" of things from the doctoral dissertation, legal writings on wood theft, and manuscripts returns. Value repeats a similar threefold process of separation from the object, activity, and being of production:

> It is no longer a table, a house, a piece of yarn or any other useful thing. All its sensuous characteristics [*Beschaffenheiten*] are extinguished [*ausgelöscht*]. Nor is it any longer the product of the labour of the joiner, the mason or the spinner, or of any other particular kind [*bestimmten*] of productive labour. With the disappearance of the useful character of the products of labour, the useful character of the kinds of labour embodied in them also disappears; this in turn entails the disappearance [*verschwinden*] of the different concrete forms [*konkreten Formen*] of labour. They can no longer be distinguished but are all together reduced to the same kind of labour, human labour in the abstract. (C, 128)

First, the practice of abstraction actually and performatively separates the process of material production from the object it produces. The table is produced to be consumed as a table for the producer, but if the object is removed, then the sensuous qualities that define it cannot be consumed. It is not what it is.

Second, the activity that produced the product is treated *as if* it were not that kind of activity, but activity "in general." Third, the concrete sensuous being of the producer is no longer distinguishable but reduced to abstract labor distinct from the product made. The beings who produce are treated as if their concrete production were not concrete at all and *as if* they were not the type of beings that they are. Concrete labor is thus treated as lacking in sensuous qualities.

THE HORROR OF VALUE

The practical creation of value involves not only a positive isolation of a discrete value distinct from nonvalue but simultaneously a paradoxical and retroactive devalorization of its own material and practical conditions. Value creation always has a specific historical and sensuous character that it aims to cover over, hence the "always already" narrative structure of value's mythically devalorized matters. This practical paradox for Marx rightfully gives rise to a genuine experience of horror in the face of such contradictory abstraction and devalorization. Marx writes:

> Let us now look at the residue [*Residuum*] of the products of labour. There is nothing left of them in each case but the same ghostly [*gespenstige*] objectivity; they are merely congealed [*Gallerte*] quantities of homogeneous human labour, i.e. of human labour-power expended without regard to the form of its expenditure. All these things now tell us is that human labour-power has been expended to produce them, human labour is accumulated [*aufgehäuft*] in them. As crystals of this social substance, which is common to them all, they are values—commodity values [*Warenwerte*]. (C, 128)

To look for the residue of a thing without sensuous qualities is to look for the appearance of that which does not appear. It is to look for the sensuous trace of the act of erasure itself. Marx's language describes precisely why this process of value creation inspires such a particularly uncanny fear or horror often associated with monsters. What is frightening about the monster of value is not so much the monster but that it feeds upon the living. Value not only devalorizes various matters but also feeds on them as its very conditions of emergence and reproduction.

Therefore devalorization is not an end in itself but the lifeblood of value. Value is composed of devalorized matters, only a discrete part of which has been given value. The parasitic or vampiric nature of this abstraction gives it a genuinely "horrible visage" (*caput horribili super*), as Lucretius puts it in lines 62-65 of book one of his *De Rerum Natura* (*The Nature of Things*). Lucretius says that for Epicurus humanity appeared (*oculos*) as a foul and rotting form of life (*Humana ante oculos foede cum vita;*), which lay fallow, idle, and inactive (*iaceret*) because it was crushed into the ground by the gravity and weight of religion (*in terris oppressa gravi sub religione*), whose horrible head (*quae caput horribili super*) stretched down from Heaven (*a caeli regionibus ostendebat*) and stood upon mortals (*mortalibus instans*). Marx follows this ancient critique of religion in his own critique of value. But there is a dually horrible or monstrous aspect to value as well.

Slime and the face of God: A residue, for example, is a strange kind of thing because it has no definite form but is still sensible in some vague or creepy sense—like a slime trail or the mysterious track of an unknown creature. The residue of the product of labor is the qualities that are still remaining once value has tried to strip them all away but cannot. What remains is the hideous waste product or fragment of the value creation process. Since value creation is a real act, we can see its traces, but we do not see what made them. The trace of the unseen creature becomes a monster of incredible power precisely because it is not fully visible. Similarly, the absolute power of Yahweh is secured by the fact that no one ever sees his face but only his traces in fire, smoke, and thunder. Both slime and Yahweh show twin aspects of the horror of abstraction. In slime there are parts without the whole, and in Yahweh there is the whole without the parts. Value turns the body into slime and value into an all-powerful God.

The zombie and the ghost: The product of labor appears to us through the concrete form of exchange-value, but value itself, Marx says, is like a "ghostly or phantom-like object" that has been abstracted form its corporeal body. This is horrible because the object is transformed into a living dead body (the zombie) and a dead living spirit (the ghost) at the same time. The commodity is thus split between two horrible figures: the zombie body and a ghostly value. Each plays on the horrible: the body without life and life without body. Value makes the body into an undead machine and makes value into a haunting specter.[11]

Blobs and crystals: The products of labor, Marx says, are "merely congealed [*Gallerte*] quantities of homogeneous human labour," because material production is in continual movement: "labour-power in its fluid state" (C, 142). In value, liquid labor congeals itself into a strange quasi-formless quantity without any differentiated qualities in it. The productive body becomes an undifferentiated mass of quivering slime. On the other hand, Marx also says that the social substance of sensuous material production is also "crystallized" into an apparently discrete unit of value. Crystals are formed by the deposition of liquid mineral flows and are by no means isolated or discrete matters. However, it is also possible to break a crystal from this liquid source of mineralization and hold it in one's hand as if it were an autonomous fragment or quantity.

Value has this horrible aspect because it requires both the support of sensuous appearance and at the same time the mutilation of that same support. Material production and human labor in particular are "accumulated" (aufgehäuft) in value, but this accumulation is not without an ongoing violence of mutilating extraction and devalorization, which Marx describes visually in the reduction of the sensuous body to a residue, slime, or zombified body. Therefore, not only is value simultaneously a value creation and devalorization, but this whole process is actually a transformative one. Treating sensuous bodies as if they had no sensation results in a transformation of their qualities. The body of the slave, for example, is not just conceptually devalorized but practically tortured, mutilated, and transformed into a body disciplined by the value creation process.[12] The migrant, the slave, and the clear-cut forest are not merely devalorized but *actively transformed* "in the hands" of value into "the wretched of the earth," as Fanon says. The bearing power of material production thus makes possible new life but also remains precariously open and vulnerable to the horrors of extraction, as Adriana Cavarero describes.[13]

The horror of value is double. What is horrible in one sense is the reduction of sensuous quality to pure quantity, but in another sense there is also a fear of the revenge of the horrible body back upon value. Value is the horror of use-value, and use-value is the horror of value. The fundamental anxiety of all value creation through primitive accumulation is that the process of material production will revolt against its accumulation and devalorization. The dead not only will rise again, but they will not go back to work. Urban worker's ghettoes will turn into war zones against the police, and suburban consumption will turn to wanton destruction—as George Romero depicted in *Dawn of the Dead* (1978). Together, they will destroy capitalist civilization. The slimy waste products of value creation will return to poison their producers through climate change. In short, the flip side of capitalist horror is that the "specter of communism" will return as a real sensuous force of revolutionary violence back upon the process of value creation that stole its body and life.

More specifically, the value creation process uses the technology of temporal measurement to strip material production of its qualities. Duration, according to Marx, is the "common unit" (*gemeinsame*) by which all others can be measured without regard to their quality:

> A use value, or useful article, therefore, has value only because abstract human labour is objectified [*vergegenständlicht*] or materialized [*materialisirt*] in it. How, then, is the magnitude of this value to be measured? By means of the quantity [*Quantum*] of the 'value-forming substance," the labour, contained [*enthaltenen*] in the article. The quantity is measured by its duration, and labour-time [*Arbeitszeit*] is itself measured on the particular scale of hours, days, etc. (C, 129)

Value is first and foremost defined by the process of material-kinetic production. Material production is made external or objective through folding, as we have seen. Matter folds over itself and externalizes itself as objective matter. Value then treats the whole continual flow of material production *as if* it were *only a discrete object*. This means first of all that only the bearing flows of soil, blood, and labor that are *materially part of the discrete object* are recognized as supporting the "form of appearance" for a value.

Second, the creation of value entails that this discrete matter be treated as a homogenous "value-forming substance"—a congealed, self-identical fluid. Value treats the continual flow and fold of matter as if it were a self-identical unity: a circle. Value, as Marx says, is treated as if it were a completely enclosed "container" that literally "holds" (*enthaltenen*) the flow of sensuous matter. Material production "holds itself" together through the fold, but value treats the sensuous hold or grasp as a sealed-up, discrete container. Just as in the Greek myth in which the first bowl was molded on Aphrodite's breast, so the container of value is not primary but modeled on the bearing flow of the matter being contained (see figure 4.2).

However, ignoring the qualities of a thing poses a problem for measurement. What are we measuring when we measure an object without qualities? Measuring according to spatial extension presupposes precisely the existence of a specific extended thing to be measured. Time, however, is used as if it can be measured without a necessary reference to any specific thing but only things in general. The nineteenth-century creation of value was based on the assumption, proven incorrect by general relativity, that time passes equally and homogeneously across space.

Space, weight, and speed are all, by necessity, relatively external measurements of external objects, requiring concrete references. Time is

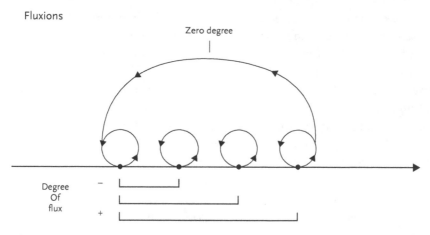

Figure 4.2 Material production versus value

treated as if it were different. Regardless of the action or inaction of a specific body, time passes *in general*. This is precisely why Kant, in the *Critique of Pure Reason*, names time the "inner sense" and space the "outer sense" of the transcendental aesthetic—or conditions for sensation. For Kant, time is our inner sense of ourselves that guarantees both the possibility of change (as sequence) and identity (as unity of the series). As pure sequence, however, time can occur independently of space (i.e., without external objects), but space must presuppose temporal differentiation. Time, for Kant, is the sense of the self or ego sensing itself. It is the ideal, formal, and mental unity of the subject itself. In other words, the transcendental primacy of time in Kant remains mired in the tradition of German idealist abstraction and bourgeois production. It is no coincidence that a philosophy such as Kant's emerged when it did in an age that believed in the universality and homogeneity of discrete temporal succession.

This theory of time follows the same model as capitalist value. Time, just like value, is defined as a series of discrete, quality-less, and extension-less moments in a totality. A unit of time is treated as a purely ideal and self-identical unity. This is complicated not just because general relativity proves that time actually occurs faster or more slowly depending on changes in gravitation, but also, more simply, because days, months, and years are highly qualitative processes that do not fully yield to discreteness or self-identity. For example, a day begins and ends differently depending on where one is on the earth and how far one has moved. Months are not all the same length. A clock at sea level runs more slowly than one in the mountains. Year-based calendars are culturally, historically, and politically diverse and have changed many times.

Marx's own theory of time, however, is radically different from those of almost every other modern philosopher, beginning with Kant, who was the first in the history of Western philosophy to have given time absolute philosophical primacy. In the ancient world, time was always just a measure of an object's motion. In the medieval world, philosophers such as Augustine contrasted time with the more primary nontemporal eternity of God. Human experience, for Augustine, occurred in time, but God's did not.[14] Marx, almost alone in modernity, returns to the ancients in asserting that time is merely the measure of motion.

However, in contrast to many ancients, Marx does not put something else before or more primary to this motion. Aristotle, for example, inserted an unmoved mover to account for the origins of motion. But Aristotle's idea was already a much older one, to be found among the early Greek philosophers such as Pythagoras, Anaximander, and others. It was only Lucretius who was bold enough to do without a more primary principle to explain movement. Even Democritus still relied on natural laws and discrete particles to explain motion. In Lucretius, such laws are fundamentally broken and motion is given full primacy. Marx, as usual, follows Lucretius on this point: "Since labour is motion, time is its natural measure" (G, 205). Material production in general and human labor in particular are motion, full stop. Movement is not derived from time, nor does it happen "in time." The "flow of time" is parasitic on the flow of matter, not the other way around.

This inversion is critical. Again, it is one of the absolutely central novelties of Marx's dissertation to have emphasized the primacy of sensuous material movement *"incerto tempore ferme incertisque locis spatio"* (in indeterminate time and indeterminate place).[15] The generative movement of matter does not occur in time and space but actually produces time and space. I have discussed the textual details of this argument in Lucretius and its contemporary support in quantum gravity theory elsewhere.[16]

Marx, however, was well aware of this original move and dedicates chapter four of his doctoral dissertation to the issue. There he argues, contra Democritus, that time is nothing other than "the absolute form of appearance. That is to say, time is determined as *accidens* of the *accidens*. The *accidens* is the change of substance in general" (DD, 132). The *accidens* here is defined by the kinetics of the swerve. Substance changes continually through motion, and since the swerve occurs *incerto tempore*, motion cannot be reduced to eternal time or even chronological time. Time, for Epicurus, cannot be independent from sensuous matter but is immanent to it. As a measure, time is a regional unit of sensuous matter in motion. What sounds like a merely scholastic issue is actually critical for understanding what value is and what philosophical consequences it has for the magnitude of value:

> However, the labour that forms the substance of value is equal human labour, the expenditure of identical human labor-power. The total labour-power of society, which is manifested in the values of the world of commodities, counts here as one homogeneous mass of human labour-power, although composed of innumerable individual units of labour-power. (C, 129)

The emergence of value is predicated on the treatment of continual material production as if it were a totality composed of individual units. From Democritus to Kant, discreteness has been a prevailing assumption of philosophy.[17] It paved the way for the effective naturalization or ontologization of value—as if value were always already there and not itself something produced through abstraction and appropriation.

SOCIALLY NECESSARY PRIMITIVE ACCUMULATION

We now have the twin conditions for the creation of what Marx calls "socially necessary labor time," that is, the average time it takes to produce a commodity. First, material production must be retroactively and constitutively devalorized or appropriated. Second, the flow of sensuous material production must be externalized and measured by a third thing (time) *as if* neither the object, nor time itself, nor the act of temporal measurement itself had any sensuous qualities. This is value.

Socially Necessary Labor Time

Only once value is first accumulated through the expulsion of sensuous qualities and then cut up into discrete bits of a whole can socially necessary labor time emerge as the "average" amount of labor it takes to produce a commodity:

> Each of these units [*individuellen*] is the same as any other to the extent that it has the character of a socially average unit of labour-power and acts as such; i.e. only needs, in order to produce a commodity, the labour time which is necessary on an average, or in other words is socially necessary. Socially necessary labour-time is the labour-time required to produce any use-value under the conditions

of production normal for a given society and with the average degree of skill and intensity of labour prevalent in that society. (C, 129)

Value produces a relative discreteness, identity, and totality from which the idea of an "average" is either approximately or arithmetically derived. Socially necessary labor time, like value, first of all assumes the precondition of all the material production necessary for the reproduction of a use-value, including everything needed "so that he can renew his life-process" (C, 276–277). However, from the perspective of sensuous matter, production is qualitatively irreducible to quantitative measure. The material conditions for production and consumption/reproduction in this sense are unlimited. This is the central dilemma of value creation: how to make value out of nonvalue.

Capitalism is often defined as "value-in-motion" or by its "melting everything solid into air," and so on. But what is less often considered is exactly how such movement relies on a very specific rigidification of movement into value in the first place. True, value is in motion, but value itself, like the atoms of Democritus, is not supposed to have any internal motion. The German word Marx uses to describe the value of socially "necessary" labor time is *nothwendige*, which literally means "not flexible" or "not moveable." Value circulates extensively but not intensively, just like Democritus's atoms. But this is perhaps too simplistic. Motion and stasis are not moral questions of good and bad. The real question is how things move.

Value is not a fixed form because what is socially necessary changes according to all kinds of factors. Therefore *nothwendig* also refers to changes between inflexible or fixed matters. It is this process of continually changing the inflexible state that gives value production its incredibly dynamic and flexible character to expand and contract its its *relatively* fixed patterns of motion.

Any material production above or below socially necessary levels is not included in this necessary value. "His labour would therefore not count as average labour, and his labour-power would not count as average labour-power. It would either be unsaleable, or saleable only at less than the average value of labour-power" (C, 441). In effect, what this means is that all the geological labor of distributing minerals for crops; all the sun's energy that supports the plants that grow from it; all the animals needed to harvest it; and all the women who birthed, bore, and raised the workers who used the animals are in dramatic excess of the minimal duration of the average unit. If their material production were included, the "average time" would soar beyond the realm of profitability.

Viewed from the perspective of the constitutive primitive accumulation that continually bears value's motion, something new comes into view. The process of value creation is a racist, sexist, and anthropocentric tool for arbitrary value creation/devalorization. The value creation of an average unit of time is actually an expression of a flexible ratio between cheap/free production and paid production. The two operate along a spectrum: "Only the labour-time which is embodied in a quantity of commodities laid down in advance and fixed by experience counts as socially necessary labour-time and is paid as such" (C, 694). Everything else *has no value* but is merely the bearer of value. As the direct appropriation of production increases, the amount of socially necessary labor time decreases. As direct appropriation decreases, the paid human worker is expected to work more and longer in order to produce at the same level that will secure a profit. Therefore the term "socially necessary" is not a technical term with any fixed or mathematical content but simply a rhetorical lever of capitalist appropriation, disguised as an economic formula.

For example, if all the materials used in production were free, necessary paid labor time would be shorter, since the paid worker is *doing less of the productive work*. If a plot of well-fertilized land is simply stolen, then there is no need to factor in the wages for workers to buy or steal fertilizer from elsewhere and fertilize the earth. The average time it takes to plant and sow is less than the time it takes to get fertilizer, plant, sow, compost, and refertilize.

However, if that extra fertilizing labor can be attained for free by using slaves, then the average paid-labor time drops back down again. The flux of "necessary" labor time is not actually about any arithmetical social average but about the fluctuating ratio of unpaid to paid production via primitive accumulation. Furthermore, it is no coincidence that the "average amount" of time to produce a commodity just happens to coincide with how much labor it takes to generate a profit from the process. As Marx says, necessary labor time always "represents an *excess* over the amount contained in wages" (C, 992). Are we to believe that it is simply a coincidence that socially necessary labor time is always by chance a profitable duration?

Such incredible inflexibility in the nonvalue/value ratio is possible precisely because, as Marx says, "Labour is the substance and immanent measure of value, but it has no value itself. . . . In the expression 'value of labour,' the concept of value is not only completely extinguished but inverted, so that it becomes its contrary. It is an expression as imaginary as the value of the earth" (C, 677). Marx is extremely clear on this point: *material production has no value*, and that is why it can be continually valued, devalorized, and revalued in all kinds of new ways. Value gains all its motion and all its flexibility from its immanent bearers in both unpaid and paid labors:

> In general, the greater the productivity of labour, the less the labour-time required to produce an article, the less the mass of labour crystallized in that article, and the less its value. . . . Inversely, the less the productivity of labour, the greater the labour-time necessary to produce an article, the greater its value. The value of a commodity, therefore, varies directly as the quantity, and inversely as the productivity, of the labour which finds its realization within the commodity. (C, 131)

This point is crucial. Value varies *directly* as a quantity and *inversely* as a process of production. Value with respect only to itself increases or decreases arithmetically. However, with respect to the process of production, value varies inversely: as production increases (including unpaid production and fixed capital), less paid labor time is required, and so the value goes down. This inversion is absolutely incredible! The more productive powers can be directly appropriated through slavery, ecocide, and unpaid women's work, the *less value the commodity actually has*. The consequences of this inversion have been absolutely devastating.

Primitive Accumulation

Socially necessary labor time is therefore not some actual economic formula but fluctuates according to a number of factors *related directly to the process of primitive accumulation*:

> The value of a commodity would therefore remain constant, if the labour-time required for its production also remained constant. But the latter changes with every variation in the productivity of labour. This is determined by a wide range of circumstances; it is determined, among other things, by the workers' average degree of skill, the level of development of science and its technological application, the social organization of the process of production, the extent and effectiveness of the means of production, and the conditions found in the natural environment. (C, 130)

Equilibrium between labor and value is absolutely out of the question. Marx is clear that the factors that determine this "average unit" are in constant flux and thus change inversely as production changes. The value creation of a discrete unit changes precisely because *production varies continually*, and direct appropriation turns out to be the most significant factor in the transformation of necessary labor time.

The degree of skill: The change in degree of skill is twofold. Either the skill of the worker can increase, causing a decrease in the labor time needed to produce a commodity (and thus the value), or the skill the job itself requires can be lowered (through technological innovation). The latter is by far more common, as Marx explores at length in part VII of *Capital*. Furthermore, and more important, lowering the skill level necessary to produce the product makes possible the introduction of the devalorized or cheapened labor of women, children, migrants, and other systematically devalorized populations. In other words, deskilling a job makes it possible to increase the amount of appropriated labor from devalorized populations.

Science and technology: Innovations in science and technology not only make it possible to increase the relative surplus value of human workers (see part VII of *Capital*), but even more important, they also make it possible to expand the reaches of direct primitive accumulation. For example, the invention of new map, compass, and shipbuilding technologies made possible colonial land appropriations in the Americas. The theft of mineral-rich native lands dramatically increased the ratio of value to devalorized unpaid production. In Europe, such fertility was long gone, and agriculture relied on imports of guano and other fertilizers. New mining and water-pump technologies allowed the English to dig deeper into mines containing the great gifts of nature, again increasing the asymmetry between unpaid and paid labor. In short, the technologically primitive accumulation of the earth itself can change the magnitude of socially necessary labor time.

Social organization: A third factor of primitive accumulation that affects socially necessary labor time is changes in social organization, including racism, xenophobia, nationalism, sexism, and anthropocentrism. The purpose of these social techniques is to systematically devalorize populations in order to appropriate their productive powers more cheaply. If white-male-national-worker labor time can be supplemented with the labor of cheaper workers, then that will reduce white-male labor time, rendering the white male more productive and efficient. This is a form of what we might call social primitive accumulation, in which what is being stolen is the social equality, dignity, and empowerment of certain matters both human and nonhuman. This is not often considered part of primitive accumulation, but here Marx includes it as one of the primary factors in determining the flux of necessary labor time. And since social oppression is a cheap or free way to decrease production time, it should be thought of as part of the broader process of devalorization.

Extent and effectiveness: This fourth factor is often treated as strictly contained within the formal economic process alone, that is, the distribution and efficient production of commodities. However, the extent of production has both valued and devalued sides. Production can be expanded domestically by opening new factories, but it can also be expanded through the colonial appropriation of new people and resources. One expands the paid extent of the means of production, the latter the unpaid extent. Effectiveness can mean getting more skilled workers or faster machines, or it can equally mean using devalorized migrant or slave labor and more of it.[18] Both options will reduce the average paid labor time of waged workers, but only the latter will increase the wretched of the earth as well.

Relation to nature: The fifth technique of primitive accumulation is perhaps one of the most obvious and dramatic. Depending on the relation to nature (*durch Naturverhältnisse*) or the natural conditions of value, average labor time increases or decreases. The more that nonvalued natural production (relative to valued products) can be appropriated for cheap or free, the lower will be the paid labor time of production and thus the lower the value and therefore the more competitive commodity, and the greater the profit. This is because nature or sensuous material production has no value. "A thing can be a use-value without being a value. Air, virgin soil, natural meadows, unplanted forests, etc. fall into this category. . . . The same quantity of labour provides more metal in rich mines than in poor" (C, 131). Rich mines, fertile soils, bountiful forests, fruit-bearing trees, and wild game are all products of nature without value and thus can supplement the necessary labor time of waged workers by making it easy to extract them. The more bountiful the earth's production, the easier it is to extract it and the less time it takes to do so, and therefore the less it is "worth" and the greater the ratio of free to paid labor time.

CONCLUSION

Primitive accumulation plays a pivotal role in the creation and reproduction of value. Value, despite its apparent abstraction and universality, is a practical activity that involves a retroactive devalorization of sensuous matters and a revaluation of itself in the wage form (see part VI of *Capital*). This is what I have called elsewhere "expansion by expulsion."

Devalorization is fundamentally a material and kinetic process. Value gets its motion from its sensuous conditions, which it must at once devalorize. Value, however, is not something other than sensuous material production. It is entirely immanent to it. The pivotal question now, then, is precisely how material production is able to continually produce and sustain both use-value and value *at the same time*. This question is addressed in chapter 6, but before moving on to this, I discuss an extremely integral concept introduced by Marx: metabolism. This is the topic of chapter 5.

CHAPTER 5
Metabolic Drift

I have held off on my discussion of Marx's theory of metabolism until this point in order to provide it with the focus and full textual analysis it deserves. The importance of metabolism in Marx's work is a relatively recent and crucial emphasis in eco-Marxism, now well-established in the literature.[1] Alongside the kinetic materialism of the doctoral dissertation and the theory of primitive accumulation, metabolism is one of the most important keys to developing a nonreductionist, nondeterministic, nonanthropocentric, and new-materialist Marxism.

Instead of repeating the work already done on the concept of metabolism in Marx's work, this chapter aims to make two novel interventions into it:

1) First, I argue that Marx's theory of metabolism does not appear suddenly or only in his "mature" philosophy.[2] Marx first knew of the term in 1950, and first used the term "metabolism" (*Stoffwechsel*) in the *Grundrisse* (1857). However, the idea of a "continuous process of nature's intra-action with itself" (MECW 3: 276) was also present from the very beginning of his work, especially in the doctoral dissertation and manuscripts, as I have shown in detail, with the terms *zusammenhängen*, *verkeren*, and *wechseln*. Metabolism thus functions as *one name among others* for a central idea that guides his materialist philosophy as a whole and secures the philosophical primacy of motion throughout his work.

2) Second, Marx's theory of metabolism is a theory of *historical* rifts, not *ontological* ones.[3] Metabolism involves more than shifts but less than ontological rifts.[4] I argue here that Marx's theory of metabolism is better

Marx in Motion. Thomas Nail, Oxford University Press (2020). © Oxford University Press.
DOI: 10.1093/oso/9780197526477.001.0001

understood as a process of "metabolic (d)rift" in which matter flows and folds itself up through an uneven process of erosion and deposition caused by humans as well as nature. The theory of metabolic drift aims to provide a new foundation for thinking about the continual, twofold process of primitive accumulation and value creation, developed in the previous chapter. This is precisely why Marx first brings up metabolism in section two of chapter one, in the context of accumulation and the production of value.

This chapter thus contains two parts. The first shows the continuity of the concept of metabolism with other key ideas in Marx's work from his dissertation leading up to *Capital*. Again, a close reading of Marx's dissertation can help offer a new rereading of key ideas in his mature work. This unique starting point provides the larger conceptual context for seeing how the concept of metabolism works in Marx's theory of value. The second, and much larger, part shows precisely how the concept of a "metabolic (d)rift" helps us think about the twofold movement of appropriation and value creation.

METABOLIC MOVEMENTS

Metabolism is first and foremost the continual movement of matter. Marx thus makes metabolism one of the largest historical-ontological categories in all of his work. Rarely does Marx write such bold and sweeping theses as the following, from section two:

> Labour, then, as the creator of use-values, as useful labour, is a condition of human existence [*Existenzbedingung*] which is independent [*unabhängige*] of all forms of society; it is a natural inflexibility [*Naturnothwendigkeit*] which mediates [*vermitteln*] the metabolism [*Stoffwechsel*] between [*zwischen*] man and nature, and therefore human life itself. (C, 133)

This is the first usage of the word *Stoffwechsel* in *Capital*.[5] It is therefore important to pause and consider in detail the centrality of this grounding concept before looking at exactly how it relates to the extremely broad concept of labor put forward here.

The idea of metabolism, although certainly connected in Marx's mind to Aristotle's use of the term μεταβολή, *metabolē*, or change, in his *Physics*, has its modern origins in the work of the Venetian physician Sanctorius (1561–1635), who described metabolism as a *"perspiratio insensibilis"* (insensible respiration) to signify "the realization that the living organism is undergoing continuous changes."[6] However, the modern German word *Stoffwechsel* did not emerge until 1815 and was not used widely until the 1830s and 1840s.

The German word *Stoffwechsel* literally means "material transformation." It is formed by combining the German word *Stoff*, meaning matter, plus the German word *Wechsel*, meaning continuous change, from the proto-Germanic *wīkwaną ("to yield, to fold"). It is no surprise that Marx latched onto this new German word for his own purpose. *Stoffwechsel* describes quite well the material-kinetic process of continual material flowing, folding, and circulating that Marx had been writing about since his 1841 dissertation. Marx had seen the term before Liebig's book was published and already had it in mind when he wrote of the material-kinetic *zusammenhängen* of Epicurus's atomism and the wood-gathering laws in Germany.[7] Even the Greek origins of this German word carry an explicitly kinetic and processual character. The ancient Greek word μεταβολή (metabolé, "change") comes from μετά (metá, between or in the midst of) plus βάλλω (bállō, "I throw"). The Greek meaning here, then, is not just "change" but rather a process of continual movement of intra-action within and between things.

When Marx writes in *Capital* of the "metabolism [*Stoffwechsel*] between [*zwischen*] man and nature," we should also hear an Epicurean and Lucretian echo of the continual kinetic transformation of subject and object and form and matter from the doctoral dissertation. The twofold sides of form and matter are dialectically reconciled in Marx *precisely* by the same continual kinetic and pedetic transformation of the two as a twofold process: in sensation. Following the insight of the doctoral dissertation, we cannot possibly read metabolism in *Capital* as an interaction between separate things. This would completely undermine the dialectical and processual nature of the strictly *twofold* nature of sensation that had guided Marx's thought up to *Capital*. In fact, the German word *zwischen*, from the Old High German word *zuiski*, means twofold. Metabolism is thus the twofold movement of matter into and out of various forms.

Again, we should also hear clear metabolic echoes from the manuscripts when Marx writes of the "continuous process of nature's intra-action with itself [*zusammenhängen*]" (MECW 3: 276). It is absolutely no coincidence that whenever Marx begins talking about metabolism and "metabolic tears [*Riss*]" in the *Capital* volumes, he is almost always talking about tears *in something that hangs together (zusammenhängen)*.[8] This is because metabolism is conceptually similar to his older and more general concept of intra-active hanging together. This is not mere conjecture. Marx says almost exactly the same thing in the line previously quoted from *Capital* that he does in the manuscripts, in which he writes of the "self-mediated [*Durchsichselbstsein*] being of nature and of man."[9] The only difference is that in the manuscripts Marx does not yet use the term *Stoffwechsel* and has to find creative ways to talk about mutual interdependent transformation.

For example, in *The German Ideology* he relies heavily on the term *verkehren*, and in the *Grundrisse*, he uses the terms *verkehren*, *zusammenhängen*, *Stoffwechsel*, and *Wechselwirkung*. *Wechselwirkung* uses *wechsel*, from *Stoffwechsel*, meaning to continuously change or fold (*wechseln*). But instead of emphasizing matter (*Stoff*), *Wechselwirkung* emphasizes that actions or effects (*Wirkung*) fold back into one another in a kind of immanent feedback loop or continual transformation of the whole (MEGA I, 5: 126).[10] Thus, we also find in the *Grundrisse* a whole theory of the *zusammenhängen* of production and consumption: the "individual produces an object and, by consuming it, returns to himself, but returns as a productive and self-reproducing individual" (G, 94). We also find there an explicit description of the *zusammenhängen* of use-value and exchange-value.[11]

Therefore *Stoffwechsel*, though absolutely crucial for rereading Marx today, is only one among at least three other core concepts that function similarly (although not identically) in his work. Not only did Marx develop a theory of material-kinetic intra-action well before the *Grundrisse*, but he also used other important terms that ought to be considered alongside one another when thinking about Marx's theory of metabolism. Metabolism, like the *zusammenhängen* of the doctoral dissertation, is the material-kinetic foundation and "earthly basis," which serves as the ultimate "source of all production and of all being."[12]

THE THREEFOLD THEORY OF METABOLISM

One of the most important developments to this concept that occurs in the *Capital* volumes is the emergence of a threefold theory of metabolism. Before moving on to show how the concept of "metabolic drift" helps us think about the twofold movement of accumulation and value creation, I need to be clear about what metabolism is for Marx. Marx's theory of metabolism is threefold: on the largest scale, there is a "metabolism of nature," within which a "human metabolism with nature" emerges and within which a further "social metabolism" emerges. Although nature obviously precedes humans, once humans emerge, all three metabolic processes become aspects or folds in the same continual metabolic process. I briefly consider each in turn.[13]

The Metabolism of Nature

This first kind of metabolism is what Marx calls the "universal metabolism" or "universal metabolic process," "nature's metabolism" or the "simple metabolism of nature" (MECW 30: 62, 63, 78; G, 271). This "universal metabolic process" consists of "elemental forces" that involve physical, chemical, or physiological transformations such as the rusting of iron, rotting of wood, fermentation of fruits, or "transposition" of matter "into a human organism" (MECW 30: 62; C II, 316; C, 323). In the *Grundrisse,* for example, Marx makes clear that his theory of production and consumption is not a strictly anthropocentric process. Nature produces and consumes itself in a continuous process or co-production and mutual metabolic transformation. Nature folds (*wechselt*) back over itself again and again. "Consumption is also immediately production, just as in nature the consumption of elements and chemical substances is the production of the plant. It is clear that in taking in food, for example, which is a form of consumption, the human being produces his own body" (G, 90).

Even in *Capital*, Marx is quite explicit that nature is productive without any assistance from humans. Human production is, strictly speaking, immanent to nature's own metabolic folding. Human production and human labor are folds within the larger metabolic process of nature's sensuous folding:

> This substratum is furnished by nature without human intervention. When man engages in production, he can only proceed as nature does herself; i.e., he can only change the form of the materials. Furthermore even in this work of modification he is constantly helped by natural forces. Labour is therefore not the only source of material wealth, i.e., of the use-values it produces. (C, 133–134)

Marx clearly says that nature, without human intervention, is productive, and when humans are involved, they are never the only source of material wealth and use-value—since they produce only as nature does. Such a position is absolutely irreconcilable with any form of anthropocentrism or social constructivism. Nature is really productive, and humans really produce only because they are a metabolic region of nature's own production process.

The Human Metabolism with Nature

This second kind of metabolism is what Marx calls the "metabolic interaction between man and nature" or the "human metabolism with nature" (C,

290; C III, 959). This is the type of metabolism found in the first chapter of *Capital*. Nature's metabolism is defined by its "elemental forces," which produce and consume themselves, just as Epicurus and Lucretius described, for example like the fermentation of grapes into wine (C II, 316). Further, since the human body is a natural body, it also has a metabolic process that is continuous with nature. For example, "It is a physiological fact that [productive activities] are functions of the human organism, and that each such function, whatever may be its nature or its form, is essentially the expenditure of human brain, nerves, muscles and sense organs" (C, 164; cf. 283). As a natural body (*Korper*), the human body is a region or subcycle of sensuous activity that in turn continually intra-acts and hangs together with nature's larger metabolic processes (C, 283–284).

This is precisely why Marx describes human sensuous activity in such elemental and natural terms. For example, he says that "labour [is] a living agent of fermentation," the "living, form-giving fire" that "awakens" certain objects "from the dead" by "breathing life into them as the elements of a 'new formation'" (C, 292; G, 361; C, 289; MECW 30: 63). Since humans are nature, they act as "a force of nature," in a "system of nature," alongside other "elemental forces," insofar as they "can only proceed as nature does herself, i.e. [they] can only change the form of the materials" and in their own corporeally specific way (C, 283, 133; GI, 37, 49).

It is precisely because humans are nature that their activity must proceed as a metabolic interchange (*Verkehr*) with nature. Human nature metabolism is thus a "nature-imposed condition of human existence," in an intra-active feedback relation between production and consumption (C, 290).

Social Metabolism

The third kind of metabolism is what Marx calls the "interdependent process of social metabolism" (C III, 949). Just as humans emerge as a continual fold in nature's metabolic process, so social metabolism emerges as a fold in both natural and human metabolic processes. Social metabolism is not just an optional subset of human activity; it is completely continuous with all human activity, which is always social activity (G, 157, 158). Material production also rests, "in one way or another, on social production," and "productive existence is possible only on this condition." Human metabolism with nature necessarily involves a "metabolism of social labor," and through this "material and mental metabolism," living human individuals "change . . . in that they bring out new qualities in themselves, develop themselves in production, transform themselves, develop new powers and ideas, new modes of intercourse [*Verkehr*], new needs and new language" (G, 489, 492, 494, 161; C II, 226).

Social metabolism, for Marx, also importantly includes nonhuman "natural agents" that "co-operate" as "creators of wealth" (MECW 34: 32; C, 752). Thus, the "process of economic reproduction[,] whatever its specific social character may be," is "always intertwined with a process of natural reproduction." The material production of nature continually bears, supports, maintains, and gives birth to all human productions. The fermentation of alcohol, the tanning of leather, the "production time" it takes for an animal or plant to grow, and so on are all nonhuman forms of productive agency that participate in social metabolism. Nonhuman productive agencies "undergo physical, chemical or physiological changes while the labour process is either completely or partially suspended" (C, 752; C II, 434, 316): the "ripening of corn, the growth of an oak," "wine that ferments in the cellar," and so forth (C II, 317, 201). The labor process can also be suspended due to "uncontrollable natural conditions, the seasons of the year, etc." (C III, 213). Social metabolism is thus differentiated in regional ways. However, as natural and social beings, humans always hang together in natural and social co-production.

It is worth noting here, as Alfred Schmitt does, that Marx "introduced a completely new understanding of man's relation to nature," one that "went far beyond all the bourgeois theories of nature presented by the Enlightenment."[14] In particular, Marx took the concept of metabolism from Daniels, Liebig, and the sciences and then transformed it into an entire historical ontology that included nature, humans, and society. Liebig and others only thought of metabolism in a relatively limited naturalistic way, but Marx completed the threefold concept by extending metabolism to the human relation to nature and to social production. Just as plants produce and consume energy, so do social patterns of motion. In Marx's theory of metabolism, any ontological division between humans and nature is impossible.

METABOLIC EXPANSION BY EXPULSION

Now that I have contextualized Marx's theory of metabolism and defined its threefold aspects or dimensions, I turn to how this theory helps us understand the dialectical process of appropriation and value creation, or what I call "expansion by expulsion."

Based on the preceding threefold account of metabolism, it seems that appropriation and value creation are not quite a ontological "breaks" or "rifts" in the metabolic process. This is the case not simply for dogmatic reasons of adhering to dialectics but because metabolism is defined by the continual intra-action, flow, and fold of material production. Marx's entire project, from his doctoral dissertation to *Capital*, was to overcome any idea that there are radical breaks or discrete cuts anywhere. In fact, every time we posit such a break in the threefold dialectical flux of matter, we end up with things like atoms and commodities.[15] These apparently discrete units try to hide the supports that bear them. Discontinuity always hides a constitutive exclusion immanent to the process of production, just as value hides primitive accumulation.

In fact, when Marx writes that value creates "conditions which cause an irreparable tear [*Riss*] in the coherence of social interchange prescribed by the natural laws of life," he uses the German word *Riss* (C III, 949), which can mean a crack or split but also "a tear" or "rough," as in *Grund-risse*, meaning "rough draft" or literally uneven or scratchy ground. The English translation of *Riss* as "break" seems to me inappropriate to the natural conditions of metabolic hanging together, and the English translation "rift" might sound too ontological.

A better translation for this term as Marx uses it would be "crack," or better "tear," since it emphasizes the uneven or rough materiality of the process (as opposed to "split," which can sound more dramatic in English). When something is torn, it undergoes a physical and kinetic redistribution along an uneven material. A tear is much more like a bifurcation in a process than it is like an ontological split or rift. Even a crack in the ground still meets at a point deeper down and is therefore a better description of the unevenness or messiness of metabolic *imbalance*. No tear or crack is absolute. A tear or crack is also never strictly repairable. This is not because two things are torn asunder forever and for all time, but because the repair will always be slightly different afterward. In the context of metabolism, a crack is closer to an unfolding. A crack, tear, or wound exposes the inside to the outside and the outside to the inside. Rough or rocky ground, or *Grundrisse*, is a better topological description of the uneven and imbalanced nature of abrupt metabolic drifts from metastable states of equilibrium. The metabolic folds unfold and refold along rough cracks or tears in a single fluctuating topological surface.

The term "metabolic shift" helps in some ways to avoid the cataclysmic sound of a metabolic "rift" but does not indicate quite as well the disruptive nature of metabolic imbalances caused by primitive accumulation. It is crucial to emphasize that "as a result [of such tears], the vitality of the soil is squandered, and this prodigality is carried by commerce far beyond the borders of a particular state" (C III, 949). Someone or something temporarily ruins the soil somewhere for some things and some people and accumulates those minerals elsewhere breaking various metabolic cycles. Metabolic transformations are somewhere between shifts and rifts. They are "shifting rifts" or "(d)rifts."

How, then, should we think of changes in metabolic processes without implying an anthropocentric division between humans and nature or a simple naturalistic continuity? Perhaps no single word will solve this problem, but in the following sections I propose a third option that aims for the middle ground of what I call a "metabolic (d)rift." A metabolic (d) rift is a metastable process caused by natural-cultural systems. Metabolic cycles can break down through regional "rifts," but these rifts can also move around or "drift." They may produce a cascade of metabolic disruption or eventually enter into a new metabolic cycle. Metabolic (d)rifts are like vortices in a fluid medium, which emerge, converge, diverge, and circulate around.

Metabolic processes take matters from one area and move them to another but in doing so also have a direct and real effect on the whole. They can also produce regional imbalances across various natural and human cycles. Some areas of the earth expand only on the condition that other areas are expelled from their regional metabolic process—producing a series of relationally constituted imbalances or asymmetries in metabolic processes. The term "drift" also refers more appropriately to the shared nonlinear, thermodynamic processes of nature and humans to generate non-equilibrium situations. This includes not only social processes of dispossession, slavery,[16] and forced migration but also natural processes of changing climatic periods (the medieval warm period and the "Little Ice Age"), animal migrations, extinctions, evolutions, environmental disasters, seasonal changes, and so on. Metabolic processes of all kinds are, like a meandering river, constantly being eroded in one location and deposited in another. The key idea of metabolic (d)rifting is that (a) it is produced by both *natural* and *social* agents and (b) it is composed of regional and *not absolute breaks* in metabolic cycles. If we want to survive in a metastable world we have to seek out metabolic balances as best we can. Unfortunately, capitalism systematically undermines all attempts at natural, human, and social metabolic balance.

Nature and humans both participate in this drift-and-deposit system. But how does this relate to the dialectic between appropriation and value creation?

Metabolic Appropriation and Value Creation

One of the first contributions of the theory of metabolism to the theory of value is that it makes it impossible to think about "free gifts" and free-floating values. Given the threefold metabolic condition, value must always come from somewhere. Value must always happen as a metabolic erosion, expulsion, or drift from somewhere else. I return to the original quote:

> Labour, then, as the creator of use-values, as useful labour, is a condition of human existence [*Existenzbedingung*] which is independent [*unabhängige*] of all forms of society; it is a natural inflexibility [*Naturnothwendigkeit*] which mediates [*vermitteln*] the metabolism [*Stoffwechsel*] between [*zwischen*] man and nature, and therefore human life itself. (C, 133)

Material production is the condition of human existence. It is the core process immanent to all forms of society and therefore is itself the material process of mediation in the twofold metabolism of humans and nature. In short, material production or labor is immanent to the metabolic process itself. Material production is fundamentally metabolic. This means that the material production of value by human societies is itself continuous with the metabolic process of nature. In addition, this requires that all value creation necessarily appropriates vastly more than it values. This includes everything from women's domestic labor to the ecological conditions of reproduction, such as drinkable water, adequate rainfall, a certain number of calories, and many other such devalorized "externalities."

Value creation is therefore like a kind of geological erosion of the production powers of the earth and a deposition of some of its pieces in highly concentrated regions of value: the European white male factory worker. Marx's theory of metabolism explicitly makes it clear that all this productive power comes from somewhere in the threefold metabolic process. The whole metabolic process is involved in every single value, because value cannot be isolated from the process as a whole.

"The earth [is] the source of all production and of all being"; it is "active as an agent of production in the production of a use-value, a material product"; and it "continuously improves, as long as it is treated correctly" (G, 106; C III, 955, 916). The earth is an active agent in production but only improves if its productions are returned in the right portions and places for its stable metabolic consumption. In the *Grundrisse*, Marx even describes the earth as a kind of "primitive instrument" or "primitive condition of production,"[17] thus connecting it to the process of primitive accumulation directly. If the earth is the primitive condition, its appropriation and accumulation are similarly primitive and devalorized.

As natural animals, humans are constantly producing and consuming the earth as part of their co-produced metabolic process. "The material of nature [is] transposed into a human organism" to become the very materiality of their bodies (C, 323). "In taking in food," Marx writes, "the human being produces his own body" (G, 90). In this way, the "living corporeity" is a subjectivity of objective essential powers whose sensuous activity is a "physical manifestation" of these powers and, as such, a "force of nature" (MECW 30: 37; C, 310, 283). "He sets in motion the natural forces which belong to his own body, his arms, legs, head and hands, in order to appropriate the materials of nature in a form adapted to his own needs. Through this movement he acts upon external nature and changes it, and in this way simultaneously changes his own nature" (C, 283). As long as the human consumption of nature is also a productive consumption that returns what was consumed to where it was produced, the metabolic cycle remains relatively stable and reproductive. Human labor "taken by itself cannot exist at all. The entire productive activity of man, through which his metabolic interchange with nature is mediated," requires "co-operation" with "the realm of natural forces" and "a conscious and rational treatment of the land as permanent communal property, as the inalienable conditions for the existence and reproduction of the chain of human generations . . . [and] of the powers of the earth" (C III, 954, 964, 948–949). The thermodynamic drift of metabolism is relatively straightforward: "Every additional expenditure of labour presupposes a corresponding additional expenditure of raw materials" (C, 752). The existence of global climate change should make further elaboration of this point unnecessary.

Metabolic Primitive Accumulation

The process of value creation, however, introduces a tear into the metabolic pattern of production and consumption. Value creation, as we have seen, treats material production as if it had no qualities and dangled from midair, detached from its conditions of production and reproduction. Practically this is impossible, but performatively it is not impossible to act *as if* all matters could be moved around without regard to the site-specific conditions of production and consumption. This also means that all value creation is simultaneously and concurrently a process of metabolic appropriation or primitive accumulation. Value creation tears one portion of a specific metabolic process away and puts it into another. Matter is eroded in one place and deposited in another without regard for any qualitative changes in the effects (*Wechselwirkung*), transforming and usually disrupting the entire process.

The appropriation of the earth: Marx is explicit on this point. "Exchange value originates in the isolated natural product separated from the earth and individualised by means of industry (or simple appropriation). This is the stage, too, at which individual labour makes its first appearance. In general, exchange does not initially arise within the original communities, but on their borders; where the communities come to an end" (MECW 29: 126). The very first step in value creation is the relative isolation of a product from the threefold metabolic flux by means of simple appropriation, that is, primitive accumulation. Unlike the production and consumption of the earth in quality-saturated use-value, value treats products *as if* they were *not* part of a larger metabolic process.

The appropriation of labor: The primitive accumulation of the metabolic products of the earth occurs at the same time as the metabolic appropriation of individual units of quality-less labor as well. Value creation and appropriation, Marx adds, historically occur on the borders of communities precisely because within "original communities" the social-metabolic process is harder to overcome. In other words, it is easier to steal things when people are not around to defend them, and it is easier to steal people when they are not around to protect one another. Rarely do communities treat their own conditions of metabolic reproduction as if they could simply be removed from their embedded context of hanging together. Most indigenous communities, for example, do not spontaneously destroy their own food or water supplies or kill their own people *as if* they had no sensuous qualities.[18]

The appropriation of the border: The primitive accumulation of metabolic products is therefore frequently a border phenomenon.[19] Appropriation always occurs at the limits of value. Wherever there is devalorized material production, there is value creation, precisely because value creation is also and simultaneously a retroactive devalorization of what does not count as value. Before the creation of value there is not a border between value and nonvalue. This is not strictly a function of quantification or objectification as such but rather a function of treating quantities *as if* they were not immanent to their qualities.

Value *is a process of bordering* that actively and practically introduces a division into the flux of material production.[20] Value-in-motion acts as if value moves from commodity A to commodity B, when in fact it is the flow of material production upon which A and B emerge in the first place. In theorizing value, we must be careful at every step to remember not to drink the water and believe that value is truly immaterial or quality-less. Value is nothing other than material production (nature) itself folded up into relatively discrete units and distributed according to specific rationales.

The border therefore is not some mental division that happens once and for all. Social borders are continually moving and shifting processes that modulate with the purpose of expanding value creation through the expulsion of devalorized matters. The thing about borders is that the line can always be drawn one more time indefinitely and asymptotically. Contrary to certain ecologists who talk about the "carrying capacity" of the earth, our "footprint" upon it, or the "natural limits of the earth," there is and can be no ontological limit to social value creation. Any such talk of ontological limits to nature's capacities is metaphysical and ahistorical. There are certainly regional limits past which certain social patterns of motion such as capitalism can no longer "effectively" produce value and past which humans will die (e.g., CO_2 levels in the atmosphere). But the bordering process of social value creation *in general* has no strict ontological or absolute limit past which nothing more can be devalorized.

METABOLIC DRIFT

Since the earth is the "primitive condition of production" and metabolic foundation, it is also the primitive source of devalorization. It is with the earth that the first metabolic drifts begin. This is not an ontological split, or break but a material and practical tear or crack. Marx, for example, explicitly uses the verb form of *riss* "to tear" to describe this process. "The earth is the reservoir, from whose BOWELS the use values are to be torn [*riss*]" (MECW 31: 465). The earthly metabolic process is treated *as if* it were a container, just as value itself is a discrete container of congealed fluid labor. Value thus creates its devalorized other in its own image: the container. What is torn from the earth is not actually quality-less or really divided in any ontological way from the earth.

Rather, devalorization relies on and is immanent to the "interdependent process of social-metabolism," which is "prescribed by the natural laws of life itself" but then treats it strictly according to the "sole driving force . . . to create surplus-value" (C III, 949; C, 342). Devalorization simultaneously "attacks the individual at the very roots of his life" and "prevents the return to the soil of its constituent elements consumed by man" (C, 484, 637). Metabolic drift produces an imbalance or asymmetrical accumulation of value over devalorization, just like the process of erosion and deposition. As water speed increases, little bits of the riverbank are eroded, or "torn" from their primitive rootedness in the ground. But these bits of soil and humus from one side of the river are not destroyed or distributed randomly; they drift through the water and are deposited and accumulated on the slower side of the river. The river enters a feedback loop of faster waters, more erosion, more deposition, until an alternating pattern of silted sandbars is visible along the river bank.

For Marx, the "exploitation and squandering of the powers of the earth" results from a metabolic drift when the cycle of production and consumption drifts out of balance, or equilibrium. On a long enough time scale, this is minor, but for human life, Marx says, it heralds "the coming degradation and final depopulation of the human race" (C III, 949; C, 381). Like a vampire, value creation "lives only by sucking living labour, and lives the more, the more labour it sucks" (C, 875, 342). Metabolic drift is a *relational and thermodynamic imbalance* such that "the future can indeed be anticipated and ruined in both cases by premature over-exertion and exhaustion, and by disturbance of the balance between expenditure and income . . . [which] in the case of the worker and the land . . . exists as power[,] and the life span of this power is shortened as a result of accelerated expenditure" (MECW 32: 442).

Although value cannot be absolutely limited, it can be regionally limited by the life of the worker and the depth of the mine, and it has tendencies toward regional exhaustion or what Jason Moore calls "the tendency of the ecological surplus to fall."[21]

Metabolic drift is a metabolic primitive accumulation that tends toward an increasing imbalance between production and consumption (the means of production). "So-called primitive accumulation, therefore, is nothing else than the historical process of divorcing the producer from the means of production" (C, 874–875). Because of its "shameless and ruthless lack of moderation, impelling it to go beyond the natural limits of labour time into the realms of madness" (MECW 33: 386), devalorization has a tendency toward self-destruction via the exhaustion of its own conditions of value creation. This is the fundamental and logical paradox of devalorization: it produces a drift or imbalance into the very cycles of metabolic production and consumption that it relies on *for its own process*.

This point is entirely passed over if we think of value creation as some kind of immaterial abstraction. It is precisely because value is *not actually immaterial and not quality-less* that it tends to actually exhaust its own metabolic conditions of concrete practice. Value creation is a material process of sensuous production like everything else and is thus affected by the metabolic processes that it is enmeshed in. The fundamental paradox and downfall of value creation is that it does not realize that (a) the values it produces are not actually discrete or quality-less and (b) its own practical conditions of action are part of the larger process of threefold metabolic circulation.

The process of devalorization is like the ouroboros that does not realize that it is eating its own tail. The ancient image of the ouroboros has stood for the idea of eternity, the perfect enclosed, discrete, Hegelian circle. But this is the history of idealism. Practically, the snake exhausts its own conditions and thus its own body by destroying them: "Nature becomes purely an object for humankind, purely a matter of utility; ceases to be recognized as a power for itself" (G, 410).

Since the threefold metabolic process is the historically primary situation, the question is not how such a continual flux was produced but rather how it became historically imbalanced into various drifts and sandbars of accumulation. As Marx writes in the *Grundrisse*:

> It is not the unity of living and active humanity with the natural, inorganic conditions of their metabolic exchange with nature, and hence their appropriation of nature, which requires explanation or is the result of a historic process, but rather the separation between these inorganic conditions of human existence and this active existence, a separation which is completely posited only in the relation of wage labour and capital. (G, 489)

Discreteness will never explain movement. Only by starting with the continual movement of material production can we then understand the emergence of relative discreteness through the process of folding. Marx first put forward this idea in his doctoral dissertation and developed it in *Capital*. What needs to be explained, then, is how we have arrived at an interpretation of the threefold metabolic process as one in which humans and nature are separate and matter and form became divided in the first place. This is, for Marx, a historical question. What are the material and historical conditions under which such a social practice has emerged and come to dominate social life? Separation and anthropocentrism are not just bourgeois delusions; they cut straight through the history of Western civilization, each epoch with its own manifestation of this division.[22]

METABOLIC COMMUNISM

The social task of communism, then, for Marx, is not to prescribe any universally right way to organize this threefold metabolic circulation but rather simply to acknowledge the primacy of material production and experiment more carefully with it. Instead of massive metabolic drifts of erosion and deposition, metabolic communism must work in closer, more sensitive feedback and "free play" with such patterns of circulation.

Metabolic communism would have to maintain an entropic "balance between expenditure and income" of material production/consumption for the proper "restoration, renewal and refreshment" of the "powers of life," the "vitality of the soil," and the "realm of natural forces" (MECW 32: 442; C, 376; C III, 949, 964).[23] Metabolic communism would need to "govern the human metabolism with nature in a rational way, bringing it under their collective control instead of being dominated by it as a blind power" (C III, 959).[24]

It should be strikingly clear at this point to all who have read Marx as a Promethean productivist, who assumed a "general material abundance" with no regard for "the liberation of nature from human domination,"[25] that such a reading is absolutely incompatible with the long list of direct quotes cited here that contradict this anthropocentric and productivist reading. It is true that Marx talks a lot about humans and production, but this alone does not make him an anthropocentric productivist. The burden of proof is on such productivist readings to show that Marx explicitly separates humans from nature; gives them special ontological, hierarchical, or epistemological priority; and thinks that nature can and should be endlessly appropriated without qualification. Any future theory of communism must include a serious consideration of the threefold kinetic and metabolic processes Marx described. Just as social metabolism is a fold within the larger threefold process, so full human social emancipation cannot take place without a threefold metabolic emancipation of nature from the process of value creation.

CONCLUSION

Anthropocentric, productivist, and social-reductionist readings of Marx still have power over the popular and even scholarly imagination. This is not because they are consistently supported in the primary texts but because of the enduring legacy of Soviet and humanist readings. Marx's writings in *Capital* can clearly be read through a strictly human- and value-centric lens, but I hope this chapter has shown the poverty of such restricted readings in the context of numerous directly nonanthropocentric citations. The threefold concept of metabolism is one of the strongest weapons we have against anthropocentric readings of Marx.

CHAPTER 6

The Patriarchy of Value

With the key ideas of kinetic materialism, devalorization, and me-tabolism in hand, I would like to look at one more major aspect of value creation. Marx *begins* his theory of value with an important refer-ence to the *gendered* nature of value creation at the start of section three. This passage is worth considering in some detail in order to make clear and expand upon the gendered nature of devalorization that occurs as a precondition and ongoing support for the movement of value more generally.

Marx begins the third section of chapter one with a crucial and illuminating foundation to his theory of value: *the appropriation of women's labor*. This brief introductory section, right before the start of Marx's ki-netic theory of value, thus links the first two sections of chapter one to the third section. It is precisely the twofold nature of the devalorization process that shapes the exchange relations of commodities. To understand value in motion, we first need to see how the source of motion itself is "home-baked" in the *patriarchy of value*. This is the aim and argument of this chapter.

HOME-BAKED VALUE

It is crucial to take seriously the continued role of devalorization and met-abolic appropriation that are played out in the theory of value in section three. In particular, Marx provides a wonderful opportunity to examine the gendered nature of the value creation process right before moving on to his theory of value:

Marx in Motion. Thomas Nail, Oxford University Press (2020). © Oxford University Press.
DOI: 10.1093/oso/9780197526477.001.0001

Commodities come into the world [*kommen zur Welt*] in the form of use-values or material goods [*Waarenkörpern*], such as iron, linen, corn, etc. This is their home-baked, [*hausbakkene*] natural form. However, they are only commodities because they have a dual nature [*Doppeltes*], because they are at the same time objects of utility and bearers of value [*Werthträger*]. Therefore they only appear [*erscheinen*] as commodities, or have the form of commodities, insofar as they possess a double form [*Doppelform*], i.e., natural form and value form. (C, 138)

In this transition, Marx explicitly reminds us that commodities first and fundamentally "come into the world" or are *born* as material *bodies* (*Körpern*) and *bearers of value* (*Werthträger*). These material and sensuous bodies are *hausbakkene*, literally home-baked. Without the movement of bearing, carrying, birthing, baking, and maintaining, there is no value, full stop. Value is something that is first and foremost a kinetic process of "coming into being" through the material conditions of the bodies of women, who bear children and bake bread. The term "home-baked" is not just about bread and pies; Marx's description about the coming-to-be of value is explicitly gendered around birth and domestic material production. The body that bears value comes from the home, and the home, in the capitalist mode of production, is defined by women's devalued domestic labor. In short, value emerges only on the condition of a *gendered devalorization* and *division of labor*.

DAME QUICKLY

Marx follows up these gendered remarks about the home-baked birth of value with an even more explicit reference to the gendered violence against women at the extractive origins of value. For Marx, the nature of the commodity is twofold (*Doppelt*), *unlike* Dame Quickly in Shakespeare's *Henry IV*. "The objectivity of commodities as values *differs* from Dame Quickly in the sense that, 'a man knows not where to have it.' Not an atom of matter enters into the objectivity of commodities as values; in this it is the direct opposite of the coarsely sensuous objectivity of commodities as physical objects" (C, 138).[1] The full meaning of this reference cannot be deciphered from Marx's footnote here unless we look at the full exchange of Falstaff, Prince Henry, and Dame Quickly in *Henry IV*, part 1, act 3, scene 3:

> DAME QUICKLY: . . . my lord, he speaks most vilely of you, like a foul-mouthed man as he is; and said he would cudgel you.
> PRINCE HENRY: What! He did not?

DAME QUICKLY: There's neither faith, truth, nor womanhood in me else.

FALSTAFF: There's no more faith in thee than in a stewed prune; nor no more truth in thee than in a drawn fox; and for womanhood, Maid Marian may be the deputy's wife of the ward to thee. Go, you thing, go.

DAME QUICKLY: Say, what thing? What thing?

FALSTAFF: What thing! Why, a thing to thank God on.

DAME QUICKLY: I am no thing to thank God on, I would thou shouldst know it; I am an honest man's wife: and, setting thy knighthood aside, thou art a knave to call me so.

FALSTAFF: Setting thy womanhood aside, thou art a beast to say otherwise.

DAME QUICKLY: Say, what beast, thou knave, thou?

FALSTAFF: What beast! Why, an otter.

PRINCE HENRY: An otter, Sir John! Why an otter?

FALSTAFF: Why, she's neither fish nor flesh; a man knows not where to have her.

The most direct surface meaning here is that for Marx, Dame Quickly is a sensuous material woman speaking the truth and should not be treated in the same way as the twofold or two-faced false commodity that hides its devalorized material conditions behind the mystified veil of value.[2] This is why she is *different from* a commodity. This is why, for Marx, Falstaff's accusation is wrong and why the commodity thus *differs* from Dame Quickly.

This reference is also vastly richer than this surface meaning. It reveals much more than Marx explicitly says about the gendered devalorization of commodity production. First of all, Marx's reference to Quickly is directly connected to the previous paragraph, where Marx had just emphasized the point that the bearing body of value is something born and home-baked. Dame Quickly is the hostess of the Boar's-Head Tavern, in which her primary role is quite literally to run around "quickly" doing such domestic labor as cooking, baking, cleaning, serving, and so on. As a wife and likely unpaid domestic worker in her husband's tavern, she is the image par excellence of exhausted and appropriated female labor. She is the bearing body (*Träger*) of kinetic value: carrying, bearing, moving, maintaining, cleaning, serving, and so on.

Second, she is also the immediate, coarsely sensuous truth of the situation. In contrast to the value of the commodity that claims to have "not an atom of matter," Dame Quickly is like the coarse kinetic materiality of the atom—moving and swerving around quickly in material production.

As devalorized producer and material condition, she is in a position to see beyond the "blinding light" of the lying and false superiority of Falstaff's merely apparent symbolic value as a "knight." Falstaff is friends with Prince Henry and so seems powerful and important but is actually a scoundrel. He is the real two-faced figure of this analgoy. Falstaff, whose name even contains "fals," falsely tells Quickly that someone in the Boar's-Head stole a valuable ring from him. Quickly points out that Henry said the ring was copper, and then Falstaff calls Henry a dog (behind his back) and threatens to cudgel him.

In short, Falstaff here plays the role of value by stealing from Quickly (running up a tab and not paying it) and so directly appropriates her unpaid labor. He then inverts the real relation of production and claims that someone in her bar *stole from him*. This is a lie. The false value of the object supposedly stolen was a worthless copper ring.

It is thus Falstaff who actually expresses the twofold nature of the commodity. On one side his value is based on a direct theft and appropriation of women's labor that supports his very presence in the tavern and on the other side a direct devalorization of that very labor in the form of an overvaluing of his own. In this scene Falstaff occupies precisely the twofold position of value, with one side facing the direct, violent, and misogynist relation to Quickly and the other side facing the value relation of fraternity to Henry. However, when Quickly speaks this truth to Henry, Falstaff attempts unsuccessfully to flip the situation and project his own twofold nature back onto Quickly herself.

Third, Falstaff launches a misogynist attack against Quickly, which dramatizes perfectly both the patriarchal structure of devalorization and the gendered subordination of material production present in the twofold structure of the commodity. Falstaff calls Quickly a stewed prune, a drawn fox, Maid Marian, a thing, and an otter. The following sections look at what each of these terms reveals about the twofold structure of gendered devalorization inherent in the commodity.

The Stewed Prune

Falstaff first calls Quickly a stewed prune. This is at once a misogynist remark about her age or wrinkled appearance and the mushy nature of her once-fertile, fruited body. The stewed or cooked prune is no longer the fertile supportive body of a fresh fruit. It is also, and perhaps more directly, a misogynist attack against her as a "false woman" or prostitute, since brothels often had bowls of stewed prunes in the windows as "remedies" for venereal disease. Quickly is said to be false because prostitutes are false, their medicine is false, they are unfaithful, and their actions are false for example, against the laws of state and religion. Another implication is that prostitutes are false because they have sex without bearing children or trying to bear children, or abort their children.

So Quickly here is both naturalized (fruit) and sterilized (whore) at the same time. "Value," the commodity says, "does not come from the agency of nature! Nature is a bunch of dead resources that men give life to." The structure of value, as shown in the next chapter, is precisely to hide the social relations of its own production. Falstaff, the commodity, discursively sterilizes nature's metabolic agency and material productivity.

The Drawn Fox

The drawn fox is a dead fox that is drawn across a hunting trail to throw off the hunting dogs. In this sense, Quickly is again called nature, but not just any nature—a dead, sterile nature. She is a false or dead nature that only deceives men as to the real self-founding nature of masculine value creation. It is men who hunt down nature, following the true guide of reason. Fox hunting is also traditionally related to the direct primitive accumulation of English forest and "waste" lands and also summons the image of the early theft of the commons and the hunting of vagabonds and runaway serfs, who would hide and live in these commons.[3]

The fox, like fruit, is also a traditionally female-gendered animal, not just because it is men who hunt it down and kill it in the woods but because historically in Europe, in the Middle Ages and Renaissance, the fox was a trickster figure. The fox was associated with fraudulent behavior, shape-shifting, cunning, and the devil.[4] The fox is beautiful, but it is a deceptive or false beauty that deceives men. The gendering of the fox thus follows the misogynist characterization of women.

Finally, both of these meanings are brought together in the image of the witch hunt. As Marx details in part VIII of *Capital*, customary land rights were dissolved during the primitive accumulation of the commons, and vagabonds (peasants who refused waged labor) were criminalized. Their bodies were mutilated by whipping and branding. Women in particular were the most devastated by the enclosure of the commons and unemployed by early restrictions on women's paid labor.[5] Women thus more often ended up sneaking into the closed-off woodlands to collect fire and building materials, begging on the streets for money, and wandering around in poverty, occasionally uttering curses upon those who did not give them money. Female vagabonds were called "witches" and often burned at the stake. So was the fox. During this time, foxes were also caught and burned at the stake because they were associated with witchcraft, metamorphosis, and the devil. The cunning of the trickster and the misogynist attack on women's knowledge go back a long way together—at least since the Greek myth of Rhea's cunning (*métis*) theft of her baby from Cronus and Zeus's direct appropriation (literal eating) of the goddess Metis.[6] Patriarchal value creation has always had a vested interest in obscuring the violent relations of social appropriation and primitive accumulation that support and maintain it.

Maid Marian

Maid Marian was originally a shepherdess figure of May Day and spring fertility festivals. She is historically associated with the fertility of animals, soil, fruits, and crops, and the husbandry practices of the peasant commons. Fertility festivals go back to the Neolithic and privilege the creative power of the earth, a powerful female goddess, and a "green man" (son/lover) who spreads fertile seed.[7] It must also be said that even though the connection is retroactive, May Day is the international workers' holiday and traditional celebration of socialism, communism, and the power of the working class.

However, during the rise of anti-pagan Puritanism in England, the figure of Maid Marian was systematically devalorized, along with the earth, the commons, and goddess worship as a necessary condition for the value and glory of the sky God and his man-son, Christ. Again, religion plays the role of abstract value, just as Falstaff plays the role of patriarchal authority over Quickly.

However, one of the most important ways Maid Marian comes to appear is in her role as the powerful and intelligent (unmarried) lover of the peasant rebel Robin Hood. Together they live as forest vagabonds, leading an army of dispossessed peasants to steal back from the rich what the rich had stolen form them. Falstaff thus slanders Quickly in the same way that religious authorities, early capitalists, and lords did. They subjugated women's power and autonomy to fight back against those who had stolen their land, criminalized their children, and burned them at the stake. Maid Marian, the once-fertile May goddess, is reduced to an unmarried criminal harlot and damned in the eyes of God. Similarly, Falstaff accuses Quickly of theft, when it is in fact he who has stolen from her. In other words, the value creation process blames metabolic exhaustion (of soil, workers, women) on the infertility of matter and deceptiveness of nature, when in fact it is value that has stolen from nature without metabolic return.

The name of Maid Marian is the perfect political synthesis of the whole historical attack on women's bodies and labor. Maid Marian combines the figure of fruit and fertility with the cunning powers of the forest-dwelling fox, who is also an unmarried criminal whore who should be burned as a witch. Most important in the case of Quickly, however, is the fact that Falstaff's misogynist attack comes by virtue of the fact that Quickly stands up to him, calls him a liar and a thief, demands compensation for her labor, and fights back. Quickly is thus, for Marx, the hero of the scene. She rejects the deceptive nature of the twofold commodity. She calls it what it is: violence, theft, dispossession, devalorization, and misogyny.

The Thing

At the culmination of this series of misogynist names, Falstaff ends by calling Quickly a "thing." Like all great Shakespearean lines, the meaning of this term operates in several registers at once. First, and perhaps most obviously, Falstaff is effectively calling Quickly a "cunt." However, below the surface of this traditional Shakespearean euphemism lies the deeper devalorization of women's domestic and reproductive labor. This also includes the devalorization of the material production of nonhuman agency more broadly as passive "things." The effect of Falstaff's attack is to devalorize Quickly from a human to a female human, then to just her vulva, and then to reduce her vulva to an inanimate thing.

The series of assumptions here is that matter is worthless, and since women are reducible to matter (via their vulvas), then they are also worthless. They are false. Falstaff's use of the term "thing" at the end of the attack reaches the ultimate core of the logic of devalorization: matter. The devalorization of matter is what ties all the other devalorization together: fruit, animal, criminal, shapechanger, and witch. Finally, he reaches the bottom of the chain of being and just calls her matter. We watch Falstaff in a single line attempt to strip Quickly of all her qualities (just as value does to use-value) until she becomes a purely passive thing upon which to sit and praise God! She is a only a passive biological means to a higher spiritual end just as the earth is merely the meaningless place where humans discover true meaning in the ultimate figure of value: God.

Here we see a perfect dramatization of the way in which the value creation process relies on a structural devalorization of women and matter as worthless and inert "bits" that can be used and exhausted to support male wages and patriarchal value. Falstaff's extreme and violent reaction occurs simply because Quickly looks him in the face and tells him he is false and violent. One cannot help but recall the real historical atrocities perpetrated by patriarchal value against women's and peasants' revolts for doing the same thing.[8]

The Otter

Finally, Falstaff calls Quickly an otter. This accusation draws on all the previous ones and reveals the ultimate source of patriarchal anxiety. Quickly's defense is above all an affront to the *masked use of violence* in the name of value. Falstaff uses his value as a man and knight of the prince to hide the fact that he is essentially *stealing from Quickly* while at the same time claiming that *Quickly is stealing from him*. *Direct* violence can be confronted and resisted, but what is so insidious about Falstaff, like the value of the commodity, is that he is essentially hiding the real relations of violence and primitive accumulation that support his value. He acts *as if* he had value in and of himself, when in fact it was attained primarily through theft and violence. By calling him a liar, Quickly is calling Falstaff two-faced, like the commodity and exposing the direct violence.

This exchange touches on the foundational anxiety of patriarchy and value creation at the same time: that they will be revealed as not being their own support. Patriarchy and social value go hand in hand in one and the same act of devalorization. Under patriarchal capitalism, every valuing of men's labor is and must be a devalorization of women's labor. If the full cost of women's labor, or ecological labor more broadly, had to be paid, the whole value creation system would crumble. The primitive accumulation of women and nature is thus revealed as primary and constitutive to value creation.

The patriarchal anxiety is that if men and value do not stand on their own, erect, and without support, then they are not what they are. They would have to depend on others who are not their formal equals (i.e., the devalorized). This patriarchal anxiety is a fear of the return or exposure of precisely what it tries to hide: the active and productive agency of matter, animals, women, and other social subordinates. To call Falstaff, who is the dramatic form of appearance of value, a two-faced liar, is to throw this fundamental anxiety (the birth of value) right in his face.[9]

In response, Falstaff attempts to project this anxiety back onto Quickly by saying that *she* is the one who is two-faced and false. His critique, however, only further exposes his own anxieties. He calls her an otter because at that time in England the otter defied the biological classification of being either a fish or a mammal. As a figure in Scottish and Celtic mythology, the otter was also a figure of transformation and witchcraft. For example, the sorceress Ceridwen transformed into an otter. The English word "otter" even comes from the shapeshifting substance par excellence: water.

Falstaff's patriarchal animalization of Quickly also takes on a directly heterosexist dimension. The reason calling her an otter is so offensive is that the otter defies sex and species categorization. The otter is a nasty animal because it is queer. The heterosexist assumption is that a man needs to know where to have the sex organ of the female. The otter is bad, for Falstaff, because it is not clear where *a man* can have it. The otter also serves to expose what Falstaff (the commodity) sees as absolutely the worst, *that a man not know* where to have it. The otter is terrible because it disrupts the epistemological foundations of heteronormative patriarchal knowledge. A man cannot know the otter's being because a man cannot know its sex or its sexual orientation or how it reproduces (fish or mammal). Its queer being defies male knowledge.

There are a number of things going on here. Falstaff first attempts to reproduce his hetero-masculinity by reducing Quickly to the materiality of her "part" (vulva). When Quickly fights back, Falstaff digs even deeper by saying that what is more, her being is so false and inferior that it is even less than female: it is queer. She literally cannot be had like a "normal woman," because she is *not even heterosexual*. She is not even fit to reproduce his hetero-masculinity. We can now see that patriarchal value introduces a two-faced gender binary just as the commodity is split between its use-value and value. Femininity is something produced as a deficient version of masculinity, just as use-value is merely the bodily feminine support for male value. The only part of women's labor that "counts" is its immediate role in the reproduction of the male worker's daily life, "something to pray to God on." A woman is an instrument in service to the higher value of God.

Beyond this limited form of patriarchal femininity lies the materiality of the body itself and its natural animality. Falstaff's "otter" remark gets directly at this next. As an otter, Quickly is stripped of her human qualities, including her female gender identity. It is not even clear what gender she is because a man does not know how to have her; her genitals are sexually ambiguous, like the otter. Quickly denies this confusion not on the basis of heteronormativity but simply on the basis of her own, as Marx says, "coarsely sensuous material body." Quickly's epistemological confidence about her own sensuous body echoes Epicurus's realist epistemology of "objective appearance." This is directly opposed to Democritus's skeptical epistemology and Falstaff's lying and skeptical commodity-value knowledge. Falstaff projects this falseness back onto Quickly.

However, masculine knowledge fails for precisely the same reason that Democritean atomism fails: it introduces a binary division between knower and known, subject and object, between the idea of atomic reality and empirical semblance. Dame Quickly, Marx, and Epicurus, on the other hand, have knowledge not through hetero-binaries but through sensuous materiality itself. Dame Quickly knows her sensuous material body, but Falstaff does not because his knowledge occurs strictly through binary models of hetero-sexuation. Falstaff can think of the singularity of sex and gender identity only as an abominable ambiguity between two preexisting sexual binaries. In *Henry IV*, the sensuous material knowledge Epicurus and Marx describe thus takes the form of a physical working-class woman speaking the sensuous truth of her own singular body. She does so against the false value of Falstaff's symbolic honor and binary heteronormative categories.

For Falstaff, the otter is also evil because its queerness defies God and makes sinners of everyone since, as the debate at the time went, one does not know whether one is allowed to eat the otter on Lent or not. If the otter is a fish it is allowed; if flesh then no. The queerness of the otter and the ambiguity of its sex organs therefore not only render the anthropocentric model of heteronormativity ambiguous but also render the human connection to God uncertain. The queer otter thus challenges the proper sexual and gustatory production/consumption relation to God and knowledge. The queerness of the otter undermines the whole epistemological foundation of abstract value.

It is also worth noting the otter's connection to the long history of misogynist mythologies of ambiguous and amphibious monsters: deathly sirens, trickster mermaids, snakes (which are seen both on land and in water), and various dragon-like female monsters. These species-queer and gender-queer creatures are in turn associated with that ultimate polymorphous and polysexual shapeshifting monster: water.

Falstaff's ultimate "otter critique" combines a host of historically patriarchal and heterosexist tropes into the single and historically rich figure of the otter, which is associated with animality, criminality (breaks laws of nature), witchcraft, queer sexualities, ambiguous genitalia, deformation, and dangerous cunning nature. In contrast to the simple heterofeminity structurally devalorized in the same stroke of hetero-male value creation, Quickly, qua otter, is said to be permanently and fundamentally devalorized and unvalorizable, contra her own sensuous knowledge of her material body.

* * *

The point is this: Marx says explicitly that Quickly *differs from the commodity*. This is the case precisely because of her strictly sensuous and materially productive body. She is not twofold, false, two-faced, binary. In *Henry IV*, it is quite clear that it is actually Falstaff who is the real two-faced liar and thus much more like the commodity. Falstaff, like the commodity, relies on the use-value stolen from Quickly and yet claims at the same time to have a falsely autonomous value independent from it. We can thus reread Falstaff's role in this scene of *Henry IV* as the dramatis persona of the commodity. In doing so, we are able to bring out more explicitly than Marx was able to in this passage and his footnote the way in which the commodity is two-sided. The commodity can also be seen as part of the longer historical tradition of using binary gender division to systematically devalorize women's labor and its connection with animal, natural, material, and queer material production.

Marx's example makes Dame Quickly the crucial dramatis persona of material production. In Falstaff's attack we see that the twofold nature of value uses anthropocentrism, heteronormativity, and patriarchy *as a way to structurally devalorize animality, women, nature, and queerness* while at the same time relying on these same bodies as its own material conditions. The scientific classification of otter sex and species for example, relies on the mutation and evolution of shapeshifting forms of sexuation and sex, just as the value of male labor depends on the hidden support of women's domestic labor, which in turn depends on the direct appropriation of changing natural metabolic processes.

The commodity appears two-sided and heterosexual, but the truth of this heterosexual twofold is both the homosexual exchange of identical values between men (Falstaff and Henry) and the queer material conditions of nature's own polymorphous perversity, within which the human animal's sex organs first evolved. As Luce Irigaray writes, "Heterosexuality is nothing but the assignment of economic roles: There are producer subjects and agents of exchange (male) on the one hand, productive earth and commodities (female) on the other. . . . Woman exists only as an occasion for mediation, transaction, transition, transference, between man and his fellow man, indeed between man and himself."[10] Women thus disappear as the structurally devalorized conditions of the kinetic transaction between patriarchal values, as discussed in the next chapter. Women, nature, animals, and racialized others play the role of "kinetic operators" or migrant supports for the exchange of values between white men.[11]

In the end, the fluid dynamics of the otter are quite different from the two-faced nature of the commodity. The figure of the queer otter has more to do with the fluid, kinomorphic, and fluctuating nature of material production upon which the division of labor, sexes, and sexuality occurs in the first place. The otter exposes a perverse or twisted queer materialism at the heart of the value creation process. Sexuation and sexuality are not a static, natural category precisely because nature itself is not static. It is a kinomorphic and perverse process of continual movement and transformation. It is within and through this material perversity that value attempts to sustain the patriarchal and anthropocentric production of heteronormative value. Matter is capable of forming itself into male, female, animal, and plant sex organs. Matter is generative, creative, and the very condition of value. This is the fact that value tries to obscure and mystify in its claim to abstract self-sufficiency.

The otter therefore reveals the true ambiguity of material production: that it is both the coarse, sensuous materiality that continually supports and maintains the creation of the value-form (and its twofold nature) and that which allows the value-form itself to act *as if* it did not come from these same conditions. Material production is the condition for both value and the abolition of value. It is what makes value possible and what resists it at the same time. As Marx says, immediately after this reference, "Everyone knows, if nothing else, that commodities have a common value-form which contrasts in the most striking manner with the motley natural forms [*bunten Naturalformen*] of their use-values" (C, 139). The German word *bunten* here means "mixed, varied, heterogeneous, multicolored; colorful; variegated." Marx thus draws our attention to the way in which the material production of use-values is *not twofold or two-faced*, like the commodity, but rather manifold, heterogenous, and diverse, like nature and the queerness of sensuous matter itself. The twofold of the commodity is thus supported by and emerges from the manifold—not the other way around.

It is for this reason that the poet Sappho writes in her *Hymn to Aphrodite* of "*poikilothron Aphrodite*" (iridescent-throned Aphrodite), because she is the goddess of bubbles and foam and heterogeneous motley desires. In contrast to the binary logic of the commodity value-form, material production is motley, queer, diverse, polymorphous, and manifold. It is precisely this polymorphous perversity of sensuous iridescent matter that makes possible the metastability of the value-form or bubble-form itself. The commodity is, as Lucretius writes, nothing more than a thing (*rerum*) made of folded up flows of matter (*corpora*) like a Venusian bubble washed up on the "shores of light" (*luminis oras*).[12] The commodity appears as an extended object in the form of the bubble, but the bubble is nothing more than the metastable moving agency of the fluid ocean itself folded up. Or, as Paul Valéry writes, echoing Lucretius, Homer,[13] and Sappho:

What grace of light, what pure toil goes to form
The manifold diamond of the elusive foam![14]

It is precisely the motley and iridescent agency of matter that produces
the form (*Naturalformen*) that supports (*tragen*) the value-form. The fundamental difference then between Quickly and Falstaff is that Quickly, like
Epicurus, knows herself to be those sensuous, material, motley, and queer
conditions capable of fighting back against the patriarchy of value, while
Falstaff remains completely deluded by the binary mystification of the patriarchal value-form itself.[15]

CHAPTER 7

Kinetic Theory of Value I

The theory of value is perhaps Marx's most important and original theoretical contribution in the whole of the *Capital* volumes. It is the theoretical core at the heart of everything that comes after it. Here Marx argues that value is not born through the devalorization process of metabolic and gendered accumulation alone (although this is a crucial precondition) but exists only in and though a process of continuous relation and *mobilization*. Capital, as Marx says quite explicitly, "can only be grasped as a movement, and not as a static thing" (C II, 185); value is always "value in motion" (C II, 211). This is a well-known point. Unfortunately, the traditional interpretation of this idea is that there are first discrete values and then they move around like atoms in the void.

In this chapter and the next I invert the standard interpretation of "value in motion" so that *value itself* is woven from a pattern of action and is not some discrete thing that merely moves from point A to point B. Value needs to "stand with its feet on the ground" again by making movement genuinely primary to its being (C, 163). That is, I show that Marx's theory of value is a fundamentally *kinetic theory of value* in which *matter-in-motion* forms the being of value. Value is not just a function of social, political, technical, and human relations. Matter-in-motion is primary to and constitutive of the being of value itself.[1]

The previous chapters have helped prepare the way for this radical rereading by showing the material-kinetic structure of the devalorization process and the primary role primitive accumulation plays in the becoming of value. In the following two chapters, the ideas of the previous chapters come together to show not only the *primacy of motion* in the birth of value

Marx in Motion. Thomas Nail, Oxford University Press (2020). © Oxford University Press.
DOI: 10.1093/oso/9780197526477.001.0001

but also the coprimacy of primitive accumulation or appropriation as the *hidden kinetic support for the internal and external movement of value.*

THE SIMPLEX-MANIFOLD OF VALUE

The first and founding concept of Marx's whole kinetic theory of value is the "simplex" or *einfachsten*—a German word combining the words *ein*, one, and *fach*, fold. If Marx had just meant to say "simple," he could have used the German words *"leicht," "simpel,"* or *"bescheiden,"* which all mean "simple" or "plain." The word *einfachsten*, however, carries the meaning of onefold or simplex.

This is a crucial point because the whole kinetic theory of value *dialectically unfolds* directly out of this onefold movement. The theory of value therefore does not have four discrete kinds of exchange (simple, expanded, general, and money) but only one continual movement that unfolds into four connected forms of motion. The goal, then, of Marx's original kinetic theory of value is not just to lay out the product of the process but to show how each of the forms of value in motion emerges dialectically from the others:

> That is, we have to show the origin of this money-form, we have to trace the development of the expression of value contained in the value-relation of commodities from its simplest [*einfachsten*], almost imperceptible outline to the, blinding money-form [*blendenden Geldform*]. When this has been done, the mystery of money will immediately disappear.... The whole mystery of the form of value lies hidden [*steckt*] in this simple form [*einfachen Werthform*]. (C, 139)

Perhaps one of the most crucial terms that Marx uses here and throughout is "expression of value." This term is so important because *Ausdruck* and similar terms in Marx's account do all the work of relating and moving commodities around. Expression, here, is not some vague metaphysical term. It is something that is directly moving or "impressing" on something else. Marx describes expression as a literal "moving" or "throwing" into relation (see later in this section).

A simplex onefold movement expresses value through its movement or unfolding. This method is in direct contrast to the blinding and mystifying nature of the value-form, which actively strives to conceal its own origins grounded in the sensuous and motley process of motion. The whole origin of value thus lies hidden, covered, and folded up in the onefold movement. In these pages, Marx wants to overcome the problem of mystification.

Political economy just looks to a single metastable region of sensuous motion and says, "Look, money!" as if money were a self-created deity. In fact, just like a religion, this view is not just simply false but a specific historical practice. To understand it, we cannot just deny it like atheists—we must critique it by showing its hidden material-kinetic conditions—like good followers of Epicurus and Lucretius.

Simplex value is also, as Marx says, pedetic (*zufällige*) insofar as it is a continual flux or flow whose origins and ends are not predetermined. *Zufällige* means "fallen" or "thrown" and is associated in German with the throw of dice and with chance. But the simplex process of value creation is, like anything thrown through the air, not random but pedetic or collectively shaped by numerous other bodies. In particular, it is the turbulence of the air through which things fall that gives them their unique and unpredictable movement. Just because the dice throw cannot be known in advance through physics does not mean that it is "random." Pure randomness means not being affected by anything else. It means just expressing a pure, spontaneous whim. The nature of bodies falling in motion, like the flux of falling matter in Lucretius, is precisely and explicitly the opposite. There is not a fall and then a swerve, but as discussed in chapter 1 of this book, matter is always swerving and sensuously affecting itself. The onefold of value is thus *zufällige* in the sense that it is a pedetic flow whose motion is not predictable in advance but develops through collective affection as it goes—like raindrops drifting and colliding in the wind. Value is neither a historical necessity nor a social a priori but rather an emergent feature of matter.

THE TWO POLES OF MOTION

The kinetic structure of value is defined by the two poles of an expressive movement. Value and devalorization are nothing other than the movement back and forth between these two aspects or regions of value. These two poles of the movement the same twofold dimensions of the commodity itself. When the commodity is set in motion through exchange, however, something new happens. Since each commodity is twofold, it can therefore relate to other twofold commodities in at least four combinatoric ways, as (1) a quality to a quality, (2) a quality to a quantity, (3) a quantity to a quality, and (4) a quantity to a quantity. These four permutations of kinetic relation between commodities are the fourfold value forms that define all social value: simplex, unfolded, general, and money.

Marx is extremely clear about the iterative nature of this movement of commodities, but we should also keep in mind that the commodity itself is already a continually born and supported fold in the flow of sensuous material production. Marx therefore does not assume the preexistence of commodities but shows how once commodities are kinetically constituted, they move around with respect to one another. This is a crucial point, since hiding it is precisely what value tries to do.

The primacy of kinetic relation: In any relation between at least two commodities, one will always be *actively related to another*. Movement is always oriented or relational in that it moves *from somewhere*, not through some empty Cartesian space:

> The value of the first commodity is represented as relative value; in other words the commodity is in the relative form of value. The second commodity fulfills the function of equivalent; in other words it is in the equivalent form. The relative form of value and the equivalent form are two insepa-rable moments [*einander gehörige*], which belong to and mutually condition [*wechselseitig bedingende*] each other; but, at the same time, they are mutu-ally exclusive or opposed extremes, i.e., poles of the expression of value. (C, 139–140)

When the first commodity moves into relation with the second, Marx calls the first the relative form and the second the equivalent form. The first is relative to the second, and the second is equivalent to the first. On their own they do not have these relative/equivalent statuses. Only when commodities change places *through motion* do they simultaneously be-come relative and equivalent to each other. In other words, there is not an interaction between two separate commodities, but an intra-action in which both become what they are only through their kinetic relation or performance.

This why Marx is always going on about how commodities "play" various "roles" (C, 139). Their material agencies mutually condition one another. In fact, the word he uses here is *wechselseitig,* from the word *wechseln,* meaning continuous change or fold, which is also used in the word *Stoffwechsel* (metabolism) and related concepts. Just as in the continuous metabolic relations that produced commodities in the first place, the commodities themselves now enter into continually transformative intra-active foldings and unfoldings. Here again the German language provides us with a won-derful linguistic way to express the inseparable unity-in-difference of one/other, as *einander.*

The primacy of motion: Commodity relations are processes. They are not merely lacking relation, nor are they prerelated. They must, as Marx says, be "moved into relation."

> They are always divided up between the different commodities moved into relation with on another [*einander bezieht*] by that expression. . . . I cannot, for example, express the value of linen in linen 20 yards of linen equals 20 yards of linen is not an expression of value. (C, 140)

Static identity cannot express value because value only becomes what it is through motion. There are not first values that then move around. Value is immanent to its movement through material exchange. Value is not merely some anthropocentric, subjective projection onto matter. Marx is extremely clear about this: human agency is only one part of material production and thus of value production. His theory of metabolism further clarifies this point: value emerges strictly within more primary metabolic movements.

The two poles of value are continuous but also locally distinct because one must always express or move into the position of the other *from a position* and *along a trajectory*. This asymmetry in kinetic expression is a practical and performative point. The production of value is above all performative. Matter must be "moved into relation." This is also an entropic point: Sensuous matter in motion changes through motion. It is not the same as it was after moving. By postulating the simple existence of money, the vulgar political economists propose the ex nihilo emergence of abstract quantities on a Cartesian plane without entropy. These abstract quantities move without changing and on a nonoriented field. The symmetric equality of exchange assumes an impossible thermodynamic equilibrium of consumption. For Marx, metabolism means there is always an energetic drift. Therefore, "whether a commodity is in the relative form or in its opposite, the equivalent form, entirely depends [*hängt*] on its actual position [*jedesmaligen Stelle*] in the expression of value" (C, 140). For Marx, we cannot assume the existence of commodities that do not depend (*hängt*) on their practical, sensuous orientation in space and *through motion*.

For example, in the first value-form (the onefold form), a quality is related to another quality: twenty yards of linen is moved into relation with one coat. However, "these two qualitatively equated commodities do not play the same part" (C, 141). "In this relation, the coat counts as the form of existence of value, as the material embodiment of value, for only as such is it the same as the linen" (C, 141). When the value of the linen is expressed in the coat, the coat is stripped of its own value and is treated as simply *equivalent to twenty yards of linen*. In other words, when two commodity qualities are brought into relation, the first quality actively colonizes the second by treating the second *as if* it had the sole quality of "being worth twenty yards of linen."

However, a mutual transformation also occurs to the linen when it is moved into relation to the coat. Since they are two different qualities, there must be some sense in which they share at least one common quality such that they can be related: labor time:

> On the other hand, the linen's own existence as value comes into view or receives an independent expression, for it is only as value that it can be related to the coat as being equal in value to it, or exchangeable with it. (C, 141)

At the very moment in which the linen acts *as if* the coat had no other qualities than to be equivalent to the linen, the linen is treated *as if* it had no other qualities than to be a duration of labor worth the duration of labor to make the coat:

> Now it is true that the tailoring which makes the coat is concrete labour of a different sort from the weaving which makes the linen. But the act of equating [*Gleichsetzung*] tailoring with weaving reduces the former in fact to what is really equal in the two kinds of labour, to the characteristic they have in common of being human labour. (C, 142)

When two heterogeneous qualities are moved into relation, their qualities no longer matter *with respect to the movement of exchange*. Weaving and tailoring are different, but if we treat their products as exchangeable, then it is as if the products and the processes of production were just equal aspects of *the same quality*: labor. This is also the sense in which the linen bears or wears (*tragen*) (C, 133) the coat. Thus the two different qualities (linen and coat) are not actually equal in any way but equal only insofar as they have a third quality: labor.

The emergence of this third quality occurs only and strictly through the act of equating (*Gleichsetzung*), bringing into line, synchronization, or coordination. This is an absolutely crucial point because

> the usual mode of procedure is the precise opposite of this: nothing is seen in the value-relation but the proportion in which definite quantities of two sorts of commodity count as equal to each other . . . under the coarse influence of the practical bourgeois, [political economists] give their attention from the outset, and exclusively, to the quantitative aspect of the question. (C, 140)

Bourgeois political economy starts, as usual, from the end, that is, the "quantity of labor," as if this object were already preconstituted. This is the source of all the political economists' errors. They treat value in motion as if there were already values moving around, when in fact it is first the movement of sensuous matter that then gets folded up into commodities, which are then moved around in a specific pattern of motion, which we call value. This whole pattern shows that the treatment of commodities as homogenous labor time is an *effect of motion*, not the source or unmoved mover of motion. This is the same atomist problem in yet another formulation. Starting with discrete atomic units of value moving around only ends up in Democretian contradiction, skepticism, and mystification:

> Human labour-power in its fluid state, or human labour, creates value but is not itself value. It becomes value in its coagulated state, in objective form. The value of the linen as a congealed mass of human labour can be expressed only as an "objectivity" [*Gegenstiindlichkeit*], a thing which is materially different from the linen itself and yet common to the linen and all other commodities. (C, 142)

Marx reminds us again here that the abstraction of discrete quantities of homogenous labor time is in fact a product of a more primary process of fluid moving labor, which has simply congealed into an objective, meta-stable, bubble-like form.

Even more important, this point about value takes on a new meaning in the context of exchange-value, namely, that the movement itself, of "fluid labor," *is not value* but the kinetic bearer and condition of the exchange of value. Commodities are "moved into relation" by a kinetic act of synchronization (*Gleichsetzung*) that itself does not count as value. Here again primitive accumulation rears its ugly head, this time *between commodities*. Material production takes place not only before the congelation of labor into commodities but also between the commodities in exchange. The change in relation between commodities is thus borne by sensuous matter in motion, which is constitutively excluded from value in motion.

Migration, for example, has historically operated as a form of unpaid labor that supports the changing structure of value creation but is essentially not included as a value per se. This is obviously the case for ancient and modern slaves but is also the case more widely for all workers whose migratory or commuting labor has no value. Although migration, according to Marx, constitutes "the primary lever of capitalist accumulation" (C, 784), it remains strictly appropriated and without value. It is the motion that supports value's mobility. Transport costs are externalities to the system of value's motion. The effects of global transport on roads, skies, and oceans are treated as if they were not part of value's mobility. The only things that matter are the points of departure and arrival. Even then, such points are treated as quality-less Cartesian coordinates. The uneven development of value around the world *seems* to be merely extrinsic to the movement of value but is in fact constitutive.

Marx's point is this: political economy acts as if all qualities had already been prestripped, when in fact we must see that apparently discrete quantities (like atoms) emerge from the qualitative kinetic relations. It is from this strictly and primarily qualitative relation between commodities that a third quality emerges:

> Franklin is not aware that in measuring the value of everything "in labour" he makes abstraction from any difference in the kinds of labour exchanged and thus reduces them all to equal human labour. Yet he states this without knowing it. He speaks first of "the one labour," then of "the other labour," and finally of "labour," without further qualification, as the substance of the value of everything. (C, 142)

Labor becomes the universal quality being exchanged through the *act of measuring* and not through anything else. The throwing into relation of different qualities is therefore the condition for the emergence of a third common quality: labor in general:

> Human labour has therefore been accumulated in the coat. From this point of view, the coat is a "bearer of value," although this property never shows through, even when the coat is at its most threadbare. In its value-relation with the linen, the coat counts only under this aspect, counts therefore as embodied value, as the body of value [*Wertkorper*]. (C, 143)

The coat bears value only *in motion*. This is why we cannot see the value in the threads of the coat. Value, contrary to its bourgeois believers, is not some subjective, immaterial, or socially constructed thing or idea. For Marx, value is completely real, completely material, *but not a substance*. Value only emerges *as a process or in motion*; thus we do not see value in itself as a discrete object. We see only patterns of motion between commodities. Value is a real kinetic process of intra-action. The only illusion or error is to think of value as existing independently of its immanent kinetic patterns or relation.

Another absolutely crucial anticonstructivist point Marx introduces here is the idea that commodities themselves have agency. Most anthropocentric readers of Marx chalk this idea up to "Marx's use of fanciful language," not to be taken too seriously by those interested in hard-nosed political economy. However, such readers have unwittingly fallen prey to the very bourgeois logic of devalorization they hoped to overcome. The agency (or lack thereof) of matter, as discussed in the previous chapter, has historically served to devalorize and appropriate women, nature, animals, and racialized humans. The devalorization of matter and matter's agency is systematically used as a tool to identify marginalized agencies as "more material" and is thus not socially valuable. As long as matter is treated as passive, it will always provide a place or attribute for devalorizing beings.

Recognition: Here, as elsewhere, Marx's language about the agency of commodities remains entirely consistent with the idea that the earth and all of nature is productive and has agency to some degree and capacity:

> Despite its buttoned-up appearance, the linen recognizes in it a splendid kindred soul, the soul of value. Nevertheless, the coat cannot represent value toward the linen unless value, for the latter, simultaneously assumes the form of a coat. An individual, A, for instance, cannot be 'your majesty' to another individual, B, unless majesty in B's eyes assumes the physical shape of A, and, moreover, changes facial features, hair and many other things, with every new "father of his people." (C, 143)

The linen *recognizes* in the coat something common to it: the common quality of labor. Just as each new king is still a king even though he looks different than the previous king, they all share in common "majesty." The crucial idea in both cases is that what is necessary for the emergence of value is an activity on the part of the first commodity and an active passivity of the second. The movement must produce its consumption and consume its production. What is common is not a "thing" but a kinetic set of relations that move the linen and coat and that support or bear a body as a king. What it means to recognize in this broad sense does not require human consciousness but is simply a material-kinetic relation or responsiveness. The coat and linen respond to each other. This is wholly consistent with Marx's Epicurean view in the doctoral dissertation that self-consciousness emerges whenever matter swerves and responds to itself. Consciousness and subjective agency are not unique to humans but occur in all sensuous matter.

Thought and language: Marx next writes that the commodity "reveals its thoughts in a language with which it alone is familiar, the language of commodities" (C, 143). Commodities, like all sensuous material things, have both active subjective dimensions and passive objective dimensions. Their "thoughts" here should be broadly defined as their intensive qualities or affections and their "language" as their extensive quantities and effects. Again, this is completely consistent with the theory of things in the doctoral dissertation and in section one of chapter one of *Capital*. All things have both qualitative and quantitative dimensions; the first is an inner self-affection, and the second is its external relation to others. They are two sides of the same fold. In the preceding passage and in others in this section, Marx simply spells this out in social terms: commodities have inner senses called thoughts and outer senses called language (C, 144). Marx notes that the active material agency of value is best brought out in the Latin word *valoir*. In *"Paris vaut bien une messe!"* Paris actively values, expresses itself, or makes itself worthy of a mass. Although most philosophers typically balk at the idea that matter has agency, there are actually a number of common linguistic constructions that show that we often act or talk this way.[2] So thought and language here are simply the active qualitative and quantitative relations between things.

Appearance: Commodities, as sensuous affections and objective external effects, therefore also appear to one another and actively reflect images back to one another. Again, this is not just fanciful language. Marx really means it:

> By means of the value-relation, therefore, the natural form of commodity B becomes the value-form of commodity A, in other words the physical body of commodity B becomes a mirror for the value of commodity A. . . . The value of commodity A, thus expressed in the use-value of commodity B, has the form of relative value. (C, 144)

A value-relation is a kinetic relation. When commodity B becomes a mirror of commodity A, there is a real material and kinetic process at work. Sensuous light actually reflects off of A and then reflects off of B and back to A and so on in a continual process of circulation. Like a hall of mirrors, the light changes slightly each time. The point here is that commodities, as light-reflecting things, actively appear and reflect one another's light. They see and are seen by one another in this general sense. They appear to one another and must appear to one another through the common medium of light and motion. In fact, this is a fundamental condition for their exchangeability as distinct and relatively discrete objects that can be exchanged in the first place.

Material practice: Marx's inversion here of the typical origins of thought and language is radical. Before human thought and language, there is in fact the sensuous material thought and language of things, albeit in a much broader sense of qualitative and quantitative relations. Human thought and language emerge through natural metabolic processes, not the other way around. The fact that Marx says that commodities speak tells us something about what his materialist and performative theory of language must be like, even if he does not spell it out here. Language must be first and foremost a kinetic structure of coordinated or patterned motions. Only much later is it possible for humans to take up this practice and then act *as if* what they did with language were representational. This, for Marx, is the primary error of philosophy: that we think that theory and language represent something else. This is nowhere more clear, as we have seen, than in his theses on Feuerbach. Theory is fundamentally practical *because* nature must already itself be practical and sensuous, such that humans emerge as practical sensuous beings in it, and such that commodities can also appear as practical and sensuous as well. The "thoughts, language, and appearance" of commodities are not like human "thoughts, language, and appearance" because both are representational (hence the initial tendency to balk at Marx's "fanciful language"), but precisely because both are *nonrepresentational, sensuous,* and *practical.*[3]

QUANTITATIVE FLUX

When qualities are put into the motion of exchange, they make possible the determination of a third quality by which the two can be commonly compared: labor. However, insofar as any given quality also comes in a given quantity, it follows that we must also say that there is a quantity of this common labor in general:

> A given quantity of any commodity contains a definite quantity of human labour. Therefore, the form of value must not only express value in general but also quantitatively determined value, i.e. the magnitude of value. (C, 144)

The quantity of this general labor in the commodity depends not on the quality itself, the linen, or even on the quantity of the linen, twenty yards, but strictly on the amount of general abstract labor that went into making that commodity. If we look only at the quality and quantity of each commodity, all its exchange relations look completely arbitrary. However, if we look at the quantitative flux in labor time it takes to produce that commodity, a strict set of inverse proportions unfolds depending on the quantitative amount of abstract labor time—and not on the quality or quantity of the commodities, twenty yards of linen, one coat, and so on.

This is an absolutely crucial point not only because it allows us to see through the mystical and apparent randomness of the exchange ratios but also because it reveals a direct relation to the devalorized conditions of metabolic appropriation. Recall that value never comes from paid humans alone; it comes from the earth, women, and the colonies. For example, Marx cites such fluctuations in labor time as "the increasing infertility of flax-bearing [*flachstragenden*] soil" and "improved looms." I could also cite here the availability of cheap slave labor and the theft of water, minerals, and other materials from colonies. All of these processes of material production do not appear in the value of "twenty yards of linen" and thus *have no value*. Rather, this underground current of metabolic flux changes the ratios of paid labor time between valued commodities. For example, as the flax-bearing (*flachstragenden*) soil is depleted, the value of flax doubles, and the "necessary labor time" of the coat remains the same, the value of the linen will then be double in relation to the coat: twenty yards of linen = two coats (C, 145).

The conclusion here should be just as startling as that of the great swindle of "necessary labor time." The quantitative change in values is a product of the more primary process of changes in devalorized material production times. The quantity of value (abstract labor time) does not float in midair or change randomly by vagaries of supply and demand alone. Exchange ratios between values fluctuate because the metabolic conditions of devalorized production expand or contract beneath the measured surface of "labor time":

> Thus real changes in the magnitude of value are neither unequivocally nor exhaustively reflected in their relative expression, or, in other words, in the magnitude of the relative value. The relative value of a commodity may vary, although its value remains constant. Its relative value may remain constant, although its value varies; and finally, simultaneous variations in the magnitude of its value and in the relative expression of that magnitude do not by any means have to correspond at all points. (C, 146)

For example, twenty yards of linen remain twenty yards of linen, but the flux of devalorized, socially necessary labor time determines the whole economic equation. This underground current remains hidden beneath the thin veneer of the apparent change in the equivalent commodity: the coat. The number of coats will vary as metabolic reproduction time fluxes, but we will never see this flux in the coat itself. The conditions that bear value are thus hidden below the surface of value if we attribute value only to the coat—and not to the earth, women, and the colonies that bore the coat.

EQUIVALENT FLUX

The introduction of a quantitative flux between commodities has a surprising and radical effect on the equivalent form. If what is being exchanged is not only the quality of labor in general but a quantity of labor time in particular, then the coat is not only stripped of its qualities as a coat, it is also stripped of its particular quantity. For example, if what is being exchanged is just labor time, then it does not matter how many coats are equivalent to the linen. All that matters is that the labor time that went into some number of coats is equal to the labor time that went into the linen:

> As soon as the coat takes up the position of the equivalent in the value expression, the magnitude of its value ceases to be expressed quantitatively. On the contrary, the coat now figures in the value equation merely as a definite quantity of some article. (C, 147)

Marx gives the example of weight to illustrate the point:

> Nevertheless, in order to express the sugar-loaf as a weight, we put it into a relation of weight with the iron. In this relation, the iron counts as a body representing nothing but weight. Quantities of iron therefore serve to measure the weight of the sugar and represent, in relation to the sugar-loaf, weight in its pure form, the form of manifestation of weight. (C, 148)

In this way the coat is not treated as a coat with qualities and quantities but simply as a total amount of labor time equal to the labor time of the linen. Just as the number of iron weights does not matter, but their total collective weight does, so the number of coats does not matter, either—or what they are made of.

It is also worth stressing again that Marx says we "put it into relation" and "we throw [werfen] both of them into the scales." What is constitutively excluded here in the value-relation is the kinetic act of putting or throwing into relation. The scale is prebalanced so the commodities can be compared, but more fundamental here is the actual setting up of the scale, the selection of the commodities to compare and the actual setting them in relation. The focus on the "value of commodities and their motion" only serves to hide the material-kinetic conditions of the throwing of things into relation. It is no coincidence that the German word *werfen* also means "to birth." Value thus comes from the birthing and bearing, *werfen und tragen* of the kinetic act, not from value alone. This is precisely why Marx is continually talking about things being "thrown into motion" (C, 184, 202, 208, 216, 224). Throwing is primary; value is what is produced. Marx says precisely this on the next page:

> The relative value-form of a commodity, the linen for example, expresses its value-existence as something wholly different from its substance and properties, as the quality of being comparable with a coat, for example; this expression itself therefore indicates that it conceals a social relation [*Verhältnis*], (C, 149)

Value is treated *as if* the quality and quantity of the linen, the coat, the kind of labor that produced them, and the metabolic conditions that supported and maintained them had nothing to do with it. Included in the social relation is precisely the act of putting things into relation. Value is treated as if it always existed, came from nowhere, and had nothing to do with all the qualities and quantities it exchanges. In other words, it seems to take on a transcendence with respect to the rest of its conditions.

Therefore, "the first peculiarity which strikes us when we reflect on the equivalent form is this, that use-value becomes the form of appearance of its opposite, value" (C, 148). Value is the opposite of all its concrete qualities and quantities. Value retroactively devalorizes what produced it at the same time that it naturalizes its own existence ex nihilo. "The coat, therefore, seems [*scheint*] to be endowed with its equivalent form, its property of direct exchangeability, by nature, just as much as its property of being heavy or its ability to keep us warm" (C, 149). Value appears as if it were the sole natural aspect of the commodity, when in fact it derived its being entirely from the kinetic conditions of being thrown into motion, which has no value.

The two other peculiarities of value follow from the first: second, "concrete labour becomes the form of manifestation of its opposite, abstract human labour," and third, "private labour takes the form of its opposite, namely labour in its directly social form" (C, 150). Value is treated as if the quality of labor did not matter and was thus merely an abstract quantity. Private labor is treated as if it were always already social or in relation with other commodities, when in fact at some point it was not.

Aristotle was the first to discover the kinetic origins of value in the asymmetrical structure of relative and equivalent forms. In the *Ethics* he writes, "This is the way exchange was before there was currency is clear, for it makes no difference to speak of five beds for a house or of the amount the five beds are worth."[4] In the exchange, the bed becomes relative, and the house becomes equivalent or simply "worth five beds."

However, and more important, Aristotle fails to see that the condition for this qualitative exchange is a quantity of abstract labor. Instead of attributing value to the labor, he jumps right into the use of currency to explain how such qualitative exchanges were equalized. For Marx, this is a *major error* because skipping over the development of a common quality (labor) and the quantity of that quality (labor time) is precisely what allows Aristotle to hide and naturalize the inequality and primitive accumulation of the material production that supports the value creation process. Aristotle treats money as if its value were strictly arbitrary and "conventional," when in fact, as Marx shows, its value fluctuates in direct proportion to the changes in "necessary labor time" and rates of metabolic appropriation.

In skipping over labor time, Aristotle draws our attention both to the arbitrary use of force necessary to appropriate production in the first place and the blinding power of money used to cover over this act of direct violence afterward. Aristotle thus ends up wrongly thinking that the value of money is just as arbitrary as the initial qualitative exchange "because it is not natural but by current custom and it is in our power to change it or make it worthless."[5] This is why, Aristotle says, currency or money is called *nomisma*, from the Greek word *nomos,* meaning "law."

Greek law and justice, for Aristotle, are like money: freely determined and universally applied among equals. In this idea, Aristotle fails to see the fundamental and primary role the kinetic power of material production itself plays. Matter flows, folds, and supports the kinetic relations of value. For Aristotle, it is the money (value) that does the work and the "bearer" (nonvalue) that merely transports the value. Aristotle thus completely inverts the real social relations that bear value.

Marx then says:

Aristotle himself was unable to extract this *fact*, that, in the form of commodity-values, all labour is expressed as equal human labour and therefore as labour of equal quality, by inspection from the form of value, because Greek society was founded on the labour of slaves, hence had as its natural basis the inequality of men and of their labour-powers. The secret of the expression of value, namely the equality and equivalence of all kinds of labour because and in so far as they are human labour in general, could not be *deciphered* until the concept of human equality had already acquired the permanence of a fixed popular opinion. This [deciphering], however, becomes possible only in a society where the commodity-form is the universal form of the product of labour, hence the dominant social relation is the relation between men as possessors of commodities. Aristotle's genius is displayed precisely by his discovery of a relation of equality in the value-expression of commodities. Only the historical limitation inherent in the society in which he lived prevented him from finding out what *"in reality"* this relation of equality consisted of. (C, 151–152)[6]

The birth of value had always been mystified by the apparently a priori existence of value in money. Only in bourgeois society, where the value of the commodity has become the dominant social form, can we see these at work to lesser degrees in previous societies. Every time the kinetic foundations of money are hidden away, we should immediately look for what *social relations are being hidden* or covered over and "made worthless" by the value-form. In Greek society, money hides a social relationship through the nomos and the *oikos*.

The nomos: Aristotle's exclusion of slaves is part of a much broader category of natural and social relations that are hidden by the supposedly conventional use of money. On the surface, money and law (nomos) both appear to be conventions of equality decided by the community. Both, however, are founded on a constitutive act of violence and primitive accumulation. We can thus see in the very Greek word for currency (nomos) itself the foundational role that primitive accumulation played for the Greek polis (city-state) and the Greek concept of *dike* (justice). The Greek word *nomos* directly appropriated from the archaic, oral, and Homeric usage that preceded classical Greece. In its archaic usage nomos, from the root word -*nem*, did not mean law at all. It meant "undivided, open, common pastureland."[7]

Just as the classical Greeks introduced systemic political divisions into the undivided common lands of peasant and "barbarian" populations through warfare, colonialism, and slavery, so they also appropriated and transformed the meaning of *nomos* to reflect their own system of colonial domination and slavery. The polis is first and foremost a division into the open pasturelands of peasants and nomads. The polis defines itself by the division of the open *chora*, or countryside. Like the process of devalorization, it then retroactively covers over its founding origins and material support and declares itself its own founding origin in the Greek myth of autochthony. According to Greek myth, the Greek people just popped out of the ground. The Greeks supposedly create their own law (nomos) out of nothing but themselves, just as they determine their own money (nomos) out of nothing, ex nihilo.

But like all ex nihilo ideologies, this hides a constitutive violence of exploitation, displacement, extraction, and appropriation. The polis remains materially and kinetically supported and borne by the countryside itself. Any polis is only as strong as its food supply. By devalorizing the material support of their *chora*, the Greeks depleted their ecosystem through deforestation and demineralization. This required expansion, and thus warfare and the expulsion of others, constant colonial extraction, and slave labor. In short, the *nomos* of law and money, like social value itself, is predicated on the expulsion, appropriation, and destruction of the very conditions that sustain the production of that value.

The *oikos*: The Greeks had a name for this region of primitive accumulation: the *oikos*. In contrast to the public polis of formal law, money, and equality, the *oikos* was the private domain of lawlessness, arbitrary exchange, theft, and inequality. Aristotle skips over the equality of labor because he connects slave labor not to the valued labor of the city-dweller but to the devalorized labor of the peripheral countryside or *oikos*. The reason the doctor in the polis and the farmer in the *oikos* (in Aristotle's example) cannot exchange equally without money is that they share no other common quality (because free and slave labor were qualitatively different), so they use money. The farmer is a figure of the *oikos*, as were women, slaves, barbarians, migrants, nomads, animals, and nature.

The *oikos* is thus a general domain of devalorization and primitive accumulation, which the Greeks plundered until they destroyed it. Aristotle can't conceptualize abstract labor time, not just because slave labor was not equal but because most material production in the *oikos* was not equal. Women, nature, slaves, and animals cannot know justice; they do not determine the value of money. They are completely outside the domain of political equality. The vast majority of material production for the Greeks was primitively accumulated from the *oikos*: the reproductive labor of women, the mining activity of slaves, the labor of animals, the transport of migrant labor, and so on. All these had to be devalorized continually so that a few property-owning male Greek citizens could exchange things with one another using money. This is what Aristotle's theory of money shows us.

Greek society divides the archaic nomos into polis and *oikos* and then needs money to bridge the gap between the two worlds. How does the polis-dwelling doctor pay the *oikos*-dwelling farmer? Aristotle needs money to make the exchange work, but since society is predicated on a natural inequality, there can be nothing but arbitrary currency and the free rule of law: the classical nomos as law. This problem, however, arises only because Aristotle devalorizes the *oikos* in the first place instead of seeing it as the material-kinetic conditions for the production of value as such, as Marx does. However, on at least one point we should give Aristotle credit: unlike bourgeois economists, Aristotle actually acknowledges the vast chasm between nonvalue and value.

In other words, today there only appears to be more equality than the Greeks had, because value is globally concentrated in a few Western countries while the vast majority of the world's population, animals, plants, and atmosphere now occupy a new global *oikos*. The delusion of formal equality does not therefore originate with the bourgeois epoch (it was already there between Greek citizens); it just reaches its highest degree of delusion necessary for the moral foundation of global capitalism today.[8] It is thus fitting that the Greek term *oikos* is the origin of both the words "economy" and "ecology," since the former is the systematic devalorization of the latter. They embody the two sides of the commodity, one facing ecological use-value and the other facing economic value.

THE EMBRYOGENESIS OF VALUE

Marx concludes his theory of the simplex form of value with a note on its insufficiency. The analysis of the onefold form of value has shown that the conditions for the emergence of value are in the movement of matter. Without "moving things into relation" there is no relation and thus no exchange, no commodities, and no value. Only by "throwing" things onto the scale can one take on a relative form with respect to the other as its equivalent. Only in treating two qualities as measures of a common quality (labor) can we then see both as measures of that quality (labor time). All this unfolds from a single kinetic exchange between qualities. From quality emerges a quantity of labor time. From the movement of matter comes the unfolded form.

This is, as Marx says, a pure embryology of value:

> We perceive straightaway the insufficiency of the simplex form of value: It is an embryonic [*Unzulängliche*] form which must undergo a series of metamorphoses before it can ripen [*heranreift*] into the price-form. (C, 154)

Following his previous language of bearing and birthing, Marx describes the onefold form of material-kinetic relation as developing embryonically into the ripened price-form. Marx thus concludes the section where he began, with the foundational role played by the kinetics of material production. Kinetic relations between qualities are not overcome but rather unfolded dialectically like an embryo.

Embryogenesis is the process by which the folded-up qualities of matter, like the albumen of the egg, unfold themselves into relatively discrete regional quantities of yolk.[9] The continuum of matter in motion unfolds, divides, and congeals into clusters or quantities of matter. Embryology has no transcendent causes but only immanent collective self-causes or transformations of the whole. Embryo subjects and objects are not drawn along species lines but are intensive regions that develop through folding and unfolding. This is the key idea at the core of Marx's kinetic theory of value: that there is first a pure flow or continuum of matter in motion. As matter folds, it produces twofold bodies defined by their qualities and quantities, which in turn are thrown into kinetic relation (relative and equivalent poles). All of this happens immanent to the continual flow and fold of material production. Despite its apparent discreteness, value is actually not discrete. In spite of its apparent autonomy and arbitrary nature, it is in fact completely immanent to material-kinetic production itself.

The task now is to see how the onefold of material production ripens into the manifold of the money form. This is the focus of the next chapter.

CHAPTER 8

Kinetic Theory of Value II

The kinetic theory of value is at the conceptual core of *Capital*. The previous chapter showed that it is not the movement *of value* that is primary but rather *the movement* of matter that bears value's mobility and is of truly central importance. Value is born of the devalorization process but is further carried along through the constitutive act of *transport* or "setting into motion" of values with one another (exchange). The previous chapter showed how the first form of value, the onefold (*einfache*) or simplex form, contained embryonically all the manifold forms of value in itself. The onefold form first and foremost establishes the entire kinetic foundation by which things are "moved into relation" with one another. These kinetic relations are what make value. Without movement and without the setting into movement, there is no value.

This chapter picks up from the previous one and argues that the other three value forms each unfold (*entfaltete*) continually from this onefold movement. Money emerges not from natural value or from divine command but strictly from the material-kinetic conditions of transport that bear and support it through each of the value-forms. The simplex form is therefore not something merely inadequate to money but in fact a constant and constitutive kinetic condition of relationality that supports and bears money as a general equivalent. Money, therefore, is not a thing but a kinetic process of value creation that emerges historically and must be continually reproduced through the devalorization process that bears its motion.

The key original thesis of this chapter is that the origins of money are not, as is commonly thought, in the "movement of value" but in the *movement of matter* that bears and transports value.

Marx in Motion. Thomas Nail, Oxford University Press (2020). © Oxford University Press.
DOI: 10.1093/oso/9780197526477.001.0001

THE UNFOLDING OF VALUE

The onefold (*einfache*) of the first value-form embryo-genetically unfolds (*entfalten*) in the second form. Unfortunately, the explicit connection between the onefold and unfolded forms is elided by Fowkes's English translation of *entfalten* as "to expand."[1] Value, for Marx, is not so much expanded as if it were just a matter of wider application but rather unfolded from the kinetic and relational patterns already established in the initial act of exchange. This is a basic dialectical point.

The Mirror of Value

Commodities are first brought into a onefold relation, in which they are set into motion as different qualities. In this simplex exchange of qualities, however, the linen "sees itself" in the coat. The coat thus becomes a "mirror" for the linen, as discussed in the first section of the previous chapter of this book (C, 144, 150). As the value-form unfolds, the mirror relation multiplies. Now that the linen sees itself as a reflection, it can find this reflection in any mirror:

> The value of a commodity, the linen, for example, is now expressed in terms
> of innumerable other members of the world of commodities [*Waarenwelt*]. . . .
> Every other physical commodity [*Waarenkörper*] now becomes a mirror [*Spiegel*]
> of the linen's value. It is thus that this value first shows itself as being, in reality,
> a congealed quantity of undifferentiated human labour. . . . As a commodity it is
> a citizen of that world. (C, 155)

Throughout section three of chapter one, the equivalent operates as a mirror for Marx. Since Marx makes use of this term many times throughout *Capital*, we should pause and consider precisely what role the mirror plays in the production of value.

A mirror is something that reflects almost all the light that it receives within a certain limited frame. A mirror, however, also actively changes the light it receives and limits the range of light returned based on the limits of its frame. The danger of the mirror, as the myth of Narcissus reminds us, is mistaking the mirror for nothing other than the image it reflects. The mirror is thus a tricky kind of object because it so easily conceals its own quality, use-value, or sensuous materiality: the frame, the tain (silver backing), as well as the agency of light itself. Narcissus dies because he mistakes the sensuous agency of nature (water, light, air) as nothing other than himself.

When a commodity acts as a mirror, the same problem arises. The concrete quality and material support of the equivalent form is treated as if it did not exist. The historical figures of women, nature, and colonial labor disappear as bodily supports or frames for the gleaming reflection of the value of the European patriarchy. The life of value is therefore a kind of undead, vampiric, or zombie life that feeds on the living, as Marx says (C, 91). Section three is thus filled with the language of "mirror play" because, for Marx, the equivalent form acts as a mirror both in its sensuous agency and, to the degree to which it tends to conceal that very agency, *as if* it were a purely passive object for the reflection of the active relative form.

The reflective transport of light between the mirror and the object is yet a third thing distinct from the relative and equivalent forms of value. The light that is transported is itself an active and constitute agent in the appearance of value. The fantasy of the reflection, like the fantasy of the male gaze, is that the light (matter) and the mirror (the feminine) are entirely passive and accurately reflect back the image of value. Marx's point in using the image of the mirror is that this fantasy is false. Value is not a static image of identity, as its bourgeois apologists say. The mirror-equivalent form, like all forms, is a form produced through motion—as is clear from Marx's kinetic theory of forms in the doctoral dissertation. The equivalent form requires and relies on the mobility, fluidity, and transport of light. It also relies on the sensuous materiality of its frame to select and deselect some matters to do the reflecting. As such, the creation of value requires the *material agency of the equivalent form itself to act, to reflect*.

All too often Marx is read as attributing some ontological "split" to the commodity between use-value and value, active and passive, relative and equivalent. But there is no such radical split, as shown in the previous chapters. Value is borne by a continual folding and unfolding. The four-fold relations between value-forms are possible because they can move and change places continually between the two poles of value. Marx continually overthrows the opposition between subject and object through the movement of folding and unfolding. Unfortunately, his explicit language of folding is obscured by such English translations as "simple" and "expanded" forms.

The point is this: mirror reflections, for Marx, cannot actually be what the value fantasy thinks they are. Rather, they are duplications or folds of light. A reflection is a folding and unfolding in which both sides and what is in between are active. Form is a kinetic fold, just as Epicurus and Lucretius described it.

Thus, in the *unfolded* form of value we can now see from the subjective side of relative value. The entire world can appear as a manifold of mirrors, each reflecting back the linen to itself. The trick of the mirror of equivalence is that once the linen sees itself in the mirror of the coat, it begins to think that its own linen-being is nothing but a reflection. It falls in love with its own image, like Narcissus, without attending to the sensuous difference and kinetic agency of the other commodity. By doing so, it then learns that it can ignore the qualities of all other commodities in the same way and treat them as mirrors of itself as well. Thus, "every other physical commodity [*Waarenkörper*] now becomes a mirror [*Spiegel*] of the linen's value" (C, 155). Marx is careful to remind us that these other commodities are corporeal (*körperlich*) and sensuous but are only treated *as if* they were not.

When the linen responds to the coat as if it were merely a mirror, what is reflected is not the linen but *an image of the linen* as abstract labor time. "It is thus that this value first shows itself as being, in reality, a congealed quantity of undifferentiated human labour" (C,155). By setting objects in motion at two poles in this manner, the coat is treated as if it had no sensuous qualities, which then generates an image of the linen as if it had no qualities, either. Accordingly, it does not matter to the linen which object it uses to reflect itself. The mirror of equivalence unfolds into a manifold of mirrors. Each mirror is unique and sensuous but is treated as if it were not.

The World of Commodities

The simplex of value bears the unfolded manifold of values in an entire "world of commodities" (*Waarenwelt*). This is a strange world of nothing but separate mirrors and one quality (linen). It is a world of "citizens" insofar as all commodities express equally one and the same quality: labor time. A single simplex commodity has been unfolded continually into manifold expressions of one and the same quality. The world of commodities is a world because it is all made of different quantities of the same quality: abstract labor time.

There are, however, several deficiencies in this *Waarenwelt*. The first is that the chain of mirrored representations (*Darstellungsreihe*) is indefinite; one more can always be added. It is never completely clear what the linen is *really* worth. The world of commodities is therefore not truly complete, total, or fully representational if it depends on the open and additive movement of new matters that have not yet been represented. This is a lack, however, only with respect to the internal logic of representation itself. Without totality, without a complete set of all mirrors, we can never know if the image reflected back as labor time is the true one or not. Its selection still appears arbitrary.

Second, the manifold of value has unfolded only into a "motley mosaic of disparate and unconnected expressions of value." Unfolding the movement of value outward has only diversified how it can be expressed, without any connection between the mirror representations (equivalent forms) themselves. All the mirrors point inward, and all appear to be unconnected, when in fact their collective action has a power much greater than the combination of their individual parts. Therefore, there must be more to the collective acts of these reflective surfaces. There must be something missing from the description of value as a mere act of unfolding from a central point (C, 156).

Third, linen has produced an entire commodity world modeled on itself, but any other commodity could do the same. "It follows that the relative form of value of each commodity is an endless series of expressions of value which are all different from the relative form of value of every other commodity" (C, 156). Therefore, there is not a single world of commodities but rather different manifold worlds of commodities. Each commodity-equivalent is defined by its own particular kind of labor (weaving, tailoring, baking, and so on), and thus there is no "exhaustive form of appearance of human labour in general" (C, 157). The world of commodities is made of the same stuff of labor time, but there still appear to be *different kinds of labor time* in each equivalent.

THE COMMON-FOLD OF VALUE

However, by inverting this relation we get a completely different outcome: the common-fold. Value begins from the basic kinetic act of setting two qualities into motion by exchange. This movement is singular, occasional, and driven by use-values. However, Marx says, once "a particular product of labour, such as cattle, is no longer exceptionally, but habitually, exchanged for various other commodities" (C, 158), then the simplex unfolds into a manifold of heterogeneous commodities, one of which becomes more common than the others. "In both cases it is the private task, so to speak, of the individual commodity to give itself a form of value, and it accomplishes this task without the aid of the others, which play towards it the merely passive role of equivalent" (C, 158). In other words, it is only through constant and habitual kinetic patterns of individual action and exchange that certain objects come to have common or general social value, such as cattle, grain, and gold. The common equivalent form is nothing other than a product of the habitual treatment of objects as if they had no sensuous qualities.

In this third value-form (common or general), however, a major inversion occurs in the movement of value. The relatively discrete product of the value creation process (a single habitually used equivalent form) now appears to be what is producing the process itself. Now instead of a single commodity reflected in a manifold of mirrors, a single mirror reflects the entire world of commodities:

> The new form we have just obtained expresses the values of the world of commodities through one single kind of commodity set apart from the rest, through the linen, for example, and thus represents the values of all commodities by means of their equality with linen. . . . Through its equation with linen, the value of every commodity is now not only differentiated from its own use-value, but from all use-values, and is, by that very fact, expressed as that which is common to all commodities. By this form, commodities are, for the first time, really brought into relation with each other as values, or permitted to appear to each other as exchange-values. (C, 158)

If there is only one mirror, then the whole world of commodities can see itself as a whole, as a truly common or shared world of abstract labor time. The whole world appears as a single quantity or totality of the same quality (abstract labor time). Quantities in this way can now be compared and exchanged as quantities or parts in a whole. This occurs, as Marx says, only on the condition that a single kind of commodity is "set apart from the rest." This single devalorization is thus constitutive of the comparative value creation of all other commodities (see figure 8.1).

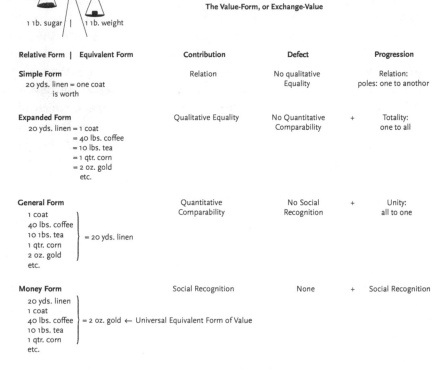

Figure 8.1 The value-form, or exchange-value. Credit: Robert Urquhart

The Common and Entangled Movement of Value

It is crucial not to lose sight of the idea that the selection and reproduction of this single equivalent form is a collective and kinetic product of the habitual exchange of motley qualities. Marx is careful to stress the common work that gives this particular equivalent the power to be the mirror of the world.

> The general form of value, on the other hand, can only arise as the joint contribution of the whole world of commodities [*gemeinsames Werk der Waarenwelt*]. A commodity only acquires a general expression of its value if, at the same time, all other commodities express their values in the same equivalent; and every newly emergent commodity must follow suit. It thus becomes evident that because the objectivity of commodities as values is the purely 'social existence' of these things, it can only be expressed through the whole range of their social relations; consequently the form of their value must possess social validity. (C, 159)

This is not just true for the common form of value. It has always been true of the entire process of value creation and mobilization:

> The one-fold relative form of value of one commodity *converts* some other commodity into an isolated equivalent. The unfolded form of relative value, that expression of the value of one commodity in terms of all other commodities, *imprints* those other commodities with the form of particular equivalents of different kinds. Finally, a particular kind of commodity acquires the form of universal equivalent because all other commodities *make it* the material embodiment of their uniform and universal form of value. (C, 160)[2]

The direction of value creation and mobilization here is crucial. The first form "converts" a commodity into an equivalent. The second form then "imprints" multiple equivalents. The third form finally "makes" one equivalent reflect the entire world. First, a flow of matter folds itself up into a relatively distinct equivalent. Second, it grants a relative hierarchy to one side over the other by using a single relative body to imprint *multiple* equivalents. Third, it then uses one of those equivalents as a way to reorganize all the relative values. Three kinetic operations are present: division, hierarchy, and reorganization.[3]

The agency here is *first* on the side of material production and only *second* on the products. This is not a binary opposition. The products of material production are nothing other than material production itself simply folded up into objects and treated *as if* they had no material qualities and were passive. Material production produces a product, but then the product seems to take on a life of its own over the production process. "The physical form of the linen counts as the visible incarnation, the social chrysalis [*Verpuppung*] state, of all human labour" (C, 159). The general or common equivalent is common only because common habitual exchange has made it so. Only because the caterpillar has made its own chrysalis does it have metamorphic powers. In other words, equivalence is nothing without the process of material production that selects it, bears it, reproduces it, and moves it around—turns itself into a pupa.

The equivalent form is the product of the relative form, but both are mutually entangled with each other (*Entwicklungsverhältniß*). Here another wonderful German conjunction shows precisely the way in which material production folds itself up like a winding coil (*Wicklung*), which brings relative and equivalent into a folded and entangled relationship (*Verhältnis*) of mutual transformation (C, 160). Since relative and equivalent are mutually entangled, one should never make the theological mistake of putting a product before the process that produced that product: "We must bear in mind that the development of the equivalent form is only the expression and the result of the development of the relative form" (C, 160).

The Magnetic Field of Value

Value is produced only through a collective social process of kinetic production. In this way, Marx says, the movement of value is like a "magnetic field":

> It is by no means self-evident that the form of direct and universal exchangeability is an antagonistic form, as inseparable from its opposite, the form of non-direct exchangeability, as the positivity of one pole of a magnet is from the negativity of the other pole. (C, 161)

The common or general form of value (nondirect exchange) is thus the inverse pole of unfolded (direct exchange) because the relationship between relative and equivalent is antagonistic like the poles of a magnet. The two sides are inseparable from each other because they are coiled or folded up with each other (*Entwicklungsverhältniß*), just like the processes of production and consumption. In the case of the mobilization of value, however, we have both the production of the form (relative/equivalent, which is derived from the kinetic fact of the relative motion of bodies) and the mobilization of those forms in various combinations that produce various patterns of value.

A magnetic field is an important comparison here because it emphasizes that the twofold difference between use-value and exchange-value or relative and equivalent forms is something that occurs in a continually fluctuating material-kinetic field. Each side of a magnetic field is just a continuation of the other. The petty bourgeois, Marx notes, want instead to think of commodities as if they were atomistic, isolated particles without relation. As such, they think that such discrete atoms can be put into any arrangement whatsoever. This is why they think value is something "accidental and purely relative," when it is actually something practically and materially produced within a social magnetic field. Value only appears to be something discrete, like an iron filing moved by the magnetic field, when in fact it is only the product of a massive collective social relation.

Therefore, as Marx writes, "Only when this exclusion becomes finally restricted to a specific kind of commodity does the uniform relative form of value of the world of commodities attain objective fixedness [*objective*

Festigkeit] and general social validity" (C, 162). The German word *Festigkeit* indicates perfectly the idea that what is fixed is not an atom in a void but rather something "steadfast, solid, firm, or holding strong" in a field of flux. The verb *festigen* means "to consolidate." Value is something neither natural nor divine but consolidated and metastable, which holds up only by the strength of the immanent support that bears it.

For example, the centralized consolidation of grain in late Neolithic societies into grain silos made possible the emergence of a central guardian and accountant of that grain. The collective social decision to centralize village grain storage was an agreement to act as if everyone's grain and thus labor was equal when it was portioned back out over the winter. Not linen but grain functioned as the first general equivalent in human societies. A *sila* of grain was one of the first equivalent forms. However, this was made possible only by reproducing a very specific social relation of centralization, which increasingly included new "socially valid" figures such as the warrior-king grain guard and the accountant-priest.[4]

The Performance of Value

Marx is not wrong to compare the production and mobilization of value with the kinetic performance of play, dance, and theater. More than anywhere else in *Capital*, Marx describes value in terms of performance in this section of the book.[5] Social equivalence, for Marx, is a role to be played precisely because of its strange status: *as if* it were a representation perfectly reflecting the value of the commodity and at the same time being itself something bodily and sensuous with its own qualities and use-value. "It becomes its specific social function, and consequently its social monopoly, to play [*spielen*] the part of universal equivalent within the world of commodities" (C, 162). In the common or general form of value, the equivalent is playacting, in the sense that it does not really or naturally have any specific value. However, by its habitual performance as such, it does really have this effect.

The German word *spielen*, from the Proto-Germanic **spilą*, means to play, dance, or move. The fact that relative and equivalent value are roles to be played means that they are aspects or dimensions continuous with one another in a whole kinetic performance, for Marx. The forms of value thus dance and exchange places with one another and trace out patterns of motion. In this way the production of value in motion is very much like the Greek *chora*, which means, "chorus, stage, space of circulation, and the generative countryside that supports the city or polis." The Greek chorus is not just a bunch of people singing in a preexisting space; the dramatic *chora* actually makes the space by kinetically performing the space. Division occurs as kinetic folds in a field of dramatic space.

Value emerges as something relatively discrete from within a more primary kinetic field of motion, performance, and circulation. Play emphasizes that value occurs only in the act of motion and not before it or above it. The exchange of commodities is also literally a dance in which the partners trade places. Through the patterns of their movement, they define social circulation.

The year king: Marx is not wrong to connect the creation of value to the origins of religion and social centralization. The historical emergence of social centralization and social value was something extremely performative and tied directly to the birth of ancient theater. One of the earliest kinetic structures of ancient performance was the emergence of a division between the central priest-king-actor and the peripheral people-chorus. By contrast, prehistoric song, dance, and ritual theater before 3500 B.C.E. were defined almost exclusively by a centripetal gathering of people without a central poet, actor, or priest-king.

After around 3500 B.C.E., ritual was stockpiled into urban, written, and theatrical forms. This occurred when a single aesthetic figure was isolated from the periphery and came to occupy the center in the form of a priest, king, actor, or poet. In lyric poetry, the periphery eventually became the audience, but in choral poetry and theater the periphery became a performative resonance chamber responding to a central point, mimicking the kinesthetic relation between the poet and audience. In Sumer, Babylon, and Egypt, the masked priest, king, and god became distinct from the people, leading the procession, performing the sacred marriage, and reciting divine texts. The single central priest said a prayer, and the multiple peripheral people responded in turn. This is the ancient chorus.

In Greece, Arion of Corinth and the dithyramb increasingly transformed the wild Dionysian festivals of immemorial past into the circular chorus. The chorus, in turn, was increasingly divided between a central *coryphaeus*— leader or head who directed the chorus—and a peripheral group that was directed. The Greek chorus, as the Greek word *chora* suggests, was an active kinetic space that made or opened a space by moving. The kinetics of the chorus here are clear: the chorus gathers around centripetally and opens up a space within which it is possible for a central figure to emerge, distinct from the periphery. Choric movement is further divided into strophic and antistrophic "turns" as the chorus moves and turns from east to west, then west to east, then finally to an epode where a single *coryphaeus* steps forward from the center and sings solo.

Since the Greek word *chora* also means "countryside," the centripetal gathering of the countryside to the center of the polis or city takes on a kino-political meaning as well: as a division or distinction between the urban and rural, center and periphery, the speaker and the singer, Dionysus and Apollo, women and men. The two are brought together and united in a single centripetal enfolding that gives birth to a central figure: the actor.[6]

Ancient ritual, religion, society, and theater were bound together in this dramatic moment in which a specific form of general equivalence emerged collectively through performance. Social, religious, and economic centralization was something socially produced through *dramatic performance*. These performances were also something deeply connected to the year king and fertility rituals, in which the center dies and must be performatively reborn through kinetic action. All this is part of the performative conditions for centralization of the modern value-form.

THE MONEY FORM

Finally, the money form can emerge only from this process because it is immanently tied to this performative movement:

> The universal equivalent form, has now by social custom finally become entwined with the specific natural form of the commodity gold. Gold confronts the other commodities as money only because it previously confronted them as a commodity. . . . It also functioned as an equivalent, either as a single equivalent in isolated exchanges or as a particular equivalent alongside other commodity-equivalents. Gradually it began to serve as universal equivalent in narrower or wider fields. (C, 162–163)

Gold has only "won a monopoly of this position" as the money form because it has fought its way up from the bottom. It has at times, Marx says, played a role in all the previous stages. Only by "social custom," and "habit" did gold attain the status of the money form for such a long time. In other words, gold only won out in the end because it played every role in the whole performance.

Marx is now finally justified in saying, "The one-fold commodity form is therefore the germ [*Keim*] of the money-form" (C, 163). The German word *Keim* means germ, seed, or sprout. Section three ends as it began, with the *birth* of value, with the generativity of matter. Society might act as if value were something beyond corporeal incarnation, but in fact value is strictly immanent to the *movement of its body* because, as shown, it is nothing other than a kinetic pattern or regime of motion. Value is not a thing but a process or relational pattern of motion. It is not an actor but a whole performance.

Material production unfolds out of itself, like a seed, split open into its relative and equivalent halves. From the onefold germ, a flow or shoot unfolds into the manifold blossom of the dazzling money flower. Money is now completely demystified. It is neither arbitrary nor divine but something constitutively produced through collective material performances both human and natural. Value and exchange fluctuate not because of the change in quantity or quality of some object but because of the temporal measure of a portion of this motion. Abstract labor time, like socially necessary labor time, is nothing other than material production treated *as if* it were "playing the role of," or "mirroring" a quality-less object made by labor in general.[7] As such, the value-form not only continues the devalorization process by ignoring the kinetic conditions that bear it but goes on to circulate values, as if they moved on their own without the kinetic support or transit of those who move and reproduce it.[8]

Elaborating this point is the purpose of section four of chapter one, on the fetishism of the commodity and the secret conditions of primitive accumulation internal to value. This is the focus of chapter 9.

CHAPTER 9

Fetishism and the Form of Motion

Value is birthed by the movement of material production, but once it is born it tries to conceal its conditions by devalorizing them. At the same time, however, this devalorization process also serves to reproduce the conditions for the continued accumulation or appropriation of devalorized matters. These are two core features of the value-form.

The argument of this chapter is that there is one final feature of value: domination. The threefold movement of the birth of value involves devalorization, appropriation, and domination. These are not developmental stages but all occur at the same time, as three aspects of the same process of value creation. Domination, in particular, occurs when a single part of the value creation process turns back against the whole process itself *as if* this single product were the cause of the very process that produced it. Marx calls this radical inversion "the fetishism of the commodity."

Through the kinetic process of production and exchange, a single commodity (money) comes to be habitually selected, as discussed in the previous chapter. Once it becomes socially selected, however, it is possible to treat it as if it had always or naturally had that value. By virtue of its relative discreteness or separation from other commodities, it seems as though value exists independently of the process that continually reproduces and bears its value (*tragen*). In short, because one cannot see directly or discretely the whole social pattern of motion that bears the value of money, it seems as though value works like a magical fetish with its own autonomous powers. The fetish thus seems to be the producer of the process that produced it. This confusion results in a strange form of domination of labor by the products of labor.

Marx in Motion. Thomas Nail, Oxford University Press (2020). © Oxford University Press.
DOI: 10.1093/oso/9780197526477.001.0001

The emergence of domination also gives rise to the double character of what Marx calls "the laws of motion of modern society" (C, 92), which are both the laws of motion that *produce* society *and* the laws of motion *produced by* society. Readers of Marx have tended to interpret these laws in either the first or the second sense but not as a twofold process of mutual transformation. However, if we interpret the laws of motion as fixed, deterministic laws of nature, we end up with classical mechanics.[1] On the other hand, if we interpret the laws of motion as fixed, deterministic laws of society, we end up with social constructivism. Both paths lead to forms of reductionism and determinism. Both also lead to a kind of fetishism in which the movement of sensuous matters is reified into either fixed natural laws or fixed social laws.

Marx's understanding of a "law," however, is neither. Moving forward from his kinetic theory of value and into his theory of fetishism and domination in section four of chapter one, it is worth taking a moment to consider his theory of the "laws of social motion." In the preface to the first edition of *Capital*, Marx says quite boldly:

> Even when a society has begun to track down the natural laws of its movement—and it is the ultimate aim of this work to reveal the economic law of motion [*Bewegungsgesetz*] of modern society—it can neither leap over the natural phases of its development nor remove them by decree. But it can shorten and lessen the birth-pangs [*Geburtswehen*]. (C, 92)

Since the ultimate aim of *Capital* is to reveal the economic law of motion of modern society, this is not an unimportant point.

Motion

First and foremost, the ultimate focus of *Capital* is to understand the nature of social *motion*. At this point in this book, it will not surprise the reader to learn that Marx's fundamental methodological orientation to modern society is a kinetic one. The aim of *Capital* is not to understand modern social laws but to understand modern social laws *of motion*. Society, like all of sensuous nature for Marx, is nothing other than matter in motion. These motions are neither predetermined nor random but pedetic and dialectical. Various patterns of motion emerge, persist, dissipate, and re-emerge historically. Modern society, like all societies, thus moves according to what

Marx calls a "*Bewegungsform*" (form of motion or motion-form) (MEGA 10: 17, 98, 103, 108). Material production moves and through its motion produces patterns, forms of circulation, or kinetic structures. Matter in motion always, following Epicurus and Lucretius, produces form, including the value-form. Form is always kinomorphic.

Law

Second, and consequently, a "law" of motion absolutely cannot be a fixed law of nature in the Newtonian sense. If the laws of motion were fixed in advance, this would posit something unchanging and thus unmoved in the universe, which Marx explicitly rejects in his doctoral dissertation. In his use of the German word *Gesetz* (law), Marx is simply following the kinetic meaning of its root word *setzen,* meaning to "to set, sit down, or settle." Law, for Marx, is something that is laid down through a process or pattern of motion. Law therefore cannot preexist its actively being laid down through motion. If Marx believed that law was natural and fixed, he would be positing an ahistorical and nondialectical "ultimate aim" for *Capital.* This is plainly not the case. The whole of part one is a careful theory of how the movement of material production becomes "settled" into patterns of habitual exchange and custom, resulting in social values. Once settled, however, these patterns can become relatively fixed. They may "seem" *as if* they had always been there or that they were natural forms of motion. We may *act as if* they were fixed social laws. As Marx says quite explicitly in the postface, after the social "forms of motion" (C, 103) have become settled historically, "only then can the real effective motion [*wirkliche Bewegung*] be determined" (C, 102). Only after the *historical movement* is complete can the *conceptual form* present the "real form of motion" in contrast to the "mystical" Hegelian logical "form of motion" (C, 103). When Marx says "law," therefore, he cannot mean either Newtonian natural law or Hegelian dialectical law.[2]

Instead, Marx gets his theory of law from Epicurus. Marx makes this entirely clear in his doctoral thesis when he writes that "*declinatio atomi a recta via* is the law, the pulse, the specific quality of the atom . . . the *arbitrium*, the specific substance, the true quality of the atom" (MECW 1: 472–473). The swerve of the atom is the *lex atomi,* or law of the atom. "The declination of the atom from the straight line is, namely, not a particular determination which appears accidentally in Epicurean physics. On the contrary, the law which it expresses goes through the whole Epicurean philosophy, in such a way, however, that, as goes without saying, the determination of its appearance depends on the domain in which it is applied" (MECW 1: 50).

These are strange definitions of law. For Marx, law is simply the tendency for matter to move pedetically and dialectically through non-predetermined motions. The swerve of movement might be unpredictable, but it is not accidental or random. On the contrary, the swerves express the law, but only in a way that depends on the domain of its appearance. Law here is explicitly immanent to the sensuous appearance and qualities of the matters in motion. "For the study of nature," Marx says, "cannot be pursued in accordance with empty axioms and laws" (MECW 1: 68). An empty law is a formal law that transcends its historical and kinetic laying or settling down. Law, for Marx, must be a kinetic form or settled pattern specific to the qualities and domain of its sensuous appearance.

Marx's theory of law is related to part of Hegel's description of law as the "source of a self-kindling movement"[3] but also goes beyond it with Epicurus's materialist and pedetic law of the atom's self-swerving movement, "That is, it is no external condition of motion but being-for-self, immanent, absolute movement itself" (MECW 1: 474). Only in Epicurean materialism do the law and form of motion become purely immanent to the matter it governs. There is not even an interaction between law and motion, but law is *nothing other than* the immanent form or pattern of motion itself: "The life process of capital consists only in its movement as value constantly expanding, constantly multiplying itself" (MECW 35: 315).

Just as the moon traces real patterns in the sky that we cannot see all at once without time-lapse photography, so there are also social forms or laws of motion that we cannot see all at once without the aid of historical concepts. As Marx says, "Just as the heavenly bodies always repeat a certain movement, once they have been flung into it, so also does social production, once it has been flung into this movement of alternate expansion and contraction" (C, 786). The patterns or laws of social motion are real and immanent, but because they are processes and not discrete things, we tend to mistake the product for the process. This is the central problem that fetishism and the domination of social value pose.

THE TRACES OF VALUE

A core problem at the heart of *Capital* is that we have mistaken discrete products for the cause of their own process. The wealth of societies appears as an immense collection of discrete individual commodities (C, 125). This is what we must try to see beneath. "A commodity appears [*scheint*] at first sight [*ersten Blick*] an extremely obvious [*selbstverständliches*], trivial thing" (C, 163). In the quick strobing flash, glance, or look (*Blick*) of an eye, the commodity shines (*scheint*) out as a single discrete thing (*Ding*). It seems as if the commodity stands still on its own (*selbstverständliches*) as an autonomous object (*Gegenstand*) hanging in midair without support, like a Democritean atom.

"But its analysis brings out that it is a very complicated thing [*vertracktes*], abounding in metaphysical subtleties and theological niceties [*Mucken*]" (C, 163). The commodity is not just "strange," as Fowkes translates the German word *vertracktes*, but "complicated." The German word *vertracktes* comes from the word *trecken*, meaning to stretch or distort (*vertrecken*) by being "drawn or pulled" over. In other words, the commodity seems like a single discrete atomic thing, but our kinetic analysis shows it to be manifolded, com*pli*cated, or folded over and folded up in *einfache* (onefolded) and *entfalten* [unfolded] forms. The commodity is full of *Mucken* (little ways) or little paths or strange little motions that disturb the shining surface appearance of the thing. What seems static is not. The commodity grumbles and moves. Marx unfolded the commodity in section three of chapter one, and now it is evident how folded-up and how mobile it really was. We saw how the value of the commodity is something produced only *through motion and in motion* and how value is immanent to the movement of matter that produces it. However, by folding itself up, it covers over and obscures its own conditions of production.

The mystical power of the commodity is therefore not a strictly psychological or epistemological delusion; it is a real, material covering or folding-over itself, like the coat. One side of the coat is something that *is worn* (*tragen*) but also something that is drawn or pulled over (*vertracktes*) the body of the wearer. Just as the movements of relative and equivalent value are two aspects of the same onefold continual movement, so is the movement of wearing and concealing performed by the coat. In other words, the process of material production that produced the linen and the coat is the same process that wears and uses the coat as a cover that obscures and folds over the wearer. The source of fetishism and domination has no other origin than the same immanent process of material production itself. We produce our own domination. This is what is so profoundly strange and mystical in the fetishism of the commodity.

There is nothing mystical in the material process of production, from the point of view of either its qualities (*Eigenschaften*) produced by nature or its qualities produced by humans (C, 163):

The form of wood, for instance, is altered [*verändert*] if a table is made out of it. Nevertheless, the table continues to be wood, an ordinary, sensuous thing. But as soon as it emerges as a commodity, it changes [*verwandelt er sich*] into a sensual, supersensible thing [*übersinnliches*]. (C, 163)

Matter, as Epicurus teaches, is continually trans*formed* and "made other" (*verändert*) through the movement of folding. The entire process is defined by a continual and sensuous self-affection of matter in motion. However, once the product of this process is treated as if it is not a product of a process but a discrete atomic individual that stands on its own (*selbstverständliches*), then it transforms itself into a sensible thing that covers over its own sensible (*übersinnliches*) form of motion (*Bewegungsform*).

Marx uses the German word *verwandelt,* which means literally "a movement of wandering, walking, strolling, which transforms" itself through motion. Fowkes's English translation, "change," does not capture the true kinetic meaning of this word and thus the specific kinetic meaning of this transformation. It is precisely in and through its motion that the commodity covers over (*über*) its own sensible qualities (*sinnliches*). Again, Fowkes's English translation of *übersinnliches* as "transcendence" obscures the kinetic foundation and material birth of the value-form, especially when Marx intentionally chose not to use the German word *transzendieren*.

The commodity does not change magically or epistemologically but practically, materially, and kinetically, by covering over the sensible tracks and traces of its kinetic history. It does this by covering its form with another form. Only when production and consumption are not collectively and intentionally organized around the threefold metabolic process is it possible to think of products as isolated, individual objects without a kinetic history. It is as though the commodity has covered itself with a coat, made itself into a mirror, or dragged (*getragen*) a branch behind it to cover over (*über*) its transformative wandering (*verwandelt*). In all these cases, the commodity practically and materially covers itself with something else to obscure the form of motion that produced it.

TURNING THE TABLES

The commodity is *sinnliches übersinnliches* (sensuously oversensible) because it is both a sensuous quality (use-value) and a folded or covered sensuous quality (value) at the same time. Marx is forced into this admittedly odd turn of phrase precisely because there is not really a magical transcendence, only a specific kinetic act of covering or overfolding that obscures the kinetic origins of the original fold. Thus, he says of the table:

> It not only stands [*steht*] with its feet on the ground [*Boden*], but, when set [*stellt*] in relation to all other commodities, it moves over and against itself onto its head [*Waaren gegenüber auf den Kopf*], and evolves out of its wooden brain grotesque ideas, far more strange [*wunderlicher*] than if it were to begin dancing of its own free will. (C, 163–164)

The commodity is twofold. On one side it stands with its feet on the soil of the earth as a kinetic product born by the earth and by its own feet in motion. It does not stand on its own in static autonomy but stands with its mobile feet in the soil of the earth that bears it. However, once it is "set in relation" or "set in motion" with other commodities, as if this movement occurred without the aid of those bearing feet, then "it moves over and against itself onto its head." It flips over or folds over itself. The metabolic movement of qualities and quantities does not necessarily do this. Objects move and stand (*gegenstand*) against themselves without mystery because they remain attached to their qualities and their kinetic conditions of folding. However, when an object moves *over and against* itself (*gegenüber*), then it seems as though it has covered over its grounding movement and borne qualities. Only when the traces of the object's habitual form of motion are covered over does it seem to have an autonomous magical motion. Only then does its motion seem to strangely originate from its own natural wooden head.

The Taiping Rebellion

The seeming autonomy of the movement of value is far stranger than if the table had actually started dancing with its own feet. This is a strange point, but Marx has something quite specific in mind, as he says in the footnote: "One may recall that China and the tables began to dance when the rest of the world appeared to be standing still—*pour encourager les autres*" (C, 164). As usual, this short footnote reveals much more about the primacy of motion in the birth of value. The first reference is to the Taiping Rebellion (1850 and 1864) in China. After the failure of the 1848 revolution in Europe, there was a revolution in China, something many Europeans did not expect. While the European Left stood still in defeat after 1848, the Taiping Rebellion encouraged Europe to get back up and continue the struggle against capitalism. Among other things, the Taiping Rebellion abolished private property; communalized land; banned foot-binding; declared a classless society and the equality of the sexes; and criminalized opium, gambling, tobacco, alcohol, and polygamy.[4] In short, the population of producers rose up against the products of Chinese domination.

However, the Taiping Rebellion also was a spiritual revolution based in Christian deism. In this sense, a kind of fetishism was still at work insofar as the real material agency of the people was seen as guided or directed by a power more primary than themselves: God. Many social problems united the rebels, but the Christian God became the single name that united, directed, and ultimately legitimated all of them. Just like the autonomously dancing table, God seems to be a power that moves on its own and commands us to act. This is strange, but the fetishism of the commodity is stranger still.

Table Turning

The second reference in the footnote is to the rise of "table turning" across Europe around the same time, after 1848. People would put their hands on a table, and a medium would speak to the spirit world by calling out letters of the alphabet or "yes" or "no" in response to a question. The spirit then would select the letter or answer the question by moving the table, just like using a Ouija board. This worked because of the now well-known "ideomotor" effect, in which slight preconscious physical movements occur in response to certain expectations. When this is done in a group, everyone thinks someone else has moved the table, when in fact it is a preconscious collective kinetic effect.

Of course charlatans also devised all kinds of clever tricks to move the table as well, but the ideomotor effect nonetheless remains demonstrably real with or without charlatans. Just as in the Taiping Rebellion, the material-kinetic conditions of production collectively rose up against the dominant social/psychological powers. By harnessing the ideomotor effect, human consciousness was exposed for what it is: an epiphenomenon of a more primary material-kinetic process of collective microaffective agencies. It is not the mind that drives the body but the body, including "background brain activity," that produces the ideological effect we call "mind."[5] Our bodies first move and act, and only milliseconds later do we "think" that we have caused the body to move. Consciousness thus becomes a kind of fetish, insofar as we act as if the mind came first when in fact the entire material, entangled, and affective milieu (the temperature of the room, the comfort of our clothes, and other such factors) participates in "the act" and "conscious product."[6]

However, just like the Taiping Rebellion, table-turning covered over its real material and kinetic conditions by attributing them to something else: a spirit. Both the rebellion and table-turning encouraged collective movement but at the same time covered over the real kinetic laws of motion by attributing them to a mystical, insensible source beyond them. This "covering over," just like the commodity, was not a purely psychological process but a real, practical one made possible by very specific sensuous structures that did the obscuring, in this case the table and the Bible.

THE OPTICS OF VALUE

The mysterious character of value comes from the commodity itself. Marx is extremely clear on this point. Fetishism is not an anthropocentric social constructivism as it is for Feuerbach. Religion is not just a subjective delusion or belief. Its basis lies in real material and kinetic practices, both human and nonhuman. The value of the commodity seems to be autonomous and causally dominant to humans because of how *the commodity itself moves* and covers its own motion.

Mysticism does not necessarily come from material production or from the forms of motion of material production but from the covering-over of these processes. "The mystical character of the commodity does not therefore arise from its use-value. Just as little does it proceed from the nature of the determinants of value" (C, 164). Material production occurs strictly within the entangled metabolic process: sensuous nature, human brains, nerves, sense organs, and so on. Even though "the duration of that expenditure or the quantity of labour . . . is quite palpably different from its quality," this measurement practice is still something humans do and know they do (C, 164). For example, there is nothing mystical in the German practice of *Tagwerk* that uses a quality (time) to measure other qualities (kinetic activity or labor) quantitatively: a day of labor time. There is nothing mystical in the social organization of this time.

The Mirror Mystery

The mysterious power of the commodity that dominates us "arises from this form itself" (C, 164). "The enigmatic character of the product of labour [arises] as soon as it assumes the form of a commodity" (C, 164). The

mysticism of value comes not from the quality, the quantity, or the movement of value but from the form specific to the commodity itself:

> The mysterious character of the commodity-form consists therefore simply in
> the fact that the commodity reflects [*zurückspiegelt*] the social characteristics
> of men's own labour as objective characteristics of the products of labour them-
> selves, as the socio-natural properties of these things. (C, 164–165)

The specifically mysterious character of the commodity-form is that it acts
not like it is the reflection of labor but *as if* it is the origin of its own natural
properties. This is the third optical error of the value-form.

(1) The first error was made in the onefold and unfolded forms by treating
    the equivalent form as a purely passive object that reflected only the
    agency and activity of the relative form. This resulted in a *devalorization*
    of the object.
(2) The second error was made by all of the value-forms insofar as they
    all treated the movement of optical transport (the act of bearing,
    migrating, setting into motion) as a completely neutral and immaterial
    motion. This resulted in an *appropriation* of transport labor.
(3) The third error is that a single object becomes the only active power,
    and the relative social process becomes entirely passive. Now the rel-
    ative form is simply a projection of a single kind of commodity. The
    result is fetishism and *domination*.

Each error is not strictly wrong but rather incomplete. The kinetic truth
is that all three forms (relative, transport, and equivalent) are threefold
motions in the same continually differentiated motion. This is the kinetic
theory of value.

The Optics of Domination

This third error, however, not only obscures its kinetic origins but reacts
back upon them so that when the relative form moves, it moves *as if* it
were nothing but the movement of the equivalent form or the money
form (which are its products). "Through this substitution [*quid pro quo*],
the products of labour become commodities, sensuous things which are
at the same time supra-sensible [*sinnlich übersinnliche*] or social" (C, 165).
In this third error, all sensuous objects now "look like" commodity-forms
of the same kind. A single commodity-form thus covers over its own

distinct sensuousness by covering over, folding over, or reflecting back over (*zurückspiegelt*) itself with another optical sensation (*sinnlich übersinnliche*). The mirror hides its tin or silver tain with glass. The mirror covers over its own material and sensuous conditions of reflection.[7] Value is sensible (*sinnlich*) because it is produced sensuously, but it is supersensible because it covers over (*übersinnliche*) its original sensuousness with another sensation that hides it. Again, this is not a social-psychological constructivism. The mirror and the commodity actually move in such a way as to obscure their conditions of production. They really look like discrete objects and not forms of motion.

Again, Marx is perfectly clear about this:

> In the same way, the impression made by a thing on the optic nerve is perceived not as a subjective excitation of that nerve but as the objective form of a thing outside the eye. In the act of seeing, of course, light is really transmitted from one thing, the external object, to another thing, the eye. It is a physical relation between physical things. (C, 165)

The relative form really emits light, light is really transmitted, and the equivalent form really reflects it. The kinetic theory of value, for Marx, works in "the same way" as optics. There is activity and material agency all the way down. Value is a physical relation (*physisches Verhältniß*) between physical things (*physischen Dingen*). The commodity-form really looks like and moves like it is autonomous because part of its appearance and motion have been covered over:

> The commodity-form, and the value-relation of the products of labour which it depicts or performs [*darstellt*], have absolutely no causal connection [*schaffen*] with the physical nature of the commodity and the material relations [*dinglich Beziehungen*] arising out of this. It is nothing but the definite social relation between men themselves which assumes here, for them, the fantastic [*phantasmagorische*] form of a relation between things. (C, 165)

In contrast to the material-kinetic and physical conditions that produce the commodity-form, the commodity-form has absolutely no causal, creative, or productive relation (*schaffen*) with the material relations that produced it. Material production is not really dominated by an external and transcendent force that impels or causes it from the outside to obey. It produces and reproduces its own immanent domination. Commodity societies simply act like or perform (*darstellt*) their social relations *as if* they were atomistic, individual, persons following predetermined laws of social motion. They perform the dance of the commodity and continually reproduce themselves as dancing commodities. Society thus becomes a "ghostly public performance" (*phantasmagorische*) of partial objects or "individuals" interacting like isolated atoms in the void.[8]

There is not some other thing outside material production that actually dominates it. "As the foregoing analysis has already demonstrated, this fetishism of the world of commodities arises from the peculiar social character of the labour which produces them" (C, 165). Any power of domination held by the fetish is only the result of the whole nonmystical material-kinetic process or form of social motion described previously. In fact, it is only because value emerges from a form or pattern of motion over time and on a larger social scale that we do not see all at once, that we mistake discrete products for the causal agents. This is why it is so absolutely crucial that Marx shows us the form of social motion that we cannot see with the eye. This is perhaps one of the earliest kinopolitical gestures in the history of philosophy: a turn to the study of the patterns or regimes of social motion that underpin fetishism, servitude, and domination.

The Fog of Religion

For Marx, a similar process of fetishism and domination occurs in religious belief:

> In order, therefore, to find an analogy we must take flight [*flüchten*] into the misty realm [*Nebelregion*] of religion. There the products of the human brain appear as autonomous figures endowed with a life of their own, which enter into relations both with one another and with the human race. So it is in the world of commodities with the products of men's hands. I call this the fetishism which attaches itself to the products of labour as soon as they are produced as commodities and is therefore inseparable from the production of commodities. (C, 165)

Religion, for Marx, is a foggy realm of flight, but not because one actually transcends the earth by flying into the clouds beyond sensation. Fog and mist are nothing but clouds that have come down to the earth. When we walk through them, it is as if we are flying through the clouds above. The fog both obscures and covers over the sensuous world but in its obscurity also easily allows us to see partial objects floating around as if they were detached from their context. We see other individuals in the fog detached from their larger kinetic-material context. Objects *seem* to come out of nowhere. The entire foggy milieu seems to shape our world of possibilities around the limited parts we can see. These reflections do not come from the mind but from the physical brain and moving body walking through the mist. Fetishism is a material social-psychological performance that has its basis in the real material-kinetic patterns of entangled exchanges:

> The private producer's brain reflects [*spiegelt*] this twofold [*doppelten*] social character of his labour only in the forms which appear in practical intercourse [*praktisehen Verkehr*], in the exchange of products. . . . Hence the socially useful character of his private labour is reflected in the form that the product of labour has to be useful to others. (C, 166)

The physical brain of the private producer in turn reflects this mirror world. In religion, the complex and entangled world of mutual interactions (*praktisehen Verkehr*) appears only in limited glimpses and fragments. The world and the brain become twofold (use-value/exchange-value) at the same time. Without being able to see or collectively control the whole social pattern of motion, individuals shape their behavior to conform to the needs of other individuals. Individuals produce "so that their character as values has already to be taken into consideration during production" (C, 166). Individuals produce for individuals in a world of fragmented and seemingly random motions.

The interactions in this fog "transform every product of labour into a social hieroglyphic," whose larger pattern of motion is unknown. Just like the invention of language, Marx says, humans created all the material-kinetic coordinations between speech and gesture, but eventually they came to think that sounds actually bore some essential relationship with things and one another. "Later on, men try to decipher the hieroglyphic, to get behind the secret of their own social product" (C, 167). The "secret," for Marx, is not God but simply the larger pattern and historical form of motion at work. This is a tricky thing to see because it is *not a thing at all* that can be directly seen all at once *but a process* or pattern of motion, seen over time. The kinetic origins of written language work in much the same way, by covering up or hiding clay tokens in a boule and then acting as if the marks on the outside of the boule had an autonomy when the tokens were removed.[9]

Atomic Fog

The same thing occurs in the fog of atomism. Instead of the flow of continually swerving pedetic matter, as in Epicurus, we find in Democritus the deterministic movement of discrete atoms in the void. So, too, in the world of commodities we find people and objects moving around as if they were independent agents when in fact they all hang together in a threefold metabolic process.

Classical atomic physics and classical political economy thus both come to similar conclusions about the discrete, passive, law-abiding nature of matter. Just as political economy starts from individuals randomly producing for other individuals in a vacuum, so classical physics begins from similarly randomly moving atoms or particles. Material production "appears to those caught up in the relations of commodity production to be just as ultimately valid as the fact that the scientific dissection of the air into its component parts left the atmosphere itself unaltered in its physical configuration" (C, 167).

The absolutely central point that unites political economy and the atmosphere for Marx is pedesis and turbulence. Marx, following Epicurus's and Lucretius's writings on meteorology, is well aware of the—still today—unresolved problem of turbulence. Neither classical nor quantum physics has been able to either model turbulence *completely*, only that it does occur. Social patterns of motion and atmospheric weather patterns are quite literally impossible to explain or model from fixed linear laws of ideal particles bouncing around.[10] For Marx, the whole process is greater than the sum of its individual static parts because what is missing in the addition of parts is the pattern or form of motion of the whole.

THE FORM OF MOTION

Value fluctuates and changes not because it is "accidental and purely relative" (C, 126) but because there is a secret form of motion (*Form einer Bewegung*) operating beneath the cover of the apparent discreteness of the commodity-form:

> These magnitudes vary continually [*wechseln beständig*], independently of the will, foreknowledge and actions of the exchangers. Their own movement [*Bewegung*] within society has for them the form of a movement [*Form einer Bewegung*] made by things, and these things, far from being under their control, in fact control them. (C, 167)

Social value is defined ultimately by the process of social metabolism or continuous interchange (*wechseln beständig*), even if it hides this fact. Values move as if they had no qualities, but they still have a specific form of motion. For example, the circulation of value still depletes the soil, kidnaps slaves from their homes, and treats women's bodies as wombs for the reproduction of labor. Social forms of motion then begin to follow the same pattern as if they, too, were quality-less values.

A social form of motion is nothing but the hanging together of collective action in interdependent patterns. What at first has appeared to political economists as a naturally "accidental and purely relative" form of motion, Marx now exposes as a specific structure with its own pattern of motion defined by the production and movement of values:

> All the different kinds of private labour which are carried on independently of one another; and yet, as spontaneously developed branches of the social division of labour, are in a situation of all-round dependence on one another [*allseitig von einander abhängigen*]. (C, 168)

Together, all these apparently random individual motions are part of a larger pattern of motion that hangs together on all sides. Material production occurs in an all-sided mutual dependence (*allseitig von einander abhängigen*) or *Zusammenhangen*. Each major historical epoch has its own dominant form of motion, but the focus of *Capital* is on the modern, "elastic" pattern of motion (C, 344, 527, 579, 752, 758).

The secret of fetishism is therefore that there are laws, forms, or patterns of motion that both structure the birth of value and hide beneath the apparent randomness and arbitrary structures of domination.

The Gravity of Value

Beneath the apparently "accidental and purely relative" social motions of exchange, there is a secret form of motion whose pattern can be discerned by following the ratios and traces of labor time:

> The reason for this reduction is that in the midst of the accidental [*zufälligen*] and ever-fluctuating [*schwankenden*] exchange relations between the products, the labour-time socially necessary to produce them asserts itself as a regulative law of nature. In the same way, the law of gravity asserts itself when a person's house collapses on top of him. The determination of the magnitude of value by labour-time is therefore a secret hidden under the apparent movements [*erscheinenden Bewegungen*] in the relative values of commodities. Its discovery destroys the semblance of the merely accidental determination of the

magnitude of the value of the products of labour, but by no means abolishes that determination's material form. (C, 168)

In response to the apparent randomness of social motion, political economy uses the determination of socially necessary labor time as if it were a fixed law of nature. Socially necessary labor time, however, as discussed in chapter 4, is not a fixed quantity but fluctuates constantly according to the availability of devalorized accumulations, among other factors. It is a determination made post festum depending on a host of shifting variables. It only looks like an explanation after the fact. Just as one invokes the law of gravity to explain the collapse of a roof, Marx says, the law is deployed both retroactively and so generally that it is not really an explanation at all. In other words, all things fall because of gravity, so it is not a helpful explanation of the roof's collapse:

> Reflection begins *post festum*, and therefore with the results of the process of development ready to hand. The forms which stamp products as commodities and which are therefore the preliminary requirements for the circulation of commodities already possess the fixed quality of natural forms of social life before man seeks to give an account, not of their historical character, for in his eyes they are immutable, but of their content and meaning. (C, 168)

The secret of such retroactive determinations as socially necessary labor time is that beneath them is a real movement of material production organized around the exchange of labor-time ratios and primitive accumulation. On the gleaming surface, the commodity-form looks like a purely natural and fixed natural law of motion that explains why things move the way they do:

> The categories of bourgeois economics consist precisely of forms of this kind. They are forms of thought [*Gedankenformen*] that are socially valid, and therefore objective, for the relations of production belonging to this historically determined mode of social production, i.e. commodity production. (C, 169)

In fact, however, what is missing is an account of how it is that the commodity-form emerged historically in the first place. Understanding these more primary motions is thus the key to understanding the semblance of "accidental and purely relative" patterns of commodity motion. What appears to be the purely arbitrary and mystical use of domination is shown to follow a specific form of motion.

In fact, all the structures of social domination, such as racism, statism, heterosexism, patriarchy, religion, and anthropocentrism are also not just arbitrary expressions of power. Nor do they emerge by necessity from any naturally legitimate or fixed source. They are patterns of motion that are collectively or socially reproduced as fetishes. They seem to have some natural or divine external power but only continue because they are continually reproduced. Furthermore, their kinetic functions are not independent from one another but are entangled at the site of social devalorization: the social border. Society expands and reproduces itself through the domination and appropriation of the devalorized. The triptych of value creation is complete: devalorization, appropriation, domination. Fetishism is the covering over of the triple determinants of value and their retroactive positioning of its power as primary.

With the threefold structure of value creation in hand, I can carefully unpack Marx's exemplification of Robinson Crusoe as a simple figure "containing all the essential determinants of value" (C, 170). This also provides the opportunity to make explicit the historically racist and colonialist nature of the birth of value under modern capitalism.

CHAPTER 10

The Colonialism of Value

This chapter looks more closely at the triple kinetic structure of the birth of value (devalorization, appropriation, and domination) in Marx's discussion of Robinson Crusoe. As is typical throughout chapter one of *Capital*, Marx's short examples and references are always much richer than the limited use he makes of them. This is especially true in the case of the book *Robinson Crusoe*, which abounds with relevant insights about the deeply interwoven nature of colonialism, racism, and primitive accumulation at the heart of value.

In section four of chapter one, "Commodity Fetishism and Its Secret," Marx reveals that the secret of the commodity fetish is a specific three-fold form of motion defined by the processes of devalorization, appropriation, and domination (described in greater detail in the previous sections). Forms or patterns of material-kinetic production create objects. However, because of the large-scale social, geographic, and durational nature of these patterns, social objects tend to hide or cover over their kinetic history. It then appears that the object itself stands on its own with a natural power to direct social motion.

The thesis of this chapter is that the secret of commodity fetishism is nothing other than "The Secret of Primitive Accumulation" of chapter twenty-six of *Capital*. It is no coincidence that the titles of chapter one, section four and chapter twenty-six are the only two in all of *Capital* to reference "the secret." They are two sides of the same twofold kinetic theory of value I have been laying out. Fetishism and primitive accumulation are entangled with each other in a way rendered explicit in the history of colonialism and in the founding mythology of capitalism itself: the story of Robinson Crusoe.

Marx in Motion. Thomas Nail, Oxford University Press (2020). © Oxford University Press.
DOI: 10.1093/oso/9780197526477.001.0001

PRIMITIVE ACCUMULATION

The story of primitive accumulation is a myth told by political economists that explains the origins of capitalist accumulation as if capitalism were always already there. Marx therefore writes, "This primitive accumulation plays approximately the same role in political economy as original sin does in theology" (C, 873). The term *ursprüngliche Akkumulation* means "first, original, or primary" and not "simple, rude, or rough." Marx develops this concept from a passage in Adam Smith's *Wealth of Nations*: "The accumulation of stock must, in the nature of things, be previous to the division of labour."[1] In other words, before humans can be divided into owners and workers, there must have already been an accumulation such that those in power could enforce the division in the first place. For Smith, the superior peoples of history naturally accumulate power and stock and then wield it to perpetuate the division of labor. This process is simply a natural phenomenon: powerful people always already have accumulated stock, *as if* from nowhere.

For Marx, however, this quote is perfectly emblematic of the historical obfuscation of political economists regarding the violence and expulsion necessary for those in power to maintain and expand their stock. Instead of acknowledging this violence, political economists mythologize and naturalize it. For Marx, however, primitive accumulation always has a material history. It is part of the original determination of value. It is the noncapitalist condition internal to capitalist production itself, its motor and becoming. Marx identifies this process in particular with the expulsion of peasants and indigenous peoples from their land through enclosure, colonialism, and antivagabond laws in sixteenth-century England:

> The discovery of gold and silver in America, the extirpation, enslavement and entombment in mines of the indigenous population of that continent, the beginnings of the conquest and plunder of India, and the conversion of Africa into a preserve for the commercial hunting of blackskins, are all things which characterize the dawn of the era of capitalist production. These idyllic proceedings are the chief moments of primitive accumulation. (C, 915)

Marx's thesis is that the condition of the social expansion of value is and always has been the prior expulsion of people from their land through devalorization, appropriation, and domination. Without the expulsion of these people, there is no expansion of private property and thus no value.[2]

However, the myth of primitive or primary accumulation described by Smith has another important aspect to it: individualism. For Smith, Ricardo,

Bastiat, Carey, Proudhon, and other political economists, the *primary* form of accumulation did not occur socially but in *isolation*. Accordingly, for them economics is not founded on social domination but on the hard work of isolated individuals in a primitive state of equality and individualism.

ROBINSON CRUSOE AND POLITICAL ECONOMY

Marx was the first to trace the rise of the popular social economic myth of the isolated individual back to the early eighteenth-century novel *Robinson Crusoe* by Daniel Defoe:

> The individual and isolated hunter and fisherman, with whom Smith and Ricardo begin, belongs among the unimaginative conceits of the eighteenth-century Robinsonades . . . [just like] Rousseau's *contrat social*, which brings naturally independent, autonomous subjects into relation connection by contract, rests on such naturalism. This is the semblance, the merely aesthetic semblance, of the Robinsonades, great and small. (G, 83)

The modern myth of primitive accumulation begins with Defoe's *Robinson Crusoe,* which became the source of inspiration for subsequent variations of the myth of "an original state of society" from which "the development in stages of the social state" emerges from individual agents (G, 83–85). The first major economic figures to take inspiration from this, Marx says, were Smith and Ricardo:

> Ricardo makes his primitive fisherman and primitive hunter into owners of commodities, who immediately exchange their fish and game in proportion to the labour-time, which is materialized in these exchange-values. On this occasion, he slips into the anachronism of allowing the primitive fisherman and hunter to calculate the value of their implements in accordance with the annuity tables used on the London Stock Exchange in 1817. (C, 169)

Ricardo retroactively casts the modern idea of an equality of exchange between isolated individuals back onto "primitive" peoples. Smith similarly posits the existence of an original "barbarous and uncivilized state,"[3] "that early and rude state of society,"[4] "that original state of things,"[5] "age of hunters,"[6] "state of hunters,"[7] "in the beginning of society," "in their primitive state."[8] Smith thus proposes an original state "of hunters and fishers, [in which] every individual who is able to work, is more or less employed in useful labour, and endeavours to provide, as well as he can, the necessaries and conveniences of life for himself, or such of his family or tribe as are either too old, or too young, or too infirm to go a hunting and fishing."[9] In the beginning, for Smith, individuals provided *for themselves* (and perhaps for the young and elderly).

Although Smith and Ricardo do not mention *Robinson Crusoe* or Defoe by name, each treats indigenous peoples as individuals fending for themselves and exchanging with other individuals. This tendency among the early economists is then amplified by later ones. Marx writes:

> Production by a solitary individual outside society—a rare event, which might occur when a civilized person who had already absorbed the dynamic social forces is accidentally cast into the wilderness—is just as preposterous as the development of speech without individuals who live together and talk to one another. It is unnecessary to dwell upon this point further. It need not have been mentioned at all, if this inanity . . . were not expressly introduced once more into modern political economy by Bastiat, Carey, Proudhon, etc.[10]

Marx says "once more" to indicate that Smith and Ricardo were the first to take it up and that Bastiat, Carey, and Proudhon took it up next.[11] This time the historical link to Defoe is explicit.

In *Economic Sophisms* (1845), the French economist Claude-Frédéric Bastiat imagines an economic dialogue between the book's characters Crusoe and Friday. Bastiat is thus explicit about the modern relevance of the Crusoe myth. Although modern conditions are more complicated, Bastiat says, "they do not change their essential nature."[12] Elsewhere, he asserts that if we "consider the nation as a collective entity . . . you will find not an iota of difference between its line of reasoning and that of Robinson Crusoe."[13]

In *Principles of Political Economy* (1837–1840), Henry Carey was the first American economist to make use of the Crusoe myth. Though Carey does not explicitly mention Crusoe, he asks the reader to consider "an individual of mature age, thrown upon and sole occupant of an island, or of an extensive body of land, fruit and flowers, in quantity that is partially unlimited."[14]

We might also add to Marx's list *An Essay on the Production of Wealth* (1821) by the British economist Robert Torrens and his example in which "a man were thrown naked and destitute upon an uninhabited shore."[15]

Numerous other economists and political philosophers have since taken up this myth in one way or another (Thomas Hobbes's "state of nature," etc.).[16] However, Marx's point in stating that "political economists are fond of Robinson Crusoe stories" (C, 169) is that all the modern myths of early societies based on exchanging individuals, often in isolation, are derived from Defoe's novel in one way or another—even if they do not explicitly reference *Robinson Crusoe*, which is an important text because it lies at the secret heart of this entire mythology. Shipwreck stories in general are quite old, but *Robinson Crusoe* is unique in the specific way it tells its shipwreck tale.[17] This is why Marx is interested not in social-origin myths or in shipwreck stories more generally but in *Robinson Crusoe* in particular. *Robinson Crusoe*, not others, shaped the way economists and political philosophers thought about the origins of society and "primitive accumulation."

What is specific about *Robinson Crusoe* and the various myths directly inspired by it is that they signify "the anticipation of bourgeois society. . . . The individual in this society of free competition seems to be rid of natural ties, etc., which made him an appurtenance of a particular, limited aggregation of human beings in previous historical epochs." The mythological and individualistic origins of society are treated by "bourgeois economists" not as products of history "but as the starting point of history; not as something evolving in the course of history, but posited by nature, because for them this individual was in conformity with nature, in keeping with their idea of human nature."[18]

In short, economists and political philosophers alike are guilty of retroactively positing a bourgeois Homo Economicus at the origin of social history in order to naturalize, justify, and mystify the true origins of modern society, which occurred through violence, colonialism, racism, sexism, and the destruction of nature. In particular, they have chosen an explicitly colonial and racist origin story befitting the true historical origins of the modern bourgeois epoch.

When Marx says that the story of primitive accumulation plays approximately the same role in political economy as original sin does in theology, Marx is deftly aware that this is the same theological narrative that Defoe *explicitly* provides about Robinson's "original sin" of leaving the feudal tutelage of his father and country to sail away to adventure.[19]

ROBINSON'S ISLAND, BATHED IN LIGHT

Defoe's *Robinson Crusoe* is the ur-myth of an entire tradition of political economy that seeks to cover over the constitutive devalorization, appropriation, and domination at the heart of economic value. Marx is explicit in his awareness of this fact when he writes, "Robinson appears first on his island" (*erscheine zuerst Robinson auf seiner Insel*) (C, 170). The importance of his use of *erscheine* here is obscured in Fowkes's English translation as "let us first look at Robinson on his island." For Marx, the fact that Robinson "appears first" on his island means precisely that his appearance is *not* the same as his entire being. Robinson only appears first on his island in the same way that the wealth of modern society *appears* as individual commodities. Robinson is an individual "first" on the island, only upon "first appearance" or at "first sight" (*ersten Blick*)—to echo the opening of section four. There is both something true in this real appearance and something hidden just below it that makes it possible, as with atoms and commodities. This is a twofold appearance of Robinson on his island bathed in light.

The Conditions of Appearance

Robinson only appears on his island under the more primary condition of the threefold natural-human-social metabolic process.

Natural: First and foremost, Robinson only *appears first* on the island from an anthropocentric perspective. The island was already a rich ecosystem filled with all kinds of minerals, plants, animals, insects, and freshwater sources before he arrived. Only by accepting the a priori devalorization of nonhuman populations can we say Robinson is in any way "isolated" or an "individual," or first. In fact, Robinson only *appears* on the island at all because of these natural metabolic conditions. Early on in his years on the island, Robinson even gives thanks in his journal for the climate, the trees, the flora, and fauna that sustain him.[20] Robinson's appearance on the island has as its condition an entire natural metabolic process of creatures and climate providing him with everything he needs for survival and happiness.

Human: Second, beyond these natural metabolic conditions, Robinson also has access to his ship's cargo, including all kinds of food, tools, building materials, weapons, books, and domestic pets (cats and a dog). The fact that he can identify familiar animals, fruits, and minerals and has tools and basic knowledge are both social products as well as the means of reproducing his natural metabolic relation to nature on the island. For example, the fact that he finds corn and barley seeds on the ship and knows how to grow them makes possible his island agriculture. Since these material conditions are strictly social products, Robinson's appearance on the island is hardly an isolated or nonmetabolic process. Early on, he gives thanks for all these material conditions that allow him to reproduce his metabolic life on the island.

Social: Robinson's *appearance as first* on the island is also made possible on the precondition of a much larger social context of international mercantilism, slavery, and colonialism. Before being shipwrecked on the island Robinson is the son of a prosperous middle-class merchant but chooses to leave his home in England to find his own fortune as a merchant—partly out of greed for something more than his standing. In his first adventures he profits from trading with Africans on the Guinea coast in exchange for more valuable gold dust worth 300 pounds. Later, he is captured and enslaved but escapes with the help of an African slave, whom he sells to the Portuguese captain who rescues them. The captain takes him to Brazil, where he uses his profits to start a tobacco plantation run on slave labor. Only when he becomes greedy for more slaves and goes out to get more does his ship wreck on "the Island of Despair."[21] He later laments this greed but not because of the immorality of slavery. In short, an entire social world of colonialism, slavery, and economic mercantilism was the precondition for Robinson's shipwreck upon the island. This is a far cry from any "original state of nature" or isolated individual.

Marx's use of the word "appears" thus means that Robinson really appears as first in the founding myth of political economy but that this founding moment of appearance is made possible only by more primary material-kinetic metabolic conditions, also described in the same founding myth. Political economists and political philosophers alike cannot admit that the foundations of modern society are not isolated individuals struggling for their own self-created wealth, but rather simply European colonists completely conditioned on a vast system of racism and metabolic drift. Colonialism, slavery, and ecocide are the real material conditions that must be covered over so that Europeans can imagine that they were always already alone on an island making their own wealth. The Robinsonade, a literary genre imitating the premise of Defoe's novel, thus functions like a fetish that covers over the real content of the actual novel itself. Just like a commodity fetish, a single individual (Robinson) is naturalized and used to cover over the real social and colonial form of motion that made his appearance possible.

This is the first point Marx makes about the myth of Robinson Crusoe: that it functions in political economy as a fetishistic myth, just like Smith's primitive accumulation. It covers over the real material and historical conditions of production.

The second point Marx makes in this passage is a more positive one. The appearance of Robinson on his island is also the place where material production appears as what it is. As Marx says, "All the relations between Robinson and these objects that form his self-created wealth are here so simple and transparent" (C, 170). Robinson's island is "bathed in light" because it reveals to him the whole material process or form of motion necessary for metabolic reproduction.

Off the island, the forms of motion are larger, more complex, less visible at once, and thus more prone to fetishism. On the island, however, Robinson sees directly the metabolic unity of his own labors and object relations on the island. Because the scale of material production is so small, Robinson is able to see the close entanglement of weather patterns, geological events, animal reproduction cycles, crop cycles, mineral compositions, his own life processes, and much else—all as aspects of the same form of motion. He sees these processes directly and consciously tries to organize their metabolic form of motion. He does not produce commodities for himself, and he does not produce fetishes to deceive himself about how things are moving. He thus produces no value. Robinson sees all the sensuous motions value tries to cover over.

Robinson comes to a number of crucial conclusions that bourgeois political economists fail to mention:

(1) **Natural:** He notes in his journal his realization that his own metabolic process is entangled or hangs together in a threefold way with the natural process of the island's weather, minerals, animals, and plants; his own biological needs; and the inorganic social artifacts he retains through his education and cargo from the boat. He even comes to see the growth of seeds, trees, and fruit as a kind of immanent productive power.[22]

(2) **Human:** He realizes that labor has no value. "But my time or labor was little worth, and so it was as well-employed one way as another."[23] Robinson realizes that there is no single value or equivalent form for material production, so labor can be freely directed in an unlimited number of ways. There is no reason or need to work toward any accumulation beyond use-value. "In a word, the nature and experience of things dictated to me upon just reflection, that all the good things of this world are no farther good to us than they are for our use; and that whatever we may heap up indeed to give others, we enjoy just as much as we can use, and no more. . . . All I could make use of was all

that was valuable. . . . The most covetous, griping miser in the world would have been cured of the vice of covetousness, if he had been in my case."[24] The greed that led Robinson away from England and from Brazil is rendered transparent in the light of the real form of motion of use-value. When one sees the direct connection between material production and enjoyment, one sees that accumulation over and above use-value has no intrinsic value but only a social value or power. Value has only the power we give it since it is nothing other than material production itself.

(3) **Social:** He realizes that money has no value. "I smiled to myself at the sight of this money. 'O drug!' said I aloud, 'what are thou good for? Thou art not worth to me, no not the taking off of the ground, one of those knives is worth all this heap; I have no manner of use for thee; e'en remain where thou art, and go to the bottom as a creature whose life is not worth saving.' "[25] Money is thus revealed for what it is: a social fetish. Money only has the value it does because it is borne by society. It is only collective social production that makes money valuable, and we can change this. "However, upon Second Thoughts, I took it away." In his first transparent thought he sees it for what it is, but in his second thought he sees it for what it could be in a possible future social context and takes it anyway.

When Marx says "Let us now transport ourselves from Robinson's island, bathed in light, to medieval Europe, shrouded in darkness" (C, 170), what he means is that when the metabolic pattern of motion becomes geographically and temporally larger and more social (than a single island), it tends to be harder to see, more covered, and thus obscure and more fetishized. To see and try to organize the whole process on this scale takes a special kind of social form, as discussed in the next chapter. There are, however, several more specific aspects of primitive accumulation rendered transparent on Robinson's island that need to be looked at more closely.

COLONIAL ACCUMULATION

Marx states only the most important conclusions on Robinson's island generally because a full treatment of them would take the text in another direction. Now, however, I can develop the details of each of the five general categories Marx lists as the essential determinants of value.

For Marx, what is important about Defoe's *Robinson Crusoe* is that it transparently lays out "in the light" how Robinson's situation "contains all the essential determinants of value" (C, 169–170). That is, Robinson produces all the essential "*determinants* of value" leading up to the production of value. Since this is precisely what sections one through three of chapter one of *Capital* had aimed to do, the story of *Robinson Crusoe* makes a significant contribution to value theory more generally. Showing all the determinants of value would demystify value by showing in detail everything that went into producing what the fetish tries to cover over.

At first, Robinson on his island only reproduces his own metabolic life process. However, once other people begin to show up on the island, the same transparency of his shining island now reveals to him firsthand the immediate social structure of colonialism, racism, patriarchy, and anthropocentrism, entangled in the process of value production more generally. Since Marx goes into specific details about the contents and narrative of the novel *Robinson Crusoe*, he has clearly read it and has in mind a more specific reading beyond a merely general critique of the myth used by political economists.[26] Since he does not develop them, let us now look into the logical extension of the five general determinants of value Marx lists as they play out in the second part of Defoe's novel, when others begin to arrive on the island:

> Necessity itself compels him to divide his time with precision between his different functions. Whether one function occupies a greater space [*Raum*] in his total activity than another depends on the magnitude of the difficulties to be overcome in attaining the useful effect aimed at. . . . His stock-book contains a catalogue of the useful objects he possesses, of the various operations necessary for their production, and finally of the labour-time that specific quantities of these products have on average cost him. (C, 169–170)

The five general determinants of value Marx finds in *Robinson Crusoe* are (1) a list of object-relations or possessions, (2) operations necessary for the production of objects, (3) the portion of space (*Raum*) required by each operation, (4) the useful effect achieved by this sensuous object, and (5) the average labor time required to produce the object. These five determinants of value pertain not only to Robinson's activities before people arrive on the island, as previously discussed, but by logical extension also pertain to them once others arrive on the island.

These five determinants can be further schematized thus: relation, production, space, consumption, and time. I consider each in the context of Robinson's island colonialism to see if I can make good on Marx's claim that *Robinson Crusoe* transparently lays out all the determinants of value (including the process of primitive accumulation) leading up to the production of value itself.

Marx seems to have something like this in mind when, only a few pages after his *Robinson Crusoe* example, he describes the constitutive and ongoing nature of primitive accumulation, specifically slavery and colonialism:

> Truly comical is M. Bastiat, who imagines that the ancient Greeks and Romans lived by plunder alone. For if people live by plunder for centuries, there must, after all, always be something there to plunder; in other words, *the objects of plunder must be continually reproduced*. It seems, therefore, that even the Greeks and the Romans had a process of production, hence an economy, that constituted the material basis [*materielle Grundlage*] of their world as much as bourgeois economy constitutes that of the present-day world. (C, 175)[27]

Marx could not be more explicit: colonialism, slavery, and plunder are ongoing processes of production and constitute the material basis of production in the ancient and the bourgeois world alike. Violence and plunder constitute aspects of the economy that are covered over by the myth of a priori accumulation by isolated individuals. *Robinson Crusoe* thus begets this myth but also lays bare its constitutive violence at the same time.

In the following sections I show how *Robinson Crusoe* demonstrates all three major forms of the determination of value (covered in section three) leading up to the production of the final money or fetish-form. Instead of their purely conceptual formulation, however, here there is a more historical and colonial theory of value.

The Onefold or Simplex Form of Colonialism

Onefold or *einfach* colonialism, just like the onefold value-form, is not simple at all but rather simplex, containing within it all the manifolds of colonial value determination. In *Robinson Crusoe* this occurs in Robinson's first personal interaction with another human on the island: Friday. Years before Friday's arrival on the island, Robinson discovers that a group of Caribbeans periodically visit the island. Instead of joining them, Robinson hides away in fear for years and feels lonely. One night, after he hears a distress shot from a ship, he has a dream that a slave escapes from a Caribbean shipwreck and becomes his servant. Years later, a Caribbean ship comes ashore, and a slave escapes. "It came now very warmly upon my thoughts and indeed irresistibly, that now was my time to get me a servant, and perhaps a companion or assistant."[28] Robinson rescues the escaped slave.

"He came nearer and nearer, kneeling down every ten or twelve steps. . . . At length he came close to me, and then he kneeled down again, kissed the ground, and laid his head upon the ground, and taking me by the foot, set my foot upon his head; this, it seems, was in token of swearing to be my slave forever."[29] Thus begins the first form of colonialism.

Relation: This is not a simple interaction or exchange between isolated individuals, as political economists imagine. The relation between Robinson and Friday is already part of a vast network of racism, colonialism, and primitive accumulation. Simplex colonialism is already manifold. Individuals are already entangled, as is clear from the fact that Friday escaped from a ship where he was a slave. Robinson thus takes care to reproduce on the personal and individual level all the material conditions of a slave relation. This includes first, and most obviously, putting his foot on Friday's head, a clear kinetic performance of asymmetry between mobility and immobility, activity and passivity, relative and equivalent forms. Next, Friday is transformed into an object when Robinson gives him the slave name "Friday" to remind him of the day Robinson saved his life and makes him an indebted object of servitude. Robinson gives him European clothes to wear that are inferior to Robinson's. These clothes cover over and devalorize his dark-skinned indigenous body while at the same time rendering visible his racialized inferiority. Robinson shows him the power of his gun to kill (a goat)—without explaining how the gun works. This scares Friday into confused, mystical obedience to Robinson, who appears to have magical control over life and death. Robinson now manages his human possession in addition to his nonhuman object relations.

Production: Robinson then teaches Friday all the practical skills necessary for the material production of their life process on the island. "I . . . made it my business to teach him everything that was proper to make him useful, handy, and helpful."[30] Robinson teaches Friday how to bake and cook; "In a little time Friday was able to do all the work for me, as well as I could do it for myself." Then Robinson makes him a kind of plantation worker on a piece of land "in which Friday not only worked very willingly and very hard, but did it cheerfully." "He appeared very sensible of that part, and let me know that he thought I had much more labor upon me on his account than I had for myself, and that he would work the harder for me, if I would tell him what to do."[31]

It is no coincidence that Robinson first teaches Friday the historically gendered forms of production associated with women's unpaid domestic labor (cooking, baking, farming). Thus, after being dehumanized as an object of possession, Friday is then feminized in his production.[32] Furthermore, Friday's "life process" becomes completely colonized through specific forms of European production. For example, Friday is made to produce European agricultural foods (corn, barely, rice, etc.) and grow them by European methods with European tools and give them European names. Robinson never once thinks to learn a word of Friday's language or consider what indigenous knowledge he has that might aid their survival. Devalorization, appropriation, and domination are thus revealed as the conditions for the reproduction of European colonial culture (work, clothing, language, custom, knowledge, etc.).

Space: Robinson also makes Friday sleep between the center of the house and the exterior. He thus introduces a spatial division between Friday and himself to secure and reproduce the asymmetrical slave relation. The degree of distance from the center of accumulation spatially marks out Friday as racially inferior. His proximity to the natural exterior indicates that he is more nature-like and animal-like. By inverse relation, this makes Robinson more human, more male, more dominant at the center of his accumulations. Robinson even sets up a burglar alarm between them, making his relation to Friday also one of lawgiver over potential criminal. However, Robinson also says, "For never man had a more faithful, loving, sincere servant than Friday was to me; without passions, sullenness, or designs, perfectly obliged and engaged; his very affections were tied to me like those of a child to a father; and I dare say he would have sacrificed his life for the saving of mine upon any occasion whatsoever."[33] Friday is thus both criminalized and infantilized at the same time, following precisely the European racist and colonial tradition.[34]

Consumption: Not only does Robinson make Friday produce as a slave, but he makes him consume as a slave as well. It is not enough for Robinson that Friday cook, bake, grow his food, and the rest; Friday must consume and internalize the racialized, feminized, animalized slave relation. Friday must become an active agent in the consumption of his own slavery. Robinson accomplishes this not only by giving Friday a slave name that reminds him of his debt relation but also by taking care "especially to make him speak and understand me when I spoke." Linguistic subjection is something produced in Friday, but Friday must then consume it by putting his own words and actions into the word and actions of the colonizer. Robinson also converts Friday to Christianity and tells him all about the all-powerful and immaterial creator God. Christianity, as Marx rightfully noted earlier, is the most fitting religion for the fetish of the value-form because it both attributes the whole creation of being to a single transcendent individual and, in Protestantism, makes the individual the fundamental subject of knowledge. Christianity, in the form of Protestantism, therefore teaches

Friday, the colonized, to consume words and actions not as natural-social products but as isolated individual products made by a God.

Time: Once Friday is enslaved, Robinson accounts not only for his own labor but for his slave's labor as well. Instructing and directing Friday becomes its own form of labor for Robinson. The measurement and management of Friday's labor time thus now becomes a new kinetic structure of domination as well. The "island of light" shows this domination directly and unfetishized. However, since the management of Friday's labor is a direct one of domination, Robinson must be constantly vigilant and watchful in case Friday does something wrong, takes long breaks, is not as efficient, is not sufficiently encouraged or punished, and so on. It is always in the back of Robinson's mind that Friday might betray him and kill him in his sleep or steal from him. He is always probing Friday for hints of betrayal and sees in him a wish to return home again and abandon God and Robinson. In short, just as Marx writes that, "the objects of plunder must be continually reproduced," so Robinson expends no small amount of his own productive labor time reproducing the transparent techniques of racialization and slavery. All of these techniques of appropriation, devalorization, and domination are necessary conditions for the emergence of colonial value.

The Unfolded or Expanded Form of Colonialism

The second colonial value-form in *Robinson Crusoe* is that of an unfolded or manifold application of the simplex form to many other individuals. This occurs when, three years after Friday arrives, twenty-one "savages" and three prisoners come ashore. Robinson wonders whether it would be right "to go and dip my hands in blood, to attack people who had neither done or intended me any wrong,"[35] but when he sees that one of the prisoners is European, he becomes "enraged to the highest degree."[36] Robinson decides to attack the men and to capture the prisoners for his own. He and Friday open fire and kill seventeen, scaring away the rest and capturing the prisoners. He thus reproduces and unfolds the determinants of colonial value onto all his people and begins to think of himself not only as a personal master over one other person but as a social master or king over all his people and owner of the whole island itself:

> My island was now peopled, and I thought myself very rich in subjects; and it was a merry reflection, which I frequently made, how like a king I looked. First of all, the whole country was my own property, so that I had an undoubted right of dominion. Secondly, my people were perfectly subjected. I was absolute lord

and lawgiver; they all owed their lives to me, and were ready to lay down their lives, if there had been occasion of it for me. It was remarkable, too, we had but three subjects, and they were of three different religions. My man Friday was a Protestant, his father was a pagan and a cannibal, and the Spaniard was a Papist. However I allowed liberty of conscience throughout my dominions.[37]

Robinson intentionally and transparently uses techniques of domination, fear, manipulation, religion, and law to work on his subjects. Later, he discovers fourteen more Spaniards and Portuguese staying with the Caribbeans, "who lived there at peace indeed with the savages." Robinson helps them escape in return for their service. Eventually an English ship comes ashore, and Robinson captures a few more men for his island. But now the original simplex form of colonial value has vastly unfolded.

Relation: With himself at the center, Robinson now unfolds his simple binary asymmetry with Friday to a more complex hierarchy and delegation of authority between his captives. Robinson thinks of the island as "his property" because now there are others there with whom he can lay claim to it and assert that claim through violence and coercion. Robison also delegates a racist and colonial social division of labor among his captives (Friday, Friday's father, and the Spaniard). "I marked out several trees which I thought fit for our work, and I set Friday and his father to cutting them down; and then I caused the Spaniard, to whom I had imparted my thought on that affair, to oversee and direct their work."[38]

Production: Robinson then has his trained slaves train the new ones, further dividing up production, expanding the hierarchies, and increasing his property, held by law and threat of violence. In order to provide food for more people, the men all work to expand the scope of production.

Space: The colonial space has now multiplied, with Robinson at the center and little structures built around him in a circle for the slaves. Robinson produces a vertical and horizontal network of circles with the entire island as the territorial limit, of which he is sole owner and king.

Consumption: The slaves then all reproduce their own material life process and accumulate more property, wealth, and slaves for Robinson, who ceased to work long ago. In order to secure the fourteen Europeans, Robinson uses their own religion against them by drawing up a contract in which they swear service to him by their God. "That they should be absolutely under my leading, as their commander and captain; and that they should swear upon the Holy Sacraments and the Gospel to be true to me and to go to such Christian country as that I should agree to, and no other; and to be directed wholly and absolutely by my orders."[39] They thus become producers and consumers of their own enslavement through their

God. This same religious belief also internalizes the racialized inferiority of Friday and other "savages" on the island, making Robinson's division of labor and delegation much easier.

Time: Robinson now delegates the accounting of labor time to others while he himself stops working.

The General Form of Colonialism

The third form of colonialism in *Robinson Crusoe* occurs when the English ship comes ashore and takes him back home to his Brazilian plantation. When the ship arrives, the captain and two other men have been taken prisoner by a mutinying crew. Robinson sides with the authority of the captain and attacks the crew, captures the two main figures responsible for the mutiny on his island colony, and sails to Brazil with Friday. This is where the major colonial inversion occurs.

Robinson leaves but commands his subjects to keep reproducing for him while he is gone. The society that he produced through institutionalized violence and racism now keeps going on as if Robinson were still there. All of his society now sees itself and its social relations as a mirror reflection of Robinson's law—just like the generalization of the equivalent form of value. Robinson returns to his Brazilian plantation to find that this same colonial inversion has actually been going on the whole time he was away! His Brazilian plantation has been kept up while he was gone, and when he returns, he is a rich man, "master all of a sudden of about 5,000 pounds sterling in money, and had an estate, as I might well call it, in Brazil, of about a thousand pounds a year, as sure as an estate of lands in England."[40]

Relation: At the same moment that Robinson finally becomes the absent king of his own colonial island, he discovers he has already been the absent king of his Brazilian plantation. The simplex form thus already contained all the colonial forms within. Robinson produced the same slave relation on his island that he was already producing in absentia on his plantation in Brazil. This is possible precisely because of the social and historical structure of private property and colonialism that was already at work the entire time. Robinson *transparently* reproduces a microcosm of the same forms of horror wreaked on the colonies but with his own transparently racist, murderous hands.

Unlike many mainland Europeans, he cannot hide behind the fetish of magically "cheap labor" or "cheap sugar" arriving in Europe because he has seen and perpetrated every horror that goes into the process of value creation. In the end, Robinson thus appears on the island and in Brazil as the natural property owner of both but from two different sides. In Brazil, the fetish lives on as the slaves work his plantation and accumulate wealth for him while he is away because of his "property right." On the island of primitive accumulation, everything is bathed in light and "dripping blood from every pore"—one side dark and mystical, the other side light and transparent.

Production: After Robinson leaves the island colony, it becomes imperialist, stealing slaves from the mainland and reproducing children on the island. "Of the improvement they made upon the island itself and of how five of them made an attempt upon the mainland, and brought away eleven men and five women prisoners, by which, at my coming, I found about twenty young children on the island." Robinson returns to the island to bring supplies, a carpenter, and a smith and later seven women "such as I found proper for service or for wives to such as would take them."

The whole social image of the island becomes a reflection of his European drive to colonialism and the domination of women. The patriarchal foundations of the colonial value-form are laid bare as nails. Robinson is now in the position of reproducing the life process of the islanders themselves through the purchasing of women's wombs. Women's bodies are used as tools for the colonial reproduction of value. In the novel, the patriarchal myth of a self-founding man is thus first undermined by his transparent dependence on nature, then by its social dependence on the domination of other men, and then finally by its gendered dependence on the domination of women and children.

Although these revelations are progressive in the novel, they are simultaneous in history. Only by the end of the novel, when Robinson has essentially reproduced all these conditions, does it become crystal clear that he could have done so only because they were *already there before him*, because what he produced was already a reproduction of that which produced him (European racism, colonialism, and patriarchy). He is, after all, the son of a merchant. The order of presentation thus differs from the order of inquiry insofar as that which is most historically primary (primitive accumulation) appears as the ultimate culmination of the conceptual schema.

Space: In the general form of colonialism the functional space (*Raum*) of activity, as Marx calls it, transforms into an action at a distance. Instead of a single center of activity with a single slave on the periphery (Robinson-Friday), or multiple centers of authority with subordinate slaves around them (master-delegates-subordinates), Robinson completely leaves the island and governs from afar through the power of law and *local* delegation.

The daily functioning of the island and its obedient reproduction of Euro-Robinsonian law, order, culture, production, and so on now goes on *as if* he were there. Just as European colonial powers used the threat of future violence, local delegates of power, and settler colonialists to reproduce European culture, power, and gender relations, so does Robinson. This allows power to operate abroad, at a distance, but still retain a mystical ownership of the land and people.

Consumption: By these techniques (threats, delegates, and settlers) the colony reproduces and consumes its own subjection to European/Robinsonian norms of production, habit, dress, religion, food, and so on. Specific material patterns of consumption, desire, and enjoyment now all appear completely natural, since the arbitrary violence of the creator has now disappeared. Myths, gods, and other fetishes move in to explain why everyone is here. Only once Robinson is gone can his colonial violence take on an apparently natural primitive origin.

Time: Finally, once Robinson leaves the island he is no longer accounting his own labor time or the labor time of the islanders, and yet their labor continues to grow *his* property. It is *as if* value mystically emerged without any labor time being expended. The general form of colonial power thus emerges when the colonizer not only lives off of but begins to accumulate wealth and property without spending any labor time at all. This is precisely what political economists do when they describe value as emanating mystically from money itself—as if money were not the product immanent to racialized, colonized, patriarchal labor time itself.[41]

* * *

The colonial origins of value are thus rendered completely transparent to Robinson because he reproduces the whole colonial value creation process in miniature. Value is revealed for what it is, the mystical product of devalorization, appropriation, and domination. Robinson devalorizes nature by treating it as his sole property, given to him by God—referring to himself often as the "king" or "emperor" of the very island that conditions his survival. He devalorizes Friday and others by racializing, feminizing, and infantilizing them. He murders and steals from others, justifying his acts through racism, classism, and patriarchy.

In short, we see in the life of Robinson Crusoe the fully transparent and systematic use of such devalorization techniques as racism, sexism, and anthropocentrism to justify and more easily, directly, and violently appropriate the material production of the others who bear and support him metabolically. On the island, Robinson's domination is initially secured by direct violence but then maintained by the use of religion and the mystical threat of damnation. After he leaves the island, he takes care to ensure that the threefold value creation process—that is, "the determinants" of value—continue on without his direct intervention. He ascends to the misty realm of colonial value and continual accumulation. The colonial fetish reaches its culmination and is forced back onto the population, which now orders its motions as colonial commodities.

The historical origins of modern value are therefore inextricable from the history of racism and colonialism. European labor and the value-form were always supported and borne by the accumulation, devalorization, and domination of the colonies. Just as with women's labor, if the costs of colonial labor and theft were actually paid, capitalism would never have gotten off the ground. Therefore, any labor theory of value that does not include the historical and ongoing appropriation of colonial labor and land is complicit in the mystification of the real birth of value. Capitalism, as Robinson's personal drama analogizes, requires the devalorization of racialized peoples in order to morally justify their direct appropriation and to perpetuate social domination over them in the form of value.

CONCLUSION

There is one final and important point to add to the colonial theory of value discussed here: Robinson acts *as if* he were independent. Since the whole colonial process (from beginning to end) appears transparently done by his own hands, he fails to see how it could have been otherwise. Off the island the process is more obviously social and not nearly as transparent; social problems are more prepared to receive social answers. According to Marx, this is the core difference between the Robinson story and all previous forms of social organization. "All the characteristics of Robinson's labour are repeated [in other historical cases], but with the difference that they are social instead of individual. . . . Here, instead of the independent man, we find everyone dependent" (C, 170–171).

Robinson's life takes place within the context of colonialism, but he personally internalizes it all *as if* he were just some isolated individual. This makes it possible for him to directly devalorize, appropriate, and dominate others *as if* he were the only one who mattered in the decision-making. If he had instead treated the threefold metabolic process as a collective one (including nonhuman agents), the story would have been quite different. Historically, the value creation process has always been a social one and therefore also has a different social form as its alternative: "an association of free men . . . working in common," or communism (C, 171).

The kinetic details of this social form are the subject of the next and final chapter.

CHAPTER 11

Kinetic Communism

Rarely does Marx have occasion to describe in any detail how communism might work. However, as a contrast to the fetishism of the commodity, he does just this in section four of chapter one. *Robinson Crusoe* illustrates but the first of four social forms of production: Robinsonian, feudal, peasant, and communist.

This chapter argues that since the fetish of value is something produced kinetically, its alternative, communism, must also be something understood kinetically. I must be understood as having its own form of motion. In particular, the previous chapters have aimed to show that what is fundamentally at stake in the difference between material production and fetishism is the transparency and direction of the form of motion. Only when the social form of motion is left fully uncovered by coats, mirrors, and fogs can it be collectively organized without devalorization, appropriation, and mystical domination. Communism is the material *social condition* in which production is treated not *as if* it were coming from what is produced but as a threefold metabolic process itself.

The thesis of this chapter then is that previous social forms of motion have always relied on a certain degree of fetishism of this motion, of which the present bourgeois epoch is the most obscured and communism is the most transparent. After *Robinson Crusoe*, Marx considers three more forms of motion, each more transparent in its own way than capitalism.

THE FEUDAL FORM OF MOTION

The first form of social motion Marx describes is the feudal form: "Here, instead of the independent man, we find everyone dependent—serfs and

Marx in Motion. Thomas Nail, Oxford University Press (2020). © Oxford University Press.
DOI: 10.1093/oso/9780197526477.001.0001

lords, vassals and suzerains, laymen and clerics" (C, 170). The whole of feudal society is defined by explicit and transparent social, legal, and hierarchical relations. "Precisely because relations of personal dependence form the given social foundation, there is no need for labour and its products to assume a fantastic form different from their reality" (C, 170). Here the relations of social devalorization, appropriation, and domination are transparently at work in the social structure of production. "Every serf knows that what he expends in the service of his lord is a specific quantity of his own personal labour-power. The tithe owed to the priest is more clearly apparent than his blessing" (C, 170). Every serf, lord, and cleric is aware that the product of the serf's labor supports the rest. The serf is taxed and tithed accordingly and with ceremony and law. Feudal society does not hide personal and social relations as if they were merely forced upon the population by the nature of the products they produce "and are not disguised as social relations between things, between the products of labour" (C, 170).

However, Marx also notes that feudal society is not completely without fetish since it is God and nature that ultimately ground and legitimate the social relations of direct and transparent domination. Feudal society is "much more simple and transparent than . . . bourgeois society [but is still] founded on direct relations of dominance and servitude" and thus still views its own social relations as natural or divine relations (C, 173). Law is still grounded in the authority of God. God and religion, as Marx described earlier in section four, always function as fetishes, even though they are not commodity fetishes. Just as in *Robinson Crusoe*'s colonial fetish, so in feudal society there is a naturalized or divine juridical fetish that mystically dictates social production above the immanent relations of material production.

THE PEASANT FORM OF MOTION

The second form of social motion Marx describes is the peasant form of motion. To see how production worked before commodity production, we do not need to look to "originary peoples" or founding mythologies: "We have one nearer to hand in the patriarchal rural industry of a peasant family which produces corn, cattle, yarn, linen and clothing for its own use. These things confront the family as so many products of its collective labour, but they do not confront each other as commodities." (C, 172). The family creates is own products, with its own methods, and "possesses its own spontaneously developed division of labour. . . . The distribution of labour within the family and the labour-time expended by the individual members of the family are regulated by differences of sex and age as well as by seasonal variations in the natural conditions of labour" (C, 171). There is no need for rural peasants to obscure or cover over the production process or the metabolic relations with nature. This would only make it more difficult to regulate and organize their own production. They do not produce commodities or any nonsensuous values that would dictate to them how they ought to produce.

However, as Marx notes, English peasant production is not without its social fetish in the form of the patriarchal division of labor and naturalized methods of customary production. Marx's concern here is that English peasant production remains limited to a naturalized and patriarchal fetish of the family that would keep it from being able to become a fully socialized and inclusive metabolic process. Society is not just a passive responsive agent to natural processes and sexuation but plays an active metabolic role as nature itself. This is not yet fully realized in English peasant production.

THE COMMUNIST FORM OF MOTION

The third and final form of social motion after the Robinsonian one is communism, which for Marx is the "association of free men, working with the means of production held in common, and expending their many different forms of labour-power in full self-awareness as one single social labour force" (C, 171). This is a major difference between all previous forms of social motion and communism. Communism treats all material production as a single, continuous, threefold form of motion and attempts to direct it as such. Accordingly, racism, patriarchy, colonialism, and anthropocentrism in principle have no place in such a society because they disrupt the threefold metabolic process described in chapter 5.

Communism is the first form of social motion to realize that it is "one single social labour force," or form of motion. This sounds like a minor point, but the realization that material production is a continual process is absolutely crucial to see that all sensuous matter as a kinetic process, and as something in motion, can be rerouted, responsive, and redirected. In short, only communism realizes the threefold unity of natural, human, and social production *as a process* of production:

> The total product of our imagined association is a social product. One part of this product serves as fresh means of production and remains social. But another

part is consumed by the members of the association as means of subsistence. This part must therefore be divided among them. (C, 171–172)

What is produced from the process of production is one ongoing socio-natural product. There are no commodities and thus no abstract values, because there is no drive for accumulation. Objects are produced to be consumed by the producers of those commodities and are completely under the direction of their own desires and use. Just as Robinson Crusoe realized that his labor and money had no value except what they could be used for, so communism creates nothing that is not meant for some sort of use by the senses. Part of the product is a novel source of social enjoyment, and another part is divided among the producers for their subsistence to maintain all three metabolic cycles.

The measurement of labor time is not itself anything mystical. It only becomes mystical when it appears as a measure independent of the process of production. Communism is the fully transparent social control over what counts as measured labor time. Some commentators have read the measurement of labor time as a kind of dehumanizing, existential reductionism of qualities to quantities. However, for Marx the measurement of quantity is not in itself an evil, nor are the sciences that use quantification in their knowledges. Antiscience humanists have tried to purge Marx of his interest and connection to the sciences. However, communism still measures labor time. This is distinct from any kind of quantitative *reductionism* insofar as such quantities are always quantities of sensuous social-natural qualities. Only when quantitative measurements try to cover over their sensuousness do they take on a fetishistic character:

> Labour-time would in that case play a double role. Its apportionment in accordance with a definite social plan maintains the correct proportion between the different functions of labour and the various needs of the associations. On the other hand, labour-time also serves as a measure of the part taken by each individual in the common labour, and of his share in the part of the total product destined for individual consumption. The social relations of the individual producers, both toward their labour and the products of their labour, are here transparent in their simplicity, in production as well as in distribution. (C, 172)

The measurement and organization of labor time, as a continual flow of collective social labor time, is the way in which the social pattern of motion appears as a whole. If material production is going to be collectively directed as a whole, it must be viewed as a whole process and not as accidental and purely relative changes among discrete individuals and objects. The measurement of labor time ceases to be strictly individual but becomes collective and social and can be directed collectively according to the desires of the free association of producers. As Marx says in the manuscripts, "The entire movement of history, just as [communism's] actual act of genesis—the birth act of its empirical existence—is, therefore, also for its thinking consciousness the comprehended and known process of its becoming" (MECW 3: 297). Value covers over the social conditions of its birth, which bears and maintains it (*tragen*), and thus hides its overt relations of appropriation, devalorization, and domination. Communism, however, sees all material production for what it is, namely, the social birthing and bearing process itself, including nature, women, and the colonies. As such, communism is the only social form in a position to recognize and transform its own conditions and desires and to count previously uncounted forms of material production.[1] In particular, a portion of communist production must always provide a "means of subsistence." That is, kinetic communism always includes at least the conditions for the universal reproduction of the social-natural metabolic cycle itself (whereas capitalism destroys it). This is not a wage but a universal support and maintenance of all humans and the conservation of nature. Marx does not say what the ratio between social enjoyment and subsistence would be, but if the widest possible understanding of material production were given, the vast majority of human and natural production would have to be returned socially and naturally rather than individually:

> Activity and enjoyment which are manifested and affirmed in actual direct association with other men will occur wherever such a direct expression of sociability stems from the true character of the activity's content and is appropriate to the nature of the enjoyment. (MECW 3: 298)

Humans become the natural-social metabolic beings they are when they socially direct their own desires and enjoyments without acting as if something else is directing them (fetishism). Only when this social-kinetic direction is not separate from nature but is seen as an expression of nature itself is the division between humans, nature, and society finally reconciled. Nature can finally enjoy itself as human (and vice versa) without the stultifying effects of various social fetishes (nature, God, the state, the commodity, racism, patriarchy, and so on) that attribute this desire to something other than the immanent metabolic process of material production itself:

> This communism, as fully developed naturalism, equals humanism, and as fully developed humanism equals naturalism; it is the genuine resolution of the

conflict between man and nature and between man and man—the true reso-
lution of the strife between existence and essence, between objectification and
self-confirmation, between freedom and necessity, between the individual and
the species. Communism is the riddle of history solved, and it knows itself to be
this solution. (MECW 3: 296)

Labor time is used as a measure to make sure that the metabolic
needs of natural and social production are reproduced (soil fertility, species diversity, social equality, and collective enjoyment). Communism is
"transparent in its simplicity, in production as well as in distribution"
insofar as it sees a whole pattern of motion, directs this pattern collectively, and does not latch onto any fetish. In other words, communism
is not a single fixed form or pattern of motion. There is no master blue-
print. It is the process of becoming and bearing without a single end
goal or telos other than the immanent one of collective self-enjoyment
and metabolic balance. At each step it directs its desires and full range of
sensation to something new, not determined in advance but dialectically
related to the present. In short, communism is the political expression
of the kinetic and pedetic dialectic that Marx first described in his doctoral dissertation.

It is therefore no coincidence that Epicurus is invoked only once in the
whole of *Capital*, in this section. Marx has in mind both Epicurus's materialist philosophy of motion and his critique of religion—the latter emerging
from the former in the same way the critique of value emerges from the
philosophy of communism.

DEUS SIVE MONETA

Marx's Epicurean critique of religion is applied to the critique of political economy, particularly the money fetish. God and money have always
functioned as fetishes. They both follow the same general logic, but historically they have diverged in the degree of dominance achieved. In the
ancient world the production of commodities was subordinated to many
other values and many other gods. The gods always exerted more power
and influence than money. However, in the bourgeois epoch, the script has
been reversed, and God has become modeled on money. God continues to
exist as a distinct fetish but also is a universal god of individual producers or
believers (Protestantism) who communicate freely as abstract individuals
with God:

Christianity with its religious cult of man in the abstract, more particularly in its bourgeois development, i.e. in Protestantism, Deism, etc., is the most fitting form of religion. In the ancient Asiatic, classical-antique, and other such modes of production, the transformation of the product into a commodity, and therefore men's existence as producers of commodities, plays a subordinate role, which how- ever increases in importance as these communities approach nearer and nearer to the stage of their dissolution. Trading nations, properly so called, exist only in the interstices of the ancient world, like the gods of Epicurus in the *intermundia*, or Jews in the pores of Polish society. (C, 172)

For Epicurus the gods are *intermundia* precisely like money used to be in the ancient world. The logic of self-sufficient gods meant that the gods, if there were any, would not care at all about human affairs and would be powerless over them. Marx is suggesting that money worked the same way in the ancient world. For Marx, ancient money was a value-fetish that had a power over its believers—but had no real power *in itself*. Just like Epicurean gods, money in itself (the greed and accumulation of money) mostly had a merely subordinate and marginal place in the ancient world. Most people in the ancient world cared more about the sensuous enjoyment of its products, festivals, excess, sacrifice, tribute, games, and luxury than accumulation for the sake of accumulation.

The Metabolic Limits of the Ancient World

One of the central limitations of the previous modes of production was that previous societies had not realized the full threefold metabolic process: nature-humans-society. Instead they held tightly to all manner of fetishes and idealisms that subordinated social metabolism to natural metabolism and thus divided one from the other:

Those ancient social organisms of production are much more simple and transparent than those of bourgeois society, but they are founded either on the immaturity of man as an individual, when he has not yet torn himself loose [*losgerissen*] from the umbilical [*Nabelschnur*] of his natural species-connection with other men [*natürlichen Gattungszusammenhangs mit Andren*], or on direct relations of dominance and servitude. They are conditioned by a low stage of development of the productive powers of labour and correspondingly limited [*entsprechend befangene*] relations between men within the process of creating and reproducing their material life [*Lebenserzeugungsprocesses*], hence also limited [*befangene*] relations between man and nature. These real limitations [*wirkliche Befangenheit*] are reflected [*spiegelt*] in the idealism [*ideell*] of older nature worship, and folk religions. (C, 173)

Ancient social motion was more transparent than bourgeois society because its relations of domination and servitude were explicit. For example, women, migrants, and slaves produced for Greek male citizens. Ancient societies did not need to *act as if* all humans were free objects following the mystical movement of commodity values. They used direct devalorization, appropriation, and domination without hiding it, although they certainly justified it in the name of various spiritual fetishes. This brings Marx to note their metabolic limits.

The ancient world and other previous social forms of motion did not see the full threefold metabolic entanglement of natural-human-social intra-action (*zusammenhängen*). This was so because they acted *as if* social metabolism were strictly subordinated and passive to nature-human metabolic processes. Nature, the gods, and human social relations were all completely naturalized, thus fixing patriarchy, anthropocentrism, racism, and colonialism as natural life conditions (*Lebenserzeugungsprocesses*). Natural and human metabolic processes were more transparent but only at the expense of completely constraining, limiting, or confining (*befangene*) "the relations between man and nature." These real metabolic limitations (*wirkliche Befangenheit*) were then reflected (*spiegelt*) or covered over by various idealist forms of nature worship and folk religion, which justified the natural hierarchies between men and women, races, classes, and so on. Ancient societies were not just "limited" but "self-constrained, prejudiced, biased, bigoted" (*befangene*). They treated arbitrary historical conventions of patriarchy, racism, and anthropocentrism as absolute natural limits of what human beings were or could be. This is precisely what communism overcomes kinetically and metabolically.

METABOLIC COMMUNISM

What I call "kinetic communism" in this chapter is simply the process by which humans treat and manage their socio-natural formations as metabolic and kinetic patterns of motion. Historically, this occurred by tearing open the closed metabolic relation between humans and nature. As Marx says in the previous section, ancient societies had yet to tear themselves loose (*losgerissen*) from a strictly naturalized metabolic entanglement with other men (*natürlichen Gattungszusammenhangs mit Andren*). To properly interpret this passage, I recall here from chapter 5 that Marx does not mean that humans need to create a metabolic "rift" (*rissen*) that tears them away from nature as such.

Marx says that the ancient world is bigoted (*befangene*) because it constrains or limits (*befangene*) the threefold metabolic form of motion to the strictly natural species hanging together (*Gattungszusammenhangs*) of humans with one another. In other words, ancient social motion treated the social-metabolic *zusammenhängen* as a strictly natural *zusammenhängen* without seeing that society is itself an active and constitutive aspect of what nature does. Nature is, among other things, human sociality, and human sociality is a natural process. Not only does nature give birth to humans, hence the umbilical relation (*Nabelschnur*), but humans also give birth (*tragen*) to one another socially and transform nature, humans, and society at the same time.

Kinetic communism thus introduces a metabolic tear into the twofold nature-human relation and in doing so discovers a new fold or dimensions in the metabolic process: society. Again, by this metabolic tearing loose Marx cannot possibly mean any kind of strictly negative or ontological division. Recall that the German word *Risse* is also a topological term indicating a rough or rocking transformation of a differentiated surface; hence the possibility of both imbalances or drifts and of new folds in the cracks —in this case social metabolism.

Once humans emerge from the earth, they become active geological and natural agents, transforming themselves and nature as one and the same earthly process. There is distinction but no separation. There are then, for kinetic or metabolic communism, no fixed natural categories or patterns. The earth is just as mutant and fluctuating as human society and vice versa. Both enter into a kind of intra-active feedback pattern in which one is not strictly modeled on the other but both mutually transform and hang together (*zusammenhängen*) metabolically.

This is the major insight directly forced upon us by the advent of climate change. Humans have never been merely subordinate to natural patterns of motion, nor has nature ever been strictly subordinate to human social patterns. The two are mutually constitutive. Kinetic communism is not just this theoretical realization but the practical collective metabolic management of the whole planetary form of motion.

Kinetic communism therefore entails abandoning all forms of idealism, nature worship, and folk religions that attempt to cover over the real metabolic forms of motion on our planet—but also is a revolutionary transformation of those same material conditions:

The religious reflections of the real world can, in any case, vanish only when the practical relations [*Beziehungen*] of everyday life [*Werkeltagslebens*] between man and man, and man and nature, generally present themselves to him in a transparent and common-sense [*vernünftige*] form. The veil [*mystischen Nebelschleier*] is not removed from the countenance of the social life-process, i.e. the process of material production [*materiellen Produktionsprocesses*], until it becomes production by freely associated [*vergesellschafteter*] men, and stands [*steht*] under their conscious and planned control. This, however, requires that society possess a material foundation [*materielle Grundlage*], or a series of material conditions of existence [*materieller Existenzbedingungen*], which in their turn are the natural and spontaneous [*naturwüchsige*] product of a long tormented historical development. (C, 173)

The core lesson of the kinetic theory of value and its fetishism is that value is not a simple or merely psychological, idealist, or anthropocentric problem in need of "ideology critique." Kinetic or metabolic communism requires the practical and material identification and transformation of the threefold patterns of natural-human-social motion at the planetary level. Only when the "practical relations [*Beziehungen*] of everyday life between man and man, and man and nature, generally present themselves to him in a transparent and rational [*vernünftige*] form" can we see how kinetically entangled humans are with nature and with one another. Only when we see the whole threefold metabolic process as one continuous and transparent hanging together (*zusammenhängen*) will we (both human and more-than-human agents) be able to collectively transform ourselves. The solution to the problem of the fetish is not just *knowing* that there is no God and that commodity-values come from material production. We actually have to transform the material conditions of *daily metabolic reproduction*.

The social metabolic transparency of real, everyday life (*Werkeltagslebens*) that Marx proposes would also entail exposing and transforming all the relations of patriarchal, anthropocentric, racist, and colonial devalorization, appropriation, and domination. If we take seriously this idea of a metabolic and entangled communism, then in principle no being should be left out of our transparent description of the threefold forms of productive motion, and none should be left out of the "common sense" (*vernünftige*) transformative or planning process. The German word *vernünftige* does not mean "rational" as in "abstract, logical calculation" but rational as in "common sense, good sense, or sensible" and thus includes much more broadly all sensible and sensuous beings in common. Humans are not the only agents in ecological or social politics. The agency of nonhumans and objects is part of the active hanging together of the whole threefold process.

The mystical and foggy veil of fetishism (*mystischen Nebelschleier*) can be removed practically and kinetically only through the collective revolutionary transformation of the whole metabolic process of material production (*materiellen Produktionsprocesses*). Since, as Marx says, the whole metabolic process includes all of nature, humans, and social formations, then the communism of "freely associated producers" (*vergesellschafteter*) must also necessarily include *all material producers*, not just humans. Human politics is always already nonhuman politics and should be collectively managed as such. To deny this is to reject the core thesis of Marx's definition of kinetic communism as the self-intra-action of nature, commonly known and practically managed as such.[2] The material grounds or conditions (*materielle Grundlage*) of natural-human-social metabolic communism are thus strictly natural (*naturwüchsige*) and historical *at the same time*. Any form of communism that does not describe and manage this natural-historical process as a whole process (including all humans and nonhuman beings) is in violation of this core thesis.

Kinetic communism is no small task, but it is the challenge of our age to rise to it.

METABOLIC CONDITIONS

The metabolic conditions for communism are the crucial and concluding ideas of chapter one of *Capital*. Material-kinetic production is the immanent foundation for the historical emergence of all social forms of motion and all their fetishes (gods, nature, the state, the commodity). Kinetic communism is nothing other than the practical and common-sense collective management of the threefold metabolic process, which avoids all the determinants of value (devalorization, appropriation, and domination) up to and including the value-fetish itself.

It is a practical and material task to make sure that the metabolic forms of motion remain collectively transparent qua processes and are not allowed to be covered over. There are not discrete individuals, only kinetic processes. The social, political, and intellectual life of humans is conditioned on the more primary foundation of these kinetic processes:

> My view is that each particular mode of production and the relations of production corresponding to it at each given moment, in short the economic structure of society, is "the real foundation [*reale Basis*], on which arises a legal and political superstructure [*Überbau*] and to which correspond definite forms of social

consciousness," and that "the mode of production of material life conditions the general process of social, political and intellectual life" (C, 175).

This is an absolutely central point for the theory of kinetic or metabolic communism. All its power hinges on the idea that the value-fetish is a material-kinetic process that can only be overthrown through practical metabolic transformation of the material conditions that produced the fetish in the first place. In this important footnote, Marx quotes the now-well-known preface to *A Contribution to the Critique of Political Economy* on the relation between the "base and superstructure."

This key idea is at the root of now well-known critiques of Marx's "economic reductionism" and "determinism." However, at the end of this careful analysis of chapter one of *Capital*, I have a new kinetic vocabulary to reinterpret this difficult passage from Marx. At stake is no less than the entire political project of communism and metabolic emancipation. There are three main points to raise here, concerning (1) the economic structure (base), (2) the social structure (superstructure), and (3) the act of conditioning.

Economic Structure

For Marx, an economic structure, following section three of chapter one, can be nothing other than a form or pattern of motion. Immediately before the preceding quote, Marx in fact gives an important description of what he thinks an economic structure is:

> For if people live by plunder for centuries there must, after all, always be something there to plunder; in other words, the objects of plunder must be continually reproduced. It seems, therefore, that even the Greeks and the Romans had a process of production, hence an economy, which constituted the basis of their world as much as bourgeois economy constitutes that of the pre-world. (C, 175)

An economy is a material process of production, which Marx has already defined in chapter one as a form or pattern of motion. Furthermore, and perhaps less obviously, the continually reproduced conditions of plunder (devalorization, appropriation, and domination)—what I have more generally called "primitive accumulation"—are also economic. Marx is direct and explicit on this point: primitive accumulation is an economic process.

This might seem odd because the tendency in bourgeois economics is to define economics strictly in terms of discrete, preexisting values. As shown in this book, this is not a definition Marx accepts, in part because it presupposes precisely what it attempts to explain: the production of value itself. For Marx, the kinetic process of producing value necessarily entails a constitutive process of primitive accumulation and plunder. This, too, is economic. It was economic for the ancients, and it's still economic for the bourgeois economy. Primitive accumulation represents the real material conditions of plunder at the heart of value production and thus is at the heart of economics through and through. It is the immanent form of motion or process that both produces value and can produce otherwise.

To interpret Marx's use of the term "economic structure" as the relations of discrete autonomous values is to completely misunderstand the whole first chapter of *Capital* and Marx's entire contribution to social and economic philosophy. Recall that in the very first sentence of *Capital* Marx took it as his starting point to overcome the idea of atomistic value. What he ended up replacing it with was a whole new kinetic theory of value and a theory of forms of motion. This is a complete rejection of a narrowly defined "economic realm" of discrete values separated from their immanent and constitutive forms of motion. Therefore there cannot be any coherent economic reductionism at work here whatsoever. Since the threefold metabolic forms of motion are also "economic," the whole division between economic and noneconomic breaks down and becomes useless reductionism, which again is not Marx's aim here and would not square with the theory of metabolism and primitive accumulation developed in *Capital*.

Social Structure

What sense can we make of Marx's distinction between the economic "base" (*basis*) and the social structure (*Überbau*)? Again, I take my cue from the lines just cited, in which Marx clearly identifies the process of primitive accumulation with the economic reproduction of primitive accumulation itself. In short, Marx collapses the whole artificial division between economic and noneconomic plunder. The consequence for theories of social, legal, political, and intellectual forms is a similar collapse.

In German, the word *Überbau* means "to build on top of." Again, there is nothing explicitly reductionistic or deterministic going on here. Building on top of something both changes what is built on and changes what is built. There is nothing spooky or metaphysical going on here. When Marx says that "the mode of production of material life conditions the general process of social, political and intellectual life," the German word *bedingen* simply means a relation that makes another possible. There is nothing in such a definition that means that a condition cannot change. Marx says that the forms of consciousness correspond to this condition, but correspondence hardly means direct one-to-one necessity. It also does not preclude a change in either conditions or conditioned. Material conditions, by Marx's own definition, are kinetic conditions. Kinetic conditions are in turn continually changing and circulating conditions.

In this sense, an *Überbau* just means something that is conditioned or built on top of something else, without any specific necessary causation. Again, recall that this was the whole basis of Marx's dialectical method taken from Epicurus and Lucretius. What comes after in the flow and fall of matter is not predetermined but is *conditioned or related* to what came before. But since matter has always been swerving, there can be no ultimate reduction or final determinism. Economic determinism directly contradicts the core contributions of Marx's doctoral dissertation.

A social structure is something in motion. It is a pattern of thought or action that is strictly immanent to the process of material production. As such, it can either hide or cover over its form of motion (ideology, religion, money) or reveal and manage its pattern of motion as a whole process (communism). Depending on how the form of motion (economic structure) moves, the social structure can either cover this over or make it transparent. In either case, the various forms of consciousness are strictly immanent expressions of one and the same form of motion. For example, the social idea of Greek racism and colonialism against the "barbarians" *corresponds* directly to the practice of plundering them and enslaving them from around the Mediterranean. Each mutually conditions the other. As I have tried to show throughout this book, devalorization and appropriation go hand in hand.

Conditioning

For Marx, condition and conditioned are distinct but enter into a mutually transformative relationship, or "hanging together." This is the explicitly stated assumption in the very first lines of the preface to A *Contribution to the Critique of Political Economy*:

> I examine the system of bourgeois economy in the following order: capital, landed property, wage-labour, the State, foreign trade, world market. The economic conditions of existence [*ökonomischen Lebensbedingungen*] of the three

great classes into which modern bourgeois society is divided are analyzed under the first three headings; the intra-action [*Zusammenhang*] of the other three headings is self-evident [*springt in die Augen*]. (MECW 29: 261)

For Marx, an economic condition (*ökonomischen Lebensbedingungen*) is a material-kinetic condition within which it is obvious that the state, foreign trade, and the world market all mutually hang or intra-act together (*Zusammenhang*) with capital, landed property, and wage labor. However, since it is only self-evident that the last three work in this way, Marx wants to show that the first three hang together in mutually conditioned interdependence with them as well. Again, the assumption here is that there is a mutual hanging together of all six areas but that only the last three (political areas) are obvious. Marx shows that the first three economic ones (capital, landed property, wage labor) hang together with everything else as well.

This is hardly a strong statement of absolute necessity, reductionism, or determinism. As I have taken great pains to show in this book, Marx uses the German word *zusammenhängen* throughout his oeuvre to describe the mutual intra-action of inextricable processes. There is not and cannot be a simple, unidirectional causality between economic and political elements that *hang together*. The "conditions of existence" all hang together. In other words, there are mutually transformative relations such that both continually change together.

Just as the emergence of fetishes is completely immanent to the process of material production, so Marx writes in *A Contribution to the Critique of Political Economy* that "material forces of production" immanently condition the relations of production and the forms of social consciousness. Marx's theory of conditioning is one of immanent causality in which different aspects can be distinguished but not separated from one another. It is we who continually reproduce the structures of domination and thus we who can do otherwise.

This is a different way of thinking about conditionality, but it is nothing mystical. For example, we can say that the movement and patterns of wind and water vapors are the condition for the emergence of a storm. But a storm is nothing other than the wind and water vapor that immanently form into the metastable spiral form of the storm. On the one hand, we can distinguish wind and water vapor from a storm, but on the other hand, these are not two separate things involved in a one-directional causality. The emergence of the storm reacts back upon the wind and reproduces its pattern of motion.

Marx's own example of this strange, immanent causality draws from nature as well. The roots are the immanent cause of the tree insofar as the roots are an inseparable aspect of the whole tree's hanging together:

> My inquiry led me to the conclusion that neither legal relations nor political forms could be comprehended whether by themselves or on the basis of a so-called general development of the human mind but that on the contrary they are rooted in [*wurzeln*] in the material conditions of life. (MECW 29: 262)

Just like a tree's branches are conditioned by its roots, so the ideas of the human mind are rooted in the material conditions of its real forms of motion. The dialectical nature of mutual transformation and immanent conditioning is also exemplified in the *Eighteenth Brumaire of Louis Bonaparte*, in which Marx writes:

> Men make their own history, but they do not make it just as they please; they do not make it under circumstances chosen by themselves, but under circumstances directly encountered, given, and transmitted from the past. (MECW 11: 103).

Human action is conditioned by metabolic process that are not completely under our control, but nonetheless humans do respond to these conditions in novel and creative ways. Historical and economic determinism here is completely without meaning for Marx unless it is strictly pedetic and dialectical, just as it is in Epicurus and Lucretius.

CONCLUSION

Kinetic communism is possible only because the material conditions of production are in continual pedetic and dialectical movement. The flow of sensuous matter in motion is a strange kind of immanent condition because it is not a fixed condition but a generative one, capable of producing numerous metastable forms of motion. Social, economic, and intellectual patterns of motion all hang together with one another because it is the whole pattern of motion that is changing.

To interpret Marx's theory of economic and social conditioning as a linear and nondialectical causal link between discrete things such as "nature," "economy," and "society" is to misunderstand entirely Marx's central philosophical orientation from the beginning of his doctoral dissertation. Material production is always in flux. There is no such thing as economy separate from the threefold metabolic process he describes. Forms of motion emerge like metastable storm systems or river eddies (as Lucretius describes), not like atomic billiard balls. We have in Marx therefore the first political philosophy grounded completely in flux: kinetic communism.

The failure of existing socialism to take seriously this philosophical point has led precisely to what Marx termed "crude" communism, which is reductionist, deterministic, and anthropocentric. Communism, for Marx, has always been kinetic and metabolic. Only by treating matter as static, discrete, or separate has it been possible to completely tear Marx from his philosophical roots in the work of Epicurus and Lucretius. In doing so, Marx has been forced into a reductionist, deterministic, and anthropocentric mold that it was his primary aim to escape, and from which it has been this book's goal to release him.

Conclusion

It is time to return to Marx again, but this time to a Marx of movement and motion. The conclusions of the method applied here are contrary to the standard story often heard about Marx's philosophy, which goes something like this: Marx believed that all of reality was made of bits of matter following ironclad dialectical laws of historical development. After centuries of such historical and economic development, the fateful day of "primitive accumulation" arrived in the sixteenth century, when English landlords enclosed peasant land and "set free" the first wave of proletarian workers. These landless workers had no other choice but to sell their labor to live, making possible a labor theory of value and the capitalist mode of production, in which the time it takes humans to produce commodities determines their value. Unfortunately, by selling their labor for money, workers became alienated from the unique essence of their human species.

This book is a refutation of several important aspects of this narrative in the texts and passages dealt with. The story may sound plausible, but it leaves out at least four crucial and interrelated aspects of Marx's thought that, if taken together, I argue significantly undermine that story: movement, nature, women, and colonialism. The aim of this book is not to add these aspects back in to Marx but to point out that they have been there all along. This book is not a claim for a true-for-all-time Marx but simply for a Marx for today.

In brief outline, the five core claims of this book are the following:

(1) Marx did not hold a labor theory of value. He never used this term, not even once. This book has tried to show that labor does not determine

Marx in Motion. Thomas Nail, Oxford University Press (2020). © Oxford University Press.
DOI: 10.1093/oso/9780197526477.001.0001

value because the theft or *appropriation* of production precedes the *exploitation* of the wage and surplus value. Since labor has no value, no arithmetical proportionality exists between labor and value. Marx wanted to abolish the value form not rehabilitate it.

(2) Primitive accumulation did not happen just once or first in sixteenth-century England, but is a constitutive process of *all value creation*. Primitive accumulation is the *becoming of value itself*.

(3) Marx did not believe in fixed developmental laws of nature and society, or at least held incompatible views on this topic. The interpretation of dialectical materialism is the invention of Engels and the Soviets, not Marx. This book has tried to show that Marx's theory of kinetic dialectics, from his doctoral dissertation to *Capital*, offers instead an open and pedetic view of nature and history.

(4) Marx was not a crude, mechanistic, or reductionist materialist and certainly not an atomist, as his doctoral dissertation makes explicit. Matter, for Marx, is not substance but kinetic process. This book has tried to show that Marx was one of the first philosophers to offer a kinetic or process materialism, well ahead of his time.

(5) Marx's theories of value, alienation, and exploitation are neither humanist nor anthropocentric concepts. Marx is clear that all three of these concepts are aspects of a larger, threefold metabolic process of natural-human-social becoming. Value never comes from humans alone, nor does alienation apply only to humans. For Marx there is, strictly speaking, no ontological division between humans, nature, and society. The problem is that capitalism introduces a historical dualism between use-value and exchange value.

THE CONSEQUENCES

There are three important consequences of these claims. The first is that if we begin our reading with Marx's earliest philosophical writings on Epicurus and Lucretius, we end up with a completely different conceptual framework than if we had started from the precepts of most Western Marxism, defined by some combination of determinism, reductionism, and anthropocentrism. In particular, this new starting point allows us to trace an alternate theory of motion from his dissertation to *Capital*. As we have seen, this has important consequences, at least for Marx's theory of objects, matter, and the kinetic nature of value. But it has consequences for other important ideas in Marx as well, not covered in this book but certainly worthy of future investigation.

The second consequence is showing that what often goes by the name "new materialism" today is actually quite old. It began at least with Lucretius and, in my view, was not taken up again until Marx in the nineteenth century.[1] It is unfortunate that the history of Western philosophy, and Marxism in particular, has so badly mischaracterized this kinetic or process materialism, which we are only now rediscovering. The key to the future of a genuinely new materialism and nonanthropocentric realism thus lies partly in the past and ought to include Marx in its pantheon of precursors.

The third consequence is that if the origins of value lie in appropriation, devalorization, and domination, then the search for a sustainable capitalism is completely out of the question. The core problem with capitalism is not exploitation (although this is certainly important) but the *appropriation* that precedes it. Furthermore, the interlocking and fundamental appropriation of women's labor, nature, and colonial labor at the heart of all value production requires the response of a much more radical form of communism than has ever existed. Today, we need a truly metabolic and kinetic communism that can repair all the natural, human, and social metabolic cracks created by capitalism.

This book has thus tried to bridge two major approaches to reading Marx and understanding capitalism: on the one hand the theory of capitalism's being founded on a system of violence and primitive accumulation, and on the other the theory of capitalism as a system of astounding idealist abstractions. "Financial," "semiotic," and "communicative" capitalisms all have at their core a profound material basis in physical violence against women, animals, the earth, and racialized/colonized others, no matter how clean their office is (their office was probably cleaned by postcolonial female immigrants anyway). This book has tried, in its own way, to paint a holistic picture of these two apparent extremes of material violence and immaterial abstraction that define twenty-first-century capitalism.

LIMITATIONS

This book has several limitations. The first is that it does not engage deeply with the history of Western Marxism, outside the all-to-brief literature review in the introduction. This is not because the history of Marxism has nothing to say about many of the issues raised in this book or is unimportant, but because there is *so much* to say that it would take another book just to survey the history of the labor theory of value, interpretations of materialism, and so on. This book does not do this because other books have already done it. I am thankful for them, have benefited greatly from them, and have cited them carefully in the footnotes for interested readers to follow up with as supplementary materials. The focus of this book has been consciously restricted in order to focus on the writings *of Marx* himself, for the methodological reasons explained in the introduction.

The second limitation is that this book has further narrowed its scope to just a close reading of chapter one of *Capital*, beginning from the theoretical framework of the doctoral dissertation. This alone is a remarkable oddity worthy of explicit qualification. Some methodological explanation was given in the introduction, but here I add that although I think the consequences beyond chapter one are large, this book has not done the textual work to prove them throughout *Capital*. In my defense, I have tried to link my close reading of chapter one to texts across Marx's corpus. But selected quotes are not a substitute for the work of close, careful reading. Therefore, although I stand by my analysis of chapter one, more work is still necessary to apply these arguments to the rest of *Capital* and Marx's oeuvre more broadly.

FUTURE DIRECTIONS

The future directions of this project reflect its current limitations. One direction worth pursuing is a book-length survey of the reception of Marx's dissertation in the history of Western Marxism. If one exists, I have not found it. Among other things, I think Marx's dissertation holds the key to a new materialist and nonanthropocentric interpretation of Marxism. So I think such a project would be worth developing further.

Another, and perhaps more obvious, direction worth pursuing is to continue this kinetic reading of Marx into the rest of *Capital*, volume 1. When I first began working on this project, I had many other chapters and themes sketched out, but in the end I was only able to work through the first chapter as carefully as I wanted to. This was disappointing because I had so much to say about circulation and surplus, but also exciting because there is so much more interesting work to do.

Finally, and more practically, another direction would be to follow up on the analysis of the primacy of primitive accumulation both historically and in contemporary politics. This is already under way in ecological,[2] feminist,[3] and postcolonial Marxism,[4] and is, to my mind anyway, one of the most interesting and important directions in contemporary Marxism. I hope that my "kinetic Marxism" can contribute in its own way to this larger effort.

NOTES

INTRODUCTION

1. Costas Douzinas and Slavoj Žižek, eds., *The Idea of Communism*, vol. 1 (London: Verso, 2010).
2. Jean-Paul Sartre, *Search for a Method*, trans. Hazel E. Barnes (New York: Vintage Books, 1958/1968), 30.
3. There would be "no future without the memory and the inheritance of Marx: in any case of a certain Marx . . . [and] at least one of his spirits." For, he added, *"there is more than one of them, there must be more than one."* Jacques Derrida, *Specters of Marx: The State of the Debt, the Work of Mourning, and the New International*, trans. Peggy Kamuf (New York: Routledge, 2011), 13 (emphasis in original).
4. "The death of nature has thus become its immortal substance; and Lucretius correctly exclaims: *Mortalem vitam mors [. . .] immortalis ademit"* (MECW 1, 62).
5. See Peter Osborn, *How to Read Marx* (New York: Norton, 2005), introduction.
6. Numerous volumes have been written criticizing each of these three axes. I offer here only a brief summary of these problems because other scholars have developed them in great depth elsewhere. I cannot list them all, so I cite here only some that have been the most influential. For a critique of determinism and humanism see Theodor Adorno, *Negative Dialectics* (London: Continuum, 2000). For a critique of reductionism and humanism see Alfred Schmidt, *The Concept of Nature in Marx*, trans. Ben Fowkes (London: Verso, 2014). For a critique of all three see John Bellamy Foster, *Marx's Ecology: Materialism and Nature* (New York: Monthly Review Press, 2000).
7. "Progress occurs where it ends," as Adorno said. "Progress means: to step out of the magic spell, even out of the spell of progress, which is itself nature, in that humanity becomes aware of its own inbred nature and brings to a halt the domination it exacts upon nature and through which domination by nature continues. In this way it could be said that progress occurs where it ends." Theodor Adorno, "Progress," in *Can One Live After Auschwitz?*, trans. Henry W. Pickford (Stanford, CA: Stanford University Press, 2003), 130.
8. Nancy Fraser, "Behind Marx's Hidden Abode: For an Expanded Conception of Capitalism," *New Left Review* 86 (March–April 2014): 71.
9. See Jason Moore, *Capitalism in the Web of Life: Ecology and the Accumulation of Capital* (London: Verso, 2016); and Saito Kohei, *Karl Marx's Ecosocialism: Capitalism, Nature, and the Unfinished Critique of Political Economy* (New Delhi: Dev Publishers & Distributors, 2018).

10. See Thomas Nail, "Theory of the Object" (unpublished manuscript); and Karen Barad, *Meeting the Universe Halfway: Quantum Physics and the Entanglement of Matter and Meaning* (Durham, NC: Duke University Press, 2007).

11. However, Bell's theorem was not taken seriously by orthodox quantum metaphysicians, who were happy to continue with the instrumentalist success of a local probability model. It was only in Alan Aspect's 1982 experiments in Paris (repeatedly confirmed over the last forty years) that entanglement (instantaneous transformation of the whole) was shown to be undeniably real. All "local realist" theories of causality have thus been proven false. See N. D. Mermin, "Is the Moon There When Nobody Looks? Reality and the Quantum Theory," *Physics Today* 38, no. 4 (1985): 38–47.

12. This does not mean that twenty-first-century quantum field theory is any more universal. This only means that it is the science of our time, where my theoretical practice begins.

13. H. J. Schellnhuber, "'Earth System' Analysis and the Second Copernican Revolution," *Nature London* 402, Supp. 2 Dec (1999): 19–23.

14. Some Marxists say that only humans can be productive creative agents. Ted Benton, "Marxism and Natural Limits: An Ecological Critique and Reconstruction," *New Left Review* 178 (1989): 51–86. But it is crucial not to conflate the "labor process" with the broader "production process." See Paul Burkett, *Marx and Nature: A Red and Green Perspective* (New York: St. Martin's Press, 1999). Marx is explicit that treating labor as the sole source of wealth is "bourgeois" insofar as it assigns "supernatural creative power to labour." Karl Marx and Friedrich Engels, *The Marx - Engles Reader*, trans. Robert C. Tucker (New York: Princeton, 2013), 536. Other Marxists have said that Marx assumes "general material abundance" with no regard for "the liberation of nature from human domination." See Andrew McLaughlin, "Ecology, Capitalism, and Socialism," *Socialism and Democracy* 10 (1990): 69–102, 95. Others argue that Marx advocates "developing the forces of production along industrial lines, both quantitatively and qualitatively." See Enzo Mingione, "Marxism, Ecology, and Political Movements," *Capitalism, Nature, Socialism* 4, no. 2 (1993): 85–92, 86.

15. For a more detailed critique and literature review of Marxist anthropocentrism and constructivism see John Bellamy Foster, "Marxism in the Anthropocene: Dialectical Rifts on the Left," *International Critical Thought* 6, no. 3 (2016): 393–421.

16. See Chris Gamble, Josh Hannan, and Thomas Nail, "What Is New Materialism?" (unpublished manuscript). See also Thomas Nail, *Being and Motion* (Oxford: Oxford University Press, 2018), chapters 3 and 4. Kinetic materialism is a new materialism distinct from previous historical varieties of older mechanistic (crude); idealist (contemplative); and newer neo-vitalist, failed, and negative materialisms.

17. See Louis Althusser, *Philosophy of the Encounter: Later Writings, 1978–87*, trans. François Matheron and Oliver Corpet (London: Verso, 2006); and Thomas Nail, *Lucretius I: An Ontology of Motion* (Edinburgh: Edinburgh University Press, 2018).

18. See Nail, *Lucretius I*.

19. See Nail, *Lucretius I*.

20. Karl Marx, introduction to "The Programme of the Parti Ouvrier," n5 (Marxists Internet Archive). https://www.marxists.org/archive/marx/works/1880/05/parti-ouvrier.htm.

21. Cited in Alfred Schmidt, *The Concept of Nature in Marx* (London: Verso, 2013), 53.

22. "It was a combination of a traditional metaphysical materialism of matter with Hegel's dialectical logic (which is a logic of process or change)." Osborn, *How to Read Marx*, 27.

23. The volume of criticism of Soviet Marxism cannot possibly all be listed here, so I refer the reader to Schmidt, *Concept of Nature in Marx*.

24. For a critique and detailed discussion of Soviet ecological efforts, see Foster, *Marx's Ecology*, 236 and throughout. See also McKenzie Wark, *Molecular Red: Theory for the Anthropocene* (London: Verso, 2016).

25. The Frankfurt school does not fit neatly into the category of "humanism." Erich Fromm called himself a humanist. Marcuse started off as a humanist but came around via Adorno and Horkheimer to a critique of the universalist idea of a shared human essence. Whether "essentialist humanism" or "real humanism," most Frankfurt school members maintained some methodological primacy for a psychoanalytic theory of the human. Martin Jay, "The Frankfurt School's Critique of Marxist Humanism," *Social Research* 39, no. 2 (1972): 285–305. See also Alfred Schmitt, "Adorno, ein Philosoph des realen Humanismus," *Neue Rundschau* 80, no. IV (1969).

26. Even if Adorno and Horkheimer rejected "anthropomorphism," they still held onto an anthropocentric methodology (social psychoanalysis). For a critique of anthropocentrism in the Frankfurt school see Foster, "Marxism in the Anthropocene," 393–421.

27. "It is impossible to know anything about men, except on the absolute precondition that the philosophical (theoretical) myth of man is reduced to ashes." Louis Althusser, *For Marx* (London: Verso, [1969]/2010), 229.

28. See Simon Choat, *Marx Through Post-Structuralism: Lyotard, Derrida, Foucault, Deleuze* (London: Continuum, 2012).

29. "However, in rejecting mechanism, including mechanistic biologism of the social Darwinist variety, thinkers in the human sciences, including Marxists, increasingly rejected realism and materialism, adopting the view that the social world was constructed in the entirety of its relations by human practice—including, notably, those aspects of nature that impinged on the social world—thereby simply denying intransitive objects of knowledge (objects of knowledge which are natural and exist independently of human beings and social constructions)." Foster, *Marx's Ecology*, 7–8.

30. See Simon Choat, "Science, Agency and Ontology: A Historical-Materialist Response to New Materialism," *Political Studies* 66, no. 4 (2018): 1027–1042; and Foster, "Marxism in the Anthropocene."

31. See Choat, "Science, Agency and Ontology," 5–7, for a summary of new materialist critiques of Marx. Bruno Latour writes that "capitalism does not exist." Bruno Latour, *The Pasteurization of France*, trans. A. Sheridan and J. Law (Cambridge, MA: Harvard University Press, 1988), 173. Jane Bennett distances her approach from that of historical materialism in J. Bennett, *The Enchantment of Modern Life: Attachments, Crossings, and Ethics* (Princeton, NJ: Princeton University Press, 2001), 116–121, and J. Bennett, *Vibrant Matter: A Political Ecology of Things* (Durham, NC: Duke University Press, 2010), 58, 129n51. Manuel DeLanda's rejection of Marxism is explicit in "Deleuze, Materialism and Politics," in *Deleuze and Politics*, ed. I. Buchanan and N. Thoburn (Edinburgh: Edinburgh University Press, 2008), 160–177.

32. Choat, "Science, Agency and Ontology"; B. Washick and E. Wingrove, "Politics That Matter: Thinking about Power and Justice with the New Materialists,"

Contemporary Political Theory 14, no. 1 (2015): 63–79; J. Cotter, "New Materialism and the Labour Theory of Value," *Minnesota Review* 87 (2016): 171–181; P. Rekret, "A Critique of New Materialism: Ethics and Ontology," *Subjectivity* 9 no. 3 (2016): 225–245; and John H. Zammito, ed., *New Politics of Materialism: History, Philosophy, Science* (New York: Taylor and Francis, 2017).

33. For a definition, typology, and critique of new materialism, see Gamble, Hanan, and Nail, "What Is New Materialism?"

34. J. Frow, "Matter and Materialism: A Brief Pre-History of the Present," in *Material Powers: Cultural Studies, History and the Material Turn*, ed. T. Bennett and P. Joyce (London: Routledge, 2010), 25–37; J. Edwards, "The Materialism of Historical Materialism," in *New Materialisms: Ontology, Agency, and Politics*, ed. D. Coole and S. Frost (Durham, NC: Duke University Press, 2010), 281–298; Matthew W. Bost, "Entangled Exchange: Verkehr and Rhetorical Capitalism," *Review of Communication* 16, no. 4 (): 334–351; Paul Cammack, "The Governance of Global Capitalism: A New Materialist Perspective," *Historical Materialism* 11, no. 2 (2003): 37–59; and Matthew T. Huber, "Value, Nature, and Labor: A Defense of Marx," *Capitalism Nature Socialism* 28, no. 1 (2017): 39–52.

35. David Harvey, *A Companion to Marx's Capital*, vol. 1 (London: Verso, 2012), 12.

36. "Dialectics [is] the science of the general laws of motion, both of the external world and of human thought." Frederick Engels, *Ludwig Feuerbach and the End of Classical German Philosophy*, ttps://www.marxists.org/archive/marx/works/1886/ludwig-feuerbach/ch04.htm.

37. See Schmidt, "Concept of Nature in Marx."

38. Worden cites Engels as saying that even in the dissertation Marx "showed complete independence of Hegel precisely in that field where Hegel was undoubtedly at his strongest, namely in history of thought." Hegel gives only "a number of careless extracts from his system [of Epicurus], whilst Marx gave a reconstruction of the immanent dialectic of Epicureanism but without in the least idealizing it." Cited in Franz Mehring, *Karl Marx: The Story of His Life* (New York: Covici, Friede, 1935), 567.

39. Karl Marx, *The First Writings of Karl Marx*, ed. Paul M. Schafer (Brooklyn, NY: Ig Publishing, 2006), 9.

40. Deleuze explicitly subordinates matter and motion to force in his book on Nietzsche, contrasting himself and Nietzsche with Lucretius's and Marx's kinetic materialism. "Only force can be related to another force. (As Marx says when he interprets atomism, 'Atoms are their own unique objects and can relate only to themselves'—Marx 'The Difference Between the Democritean and Epicurean Philosophy of Nature.' But the question is; can the basic notion of atom accommodate the essential relation which is attempted to it? The concept only becomes coherent if one thinks of force instead of atom. For the notion of atom cannot in itself contain the difference necessary for the affirmation of such a relation, difference in and according to the essence. Thus atomism would be a mask for an incipient dynamism)." Gilles Deleuze, *Nietzche and Philosophy* (New York: Columbia University Press, 1983), 6–7.

CHAPTER 1

1. This is an ambitious claim, defended elsewhere. In fact, each area (politics, science, and art) requires its own book-length argument showing the historical and contemporary importance of motion: Thomas Nail, *The Figure of the Migrant* (Stanford, CA: Stanford University Press, 2015); Thomas Nail, *Theory of the*

Border (Oxford: Oxford University Press, 2016); Thomas Nail, *Theory of the Image* (Oxford: Oxford University Press, 2019); Thomas Nail, *Being and Motion* (Oxford: Oxford University Press, 2018); and Thomas Nail, "Theory of the Object" (unpublished manuscript).

2. "There are, effectively, features [flows] that justify calling Deleuze the ideologist of late capitalism." Slavoj Žižek, *Organs Without Bodies: Deleuze and Consequences* (New York: Routledge, 2004), 184.

3. See Nail, *Figure of the Migrant*; and Nail, *Theory of the Border*.

4. "Since labour is motion, time is its natural measure" (G, 205).

5. Indeed, Marx was the first to discover what modern scholarship has confirmed: that as Farrington observed in *Science and Politics in the Ancient World* (1939), Epicureanism was "not a purely mechanical system; it was the specific originality of Epicurus in the domain of physics to have defended freedom of the will in man as a product of evolution." Cited in John Bellamy Foster, *Marx's Ecology: Materialism and Nature* (New York: Monthly Review Press, 2000), 53.

6. See Thomas Nail, *Lucretius I: An Ontology of Motion* (Edinburgh: Edinburgh University Press, 2018), 36.

7. "Commentators have exaggerated the degree to which Marx had to experience a 'break' with the assumptions of the dissertation in order to become a full-blown 'Marxist.' What is missing from Marx's dissertation is (contrary to the humanists) neither materialism nor (contrary to virtually all commentators) a move to praxis. What is missing is the particular identity of the revolutionary proletarian actor in place of the generalized *zoon politikon* of the dissertation." John Stanley, "The Marxism of Marx's Doctoral Dissertation," *Journal of the History of Philosophy* 33, no. 1 (January 1995): 133–158, 139.

8. "In opposition to the standard interpretation, it will be argued below that Marx's doctoral thesis is not merely an anomaly left over from his Hegelian period but constituted an effort to come to terms with the implications of the materialist dialectic of the ancient Greek philosopher Epicurus, both from the standpoint of the Hegelian philosophical system, and to some extent going beyond the latter. More than that, it was an indirect attempt to come to grips with the problem that the materialist tradition of the English and French enlightenments, which drew heavily upon Epicurus for their inspiration, raised for Hegelian philosophy. Given its importance for British and French materialism, 'atomistic philosophy,' as James White has observed, had strong political overtones, and these were well known to Marx when he embarked on his dissertation . . . in 1840." Foster, *Marx's Ecology*, 33.

9. Here my reading breaks with the vast majority of readers of the doctoral dissertation. While I am not alone in believing that the thesis provides the key to overcoming the three axes of criticism (see Stanley, "Marxism of Marx's Doctoral Dissertation," and Foster, *Marx's Ecology*), I believe that my interpretation of *exactly how* the dissertation does this is original.

10. See Nail, *Being and Motion*, book I.

11. As I have argued in *Lucretius I*.

12. Roy Bhaskar, *Reclaiming Reality: A Critical Introduction to Contemporary Philosophy* (London: Routledge, 2011); and Foster, *Marx's Ecology*.

13. Karen Barad, *Meeting the Universe Halfway: Quantum Physics and the Entanglement of Matter and Meaning* (Durham, NC: Duke University Press, 2007).

14. This new-realist or new-materialist theory is what Foster calls the "strange character" of Epicurus's method. In his doctoral dissertation, Marx discovers

that the apparent "abstraction" of Epicurean and Lucretian materialism is an immanent and concrete abstraction, a new historical and regional ontology of matter. "Marx writes with reference to Lucretius' great poem—celebrates sensation, but herein lies the strange character of Epicurus' natural philosophy, in that it 'proceeds from the sphere of the sensuous' and yet posits 'as principle such an abstraction . . . as the atom.' . . . This tension is never fully resolved, though Epicurus, as Marx himself emphasized in his doctoral thesis, rose beyond mechanistic materialism to a considerable extent." Foster, *Marx's Ecology*, 59.

15. See Barad, *Meeting the Universe Halfway*.

16. Many of Marx's definitions of the difference between humans and animals are factually incorrect.

17. (*menschliche Wesen*) (MEGA 2: 264).

18. I am here using the English translation of the German *entfremden* as "separation" instead of "alienation" or "estrangement" in order to emphasize the material and kinetic structure of *entfremden* and not the humanist and existentialist emphasis on the psychological experience of *entfremden*. Both are two sides of the same process.

19. Marx often uses the words *Entäußerung* and *entfremden* interchangeably. *Entäußerung* is important because it means not only the strict "separation from" as if it were a real "cutting-off" but more a continual process of relocating, externalization, or divestment, in which something is not strictly "cut" but rather bifurcated and redistributed. Something opens up out of itself and is removed from itself elsewhere. Therefore "separation" should not be thought of as an "ontological rift" (see Jason Moore, *Capitalism in the Web of Life* [London: Verso, 2016]) but simply a relative or regional extraction or divestment from one place to another.

20. See Moore, *Capitalism in the Web of Life*; and John Bellamy Foster, "Marxism in the Anthropocene: Dialectical Rifts on the Left," *International Critical Thought* 6, no. 3 (2016): 393–421.

21. It must be noted that Marx's definition of the difference between humans and animals and even between animals is factually incorrect by the standards of contemporary animal studies. This is not the place to develop this critique, since others have already done so quite well. However, it is also important to note that there is a difference between anthropocentrism and being wrong about the differences between capacities in animals and humans. Although the two issues are often historically related, they are not identical. In Marx, the human is not an ontologically privileged point but just one region of a larger metabolic process. See Foster, *Marx's Ecology*, 9–10, and for a convincing denunciation of Marx's supposed anthropocentrism, 16–20. See also Ted Benton, "Marxism and Natural Limits: An Ecological Critique and Reconstruction," *New Left Review* 178 (1989): 51–86. See P. Drake, "Marxism and the Nonhuman Turn: Animating Nonhumans, Exploitation, and Politics with Ant and Animal Studies," *Rethinking Marxism* 27, no. 1 (2015): 107–122. For the earliest critique of Marx's anthropocentrism, see Leszek Kolakowski, *Main Currents in Marxism*, vol. 1, *The Founders* (Oxford: Oxford University Press, 1978), 401; and Reiner Grundmann, "The Ecological Challenge to Marxism," *New Left Review* I, no. 187 (May–June 1992):1.

22. My translation.

23. See Matthew Bost, "Entangled Exchange: Verkehr and Rhetorical Capitalism," *Review of Communication* 16, no. 4 (2016): 344–351.

24. See Nail, *Being and Motion*.

CHAPTER 2

1. See Thomas Nail, *Being and Motion* (Oxford: Oxford University Press, 2018); and Thomas Nail, *Lucretius I: An Ontology of Motion* (Edinburgh: Edinburgh University Press, 2018).
2. Emphasis added.
3. Paul Valéry, *Collected Works of Paul Valéry*, vol. 15, *Moi* (Princeton, NJ: Princeton University Press, 2015), 291.
4. MECW 1: 85; and C, 101.
5. Michel Foucault, "Nietzsche, Genealogy, History," in *The Foucault Reader*, ed. Paul Rabinow (New York: Vintage Books, 2010), 76.
6. Unlike Kant's, Marx's critique is neither humanist nor idealist. The conditions of human sensation are themselves not human, nor do they only condition human sensation alone. If the human is a sensitive object and senses are objective, then what must nature be like such that the human body is a region of this nature that can sense itself and other objects?
7. Georg Wilhelm Friedrich Hegel, *Hegel's Philosophy of Nature: Being Part Two of the Encyclopedia of Philosophy*, trans. Arnold V. Miller (Oxford: Clarendon Press, 2004), 443.
8. See Foucault, "Nietzsche, Genealogy, History."

CHAPTER 3

1. See also Jacques Lezra, *On the Nature of Marx's Things: Translation as Necrophilology* (New York: Fordham University Press, 2018).
2. Alfred Schmidt, *The Concept of Nature in Marx* (London: Verso, 2014), 49.
3. "Nature is, and remains, the only substance 'by means of which and in which man's labour can be embodied.'" Cited in Schmidt, *Concept of Nature in Marx*, 76.
4. Lucretius, *De Rerum Natura*, Book I, lines 992–994.
5. Cited from the *Economic and Philosophical Manuscripts* by Schmidt, *Concept of Nature in Marx*, 64.
6. Cited by Schmidt, *Concept of Nature in Marx*, 65.
7. See Jason Moore, *Capitalism in the Web of Life* (London: Verso, 2015).
8. John Bellamy Foster and Brett Clark suggest that Marx got the terms for metabolic "drift" and "rift" from a 1884 translation of Lucretius's poem *De Rerum Natura*, by Thomas Charles Baring, who translated Lucretius' famous lines as: "A property is that which ne'r can cut itself adrift?, nor can be sundered anyhow, without a fatal rift" (I. 450-52). See John Bellamy Foster and Brett Clark, *The Robbery of Nature* (New York: Monthly Review Press, 2020), 23.
9. For a full historical review of this issue in Marx's theory of value see: John Bellamy Foster and Paul Burkett, "Value Isn't Everything," *Monthly Review* 70, no. 6 (November 2018): 1–17.
10. Moishe Postone, *Time, Labor, and Social Domination: A Reinterpretation of Marx's Critical Theory* (Cambridge: Cambridge University Press, 1993), 27.
11. Compare this to Lucretius's theory of drawing (*figuris*) tracks (*tractu*) in *De Rerum Natura*, Book II, lines 100–104. See also Thomas Nail, *Lucretius I: An Ontology of Motion* (Edinburgh: Edinburgh University Press, 2018), chapter 12.

CHAPTER 4

1. In a number of passages Marx seems to limit primitive accumulation to just being a one-time event in the history of capitalism (C, 925, 928–929). In these passages, Marx is simply referring to the historical conditions for capitalism, not primitive accumulation more generally, which he clearly recognizes as going back to the Greeks (C, 175n35). In other words, capitalism does not emerge everywhere there is primitive accumulation. Marx wants to make that clear.

2. Most versions of Marx's "labor theory of value" assume some direct or proportional relation between a quantity of labor time and its value and/or price. But value, for Marx, cannot be labor time plus constant capital, plus surplus value. On this point I agree with G. A. Cohen that "the fact that labour creates what has value" does not mean "that the amount of value in what it creates varies directly and uniformly with the amount of labour expended." G. A. Cohen, "The Labour Theory of Value and the Concept of Exploitation," in *Critiques and Alternatives*, ed. Will Kymlicka (Aldershot, Hants: Elgar, 1992), 359. However, I agree with him for totally different reasons. I think that labor has no value precisely because it is appropriated as such through the violent process of primitive accumulation. The magnitude of value therefore has no proportionality with the process of material production because of the more primary act of theft. For a full debate on the relation between labor and value, see Ian Steedman, ed., *The Value Controversy* (London: New Left Books, 1981). Furthermore, I agree with Diane Elson that value also reacts back on labor and that surplus value also affects the magnitude of value. However, my argument is a much more foundational one. The existence of surplus labor already assumes the birth of value and therefore must first grapple with the more primary process of violent appropriation. Diane Elson, *Value: A Representation of Labor in Capitalism* (London: Verso, 2015).

3. The material-kinetic conditions of value do not resemble value, not because value is a "spectral void" or "metaphysical form" "opposed to all materiality," as Christopher Arthur says (the spectral ontology of value), but rather because the condition of the value form is fundamentally social in nature, as Elena Louisa Lange argues in "Form Analysis and Critique: Marx's Social Labour Theory of Value," in *Capitalism: Concept, Idea, Image: Aspects of Marx's Capital Today*, ed. Peter Osborne, Eric Alliez, and Eric-John Russell (London: Centre for Research in Modern European Philosophy Books, 2019), 21–53. The problem with the "new interpretation" of value-form theory, as Lange pinpoints accurately, is similar to the traditional Sraffian one: both assume the a priori existence of capitalism *petito principii*. "Regarding the analysis of the value form, two crucial interventions Marx aimed at go completely unnoticed (or even rejected) by these [value-form] authors: the necessity of presupposing the totality of the capital relation from the beginning, in which the category of the 'commodity' with which the analysis starts signifies by no means the 'simplest' but the most complex determination, a 'relation of totality', and the function of value-form analysis as deducing the fetishistic semblance of simple circulation from the development of the commodity into money in their common ground of abstract labour. By refusing to see the critical intent already inherent in Marx's very first, allegedly 'innocuous' analysis—that of the commodity—the commentators mentioned above become accomplices to an ideological approach, legitimizing the mere appearance of the capital relations" (28). "Chris Arthur, for example, insists that in the architecture of Capital the 'pure forms' of capital should be

studied first—and especially 'the value form (as the germ of capital)' before its 'grounding in labour' is analysed. He claims that 'the question of form is so crucial that the presentation starts with the form of exchange, bracketing entirely the question of the mode of production [sic], if any, of the objects of exchange" (24).

For a wonderful survey and similar critique of the traditional Richardian embodied theory of labor and more recent value-form theories of labor debates (including the work of Backhaus, Bellofiore, Bonefeld, and more recent scholars like Tomba), see Alfredo Saad-Filho, *The Value of Marx: Political Economy for Contemporary Capitalism* (London: Routledge, 2007), 21–34.

My own kinetic analysis of value here is distinct from both of these interpretations and is much closer to the "truly social" and "historical" one developed by Patrick Murray in *The Mismeasure of Wealth: Essays on Marx and Social Form* (Chicago: Haymarket Books, 2018) when he writes that "labour is always situated in space and time." The question of the birth of value is a historical one: "How many wage earners move? How often? How far? How do they feel about it? How do they settle in (or not settle in) to the places where they live and work?" (163). I agree with Murray that "*Capital* is largely a study of the nature, inner connections, and powers of value forms (commodity, money, capital, wages, etc.), that is, the specific social forms constitutive for the capitalist mode of production. This means that *Capital* is not a work in economics—'Marxist economics' is a misnomer—rather, *Capital* is what Marx said it was: a critique of economics" (121).

My analysis adds to these general sociological and political conditions a number of ecological, gendered, colonial, and *material-kinetic* conditions for the birth of value with an *explicit emphasis* on the violent but constitutive historical process of *primitive accumulation* in producing value. I do not treat chapter one of *Capital* as a strictly "logical" starting point distinct from the historical inquiry found in part eight—in contrast to certain Hegelian approaches to the theory of value such as Tony Smith, *The Logic of Marx's Capital: Replies to Hegelian Criticisms* (Albany: State University of New York Press, 1990).

4. See Steedman, *Value Controversy*; and Elson, *Value*.
5. MECW 5: 293. Cited in Michael Perelman, *Classical Political Economy: Primitive Accumulation and the Social Division* (London: Bloomsbury Publishing, 2013), 8 (emphasis added).
6. Thomas Nail, *The Figure of the Migrant* (Stanford, CA: Stanford University Press, 2015); and Thomas Nail, *Theory of the Border* (Oxford: Oxford University Press, 2016).
7. Matthew T. Huber, "Value, Nature, and Labor: A Defense of Marx," *Capitalism Nature Socialism* 28, no. 1 (2017): 39–52.
8. Thomas Nail, "Theory of the Object" (unpublished manuscript).
9. See Catherine Keller, *Face of the Deep: A Theology of Becoming* (London: Routledge, 2007).
10. Louis Althusser and Étienne Balibar, *Reading Capital* (London: Verso, 2009), 20.
11. Jacques Derrida, *Specters of Marx: The State of the Debt, the Work of Mourning, and the New International*, trans. and ed. Peggy Kamuf (New York: Routledge, 2011).
12. For a detailed argument for the racist nature of capitalist value creation see Cedric J. Robinson, *Black Marxism: The Making of the Black Radical Tradition* (Chapel Hill: University of North Carolina Press, 2000).

13. Adriana Cavarero, *Horrorism: Naming Contemporary Violence*, trans. William McCuaig (New York: Columbia University Press, 2011).
14. See Thomas Nail, *Being and Motion* (Oxford: Oxford University Press, 2018).
15. Lucretius, *De Rerum Natura*, Book II, lines 216–220.
16. This is not the place to go into this. See Thomas Nail, *Lucretius I: An Ontology of Motion* (Edinburgh: Edinburgh University Press, 2018), chapter 11.
17. Nail, *Being and Motion*.
18. See Walter Johnson, *River of Dark Dreams: Slavery and Empire in the Cotton Kingdom* (Cambridge, MA: Harvard University Press, 2017).

CHAPTER 5

1. The significance of Marx's use of the concept of metabolism to designate the material-energetic interchanges between humans and the rest of nature, as mediated by the labor process, has been well-established. See Alfred Schmidt, *The Concept of Nature in Marx* (London: Verso, 2014), 76–93; Marina Fischer-Kowalski, "Society's Metabolism: The Intellectual History of Materials Flow Analysis, Part I—1860–1970," *Journal of Industrial Ecology* 2, no. 1 (1998): 61–78, 64. John Bellamy Foster, "Marx's Theory of Metabolic Rift: Classical Foundations for Environmental Sociology," *American Journal of Sociology* 105, no. 2 (1999): 366–405; John Bellamy Foster, *Marx's Ecology: Materialism and Nature* (New York: Monthly Review Press, 2000), 141–177; Peter Dickens, *Society and Nature: Changing Our Environment, Changing Ourselves* (Cambridge, UK: Polity, 2004), 62–93; and Erik Swyngedouw, "Circulations and Metabolisms: (Hybrid) Natures and (Cyborg) Cities," *Science as Culture* 15, no. 2 (2006): 105–121.
2. Foster, *Marx's Ecology*, ix.
3. Foster has emphasized the "rift" language.
4. Jason Moore, "Metabolic Rift or Metabolic shift? Dialectics, Nature, and the World-Historical Method," *Theory and Society* 46, no. 4 (2017): 285–318.
5. Ben Fowkes' translation errors in saying that metabolism is only first mentioned on page 198 of Karl Marx, *Capital* volume 1, trans. Ben Fowkes (New York: Penguin, 1976).
6. Franklin Bing, "The History of the Word 'Metabolism,'" *Journal of the History of Medicine and Allied Sciences* 26, no. 2 (1971): 158–181, 158–159.
7. Kohei Saito provides an extensive discussion of Roland Daniels and his role in introducing Marx to metabolism (Stoffwechsel) in his *Karl Marx's Ecosocialism* (New York: Monthly Review Press, 2017), 72–74, 82, 88. I thank John Foster for bringing this to my attention when I ran into him by chance at the University of Oregon one day.

    Marx's close friend, Roland Daniels (1819–1855) was a medical doctor and scientist as well as a communist. Daniels' great work was *Mikrokosmos* (completed in 1850), but it was not published then due to his untimely death. However, one other person had read the manuscript: Karl Marx. Daniels made use of the concept of *Stoffwechsel* (metabolism) to discuss plant and animal systems and Marx was influenced by this idea. Marx even dedicated *The Poverty of Philosophy* to Daniels.
8. "Die einen unheilbaren Riß hervorrufen in dem Zusammenhang des gesellschaftlichen und durch die Naturgesetze des Lebens vorgeschriebnen Stoffwechsels" (MEGA² II.15: 788); "Zusammenhang endgültig zerrissen" Karl Marx and Frederic Engels, Marx-Engels-Gesamtausgabe Second edition volume 15 (Berlin: De Gruyter Akademie Forschung, 2017), 804.

9. Karl Marx, *Early Writings*, ed. Quintin Hoare (New York: Vintage Books), 356.
10. "Their own collisions with one another produce alien social power standing above them, produce their mutual interaction as a process and power independent of them" (G, 197).
11. "Zusammenhang mit der natürlichen Daseinsform [use-value hangs together with value]" (MEGA² II.1: 81).
12. (GI, 48; G, 106).
13. I owe great thanks to Jason Schreiner and his excellent dissertation on Marx and metabolism for clarifying this distinction for me. Jason Schreiner, "The Roots of Life: Marx's Concept of Social Metabolism and the Dialectics of Corporeal Praxis" (PhD diss., University of Oregon, 2017).
14. Schmidt, *Concept of Nature in Marx,* 78–79.
15. Deleuze and Guattari fall prey to precisely this trap in *Anti-Oedipus*, where desiring machines are defined by flows *and breaks*. Gilles Deleuze and Félix Guattari. *Anti-Oedipus: Capitalism and Schizophrenia* (Minneapolis: University of Minnesota Press, 1983).
16. See Walter Johnson, *River of Dark Dreams: Slavery and Empire in the Cotton Kingdom* (Cambridge, MA: Harvard University Press, 2017); and Raj Patel and Jason W. Moore, *A History of the World in Seven Cheap Things: A Guide to Capitalism, Nature, and the Future of the Planet* (Berkeley: University of California Press, 2017).
17. Cited in Schmidt, *Concept of Nature in Marx,* 88.
18. David Graeber, *Debt: The First 5,000 Years* (New York: Melville House, 2014).
19. See Thomas Nail, *Theory of the Border* (Oxford: Oxford University Press, 2016).
20. See also Nail, *Theory of the Border*. On the same point, see also Moore, *Capitalism in the Web of Life*, 222. "Abstract social labor does not create frontiers so much as it is a frontier process itself."
21. Moore, *Capitalism in the Web of Life*, 91.
22. See Nail, *Being and Motion* for a full historical account of the emergence of the idea of discreteness and separation.
23. See Paul Burkett and John Bellamy Foster, "Metabolism, Energy, and Entropy in Marx's Critique of Political Economy: Beyond the Podolinsky Myth," *Theory and Society* 35 (2006): 109–156.
24. Istvan Mészáros, *Beyond Capital* (London: Merlin Press, 1995), 45–46.
25. Andrew McLaughlin, "Ecology, Capitalism, and Socialism," *Socialism and Democracy* 10 (1990): 69–102, 95; and Enzo Mingione, "Marxism, Ecology, and Political Movements," *Capitalism, Nature, Socialism* 4, no. 2 (1993): 85–92.

CHAPTER 6

1. Emphasis added.
2. Crystal Bartolovich, David Hillman, and Jean E. Howard, eds., *Marx and Freud: Great Shakespeareans*, vol. X (London: Bloomsbury Publishing, 2014), 23. The authors mistakenly compare Dame Quickly to the commodity, when Marx's point is the opposite!
3. See Grégoire Chamayou, *Manhunts: A Philosophical History,* trans. Steven Rendal (Princeton, NJ: Princeton University Press, 2012), chapter 10.
4. Janetta Benton, *Holy Terrors: Gargoyles on Medieval Buildings* (New York: Abbeville Press, 1997), 82.
5. Silvia Federici, *Caliban and the Witch: Women, the Body and Primitive Accumulation* (New York: Autonomedia, 2014).

6. See Thomas Nail, *Lucretius I: An Ontology of Motion* (Edinburgh: Edinburgh University Press, 2018), 240–241.
7. See Thomas Nail, *Theory of the Image* (Oxford: Oxford University Press, 2019); Anne Baring and Jules Cashford, *The Myth of the Goddess: Evolution of an Image* (London: Arkana, 2000); and Thomas Nail, *Being and Motion* (Oxford: Oxford University Press, 2018).
8. Federici, *Caliban and the Witch*; A. L. Beier, *Masterless Men: The Vagrancy Problem in England 1560–1640* (London: Methuen, 1987); and Raj Patel and Jason Moore, *History of the World in Seven Cheap Things* (London: Verso, 2018).
9. For an important theory of birth, care, rectitude, and critique of patriarchy see Adriana Cavarero, *Inclinations* (Stanford, CA: Stanford University Press, 2016)
10. Luce Irigaray, *This Sex Which Is Not One* (New York: Cornell University Press, 2010), 192–193.
11. The idea of a "kinetic operator" is developed extensively in Thomas Nail, "Theory of the Object" (unpublished manuscript).
12. Lucretius, *De Rerum Natura*, Book I, lines 10–22.
13. Hesiod, "Works and Days," in *The Homeric Hymns and Homerica*, with an English translation by Hugh G. Evelyn-White (Cambridge, MA: Harvard University Press; London: William Heinemann, 1914). "Muse, sing to me the deeds [*ergon*] of golden Aphrodite of Cyprus, who roused sweet longing in the gods and overwhelmed the tribes of mortal men and the birds of the air and all the beasts . . . for the deeds of fair-wreathed Kytherea are a care to all."
14. "Quel pur travail de fins éclairs consume Maint diamant d'imperceptible écume, Et quelle paix semble se concevoir!" Paul Valéry, *The Graveyard by the Sea*, trans. C. Day Lewis, http://unix. cc.wmich.edu/~cooneys/poems/fr/valery.daylewis. html (accessed July 29, 2017).
15. Federici, *Caliban and the Witch*.

CHAPTER 7

1. For excellent *social* and *political* interpretations of value see William Roberts, *Marx's Inferno: The Political Theory of Capital* (Princeton, NJ: Princeton University Press, 2018); and Jason Read, *The Micro-Politics of Capital: Marx and the Prehistory of the Present* (Albany: State University of New York Press, 2003). I do not substantially disagree with the "social" and "relational" readings of value but want to add a missing dimension to this story that includes nonhuman and natural agencies as constitutive part of the social/relational theory. Gilbert Simondon was also interested in the materiality of the labor process in the production of value, and his theory of technicity adds an important analysis of the agency and activity of nonhuman objects in the production of value. However, his analysis of technical objects still does not theorize the emergence of *kinetic patterns* and *laws of motion* from these objects. Instead his focus remains on the anthropocentric "technical organization where the human meets the human" through the "mediation" of technology. Simondon writes, "We should discover a social and economic mode where the user of the technical object would be not only the owner of the machine but also the person who chooses it and maintains it. [. . .] The bases of norms and laws in the industrial realm is neither work nor property but technicity. Communication should go towards the technical activity, not through values of work of economic criteria. Social conditions and economic factors cannot be harmonized since they belong to different worlds: they can find mediation only through a technically

dominated organization. This level of technical organization where the human meets the human, not as member of a class but as being that expresses itself through the technical object, which is homogenous to its activity, is the level of collective that goes beyond interindividuality and a given social order." Gilbert Simondon, *Du mode d'existence des objets techniques* (Paris: Aubier, 1958), 342.

2. Language often assumes the animacy of nonhuman agents and of how the stripping of agency from oppressed human groups coincides with the denigration of them as "more" material bodies than others. The stripping of agency from matter is directly connected to the devalorization of certain "more" material bodies (raced, classed, disabled, queer, etc.). For a full discussion see Mel Chen, *Animacies: Biopolitics, Racial Mattering, and Queer Affect* (Durham, NC: Duke University Press, 2012).

3. For a more developed material-kinetic theory of language see Thomas Nail, *Being and Motion* (Oxford: Oxford University Press, 2018); for material theory of appearance see Thomas Nail, *Theory of the Image* (Oxford: Oxford University Press, 2019).

4. Aristotle, *Physics*, Book V, chapter 5, lines 1133b, 26–29. Translation by Joe Sachs.

5. Aristotle, *Physics*, Book V, chapter 5, lines 1133a, 28–30. Translation by Joe Sachs.

6. Emphasis added.

7. See Emmanuel Laroche, *Histoire de la racine NEM- en grec ancien* (Paris: Klincksieck, 1949), 255.

8. See also Joshua S. Hanan, "The Oikos as Economic Rhetoric: Toward an Ontological Investigation of Rhetorical Biopolitics," in *Rhetoric's Change: 2016 Rhetoric Society of America Conference Proceedings*, ed. J. Rice and C. Graham (Anderson, SC: Parlor Press, forthcoming). For a full-length treatment of the *oikos*, see Josh Hanan, "The Rhetorical Politics of the Household: Economic Imaginaries and the Rhetorical Criticism of Biopolitics" (unpublished manuscript).

9. See Ryan Johnson, "*The Egg* on Deleuze and the Stoics" (unpublished manuscript).

CHAPTER 8

1. Karl Marx, *Capital*, trans. Ben Fowkes (London: Penguin Books, 1976).

2. Emphasis added.

3. I now offer a brief historical and kinetic typology of this sequence, developed at length elsewhere. See Thomas Nail, "Theory of the Object" (unpublished manuscript).

4. See Lewis Mumford, *The City in History: Its Origins, Its Transformations, and Its Prospects* (San Diego: Harcourt, 2014); and Nail, "Theory of the Object."

5. "Play two different parts" (C, 139); "play the same role" (C, 141); "coat here plays the part of equivalent" (C, 147); "This part is played by the iron only within this relation" (C, 148); "commodities which have played the role of the equivalent" (C, 150); "play towards it the merely passive role of equivalent" (C, 159). "Play" is a crucial term.

6. For a full kinetic theory of the theater see Thomas Nail, *Theory of the Image* (Oxford: Oxford University Press, 2019), chapter 7.

7. The logic of the *Keim* here, I must note, is taken from Lucretius's robust vocabulary of seeds, sprouts, fruits, and bodies, or corpora. The emergence of

value from metabolic process is explicit here. Metabolism is natural, human, and social.

8. For relevant theories of the "real abstraction" of the value-form see A. Sohn-Rethel, *Intellectual and Manual Labour* (Atlantic Highlands, NJ: Humanities Press, 1978); and A. Toscano, "The World Is Already Without Us," *Social Text* 34, no. 2 (2016): 109–124.

CHAPTER 9

1. Alfred Schmidt, *The Concept of Nature in Marx*, trans. Ben Fowkes (London: New Left Books), 191.
2. John P. Burkett, "Marx's Concept of an Economic Law of Motion," *History of Political Economy* 32, no. 2 (2000): 381–394.
3. Law is "the peculiar determination of pure individuality or of the Notion which is for itself: as distinction in itself it is the imperishable source of a self-kindling movement; and, relating itself to itself alone in the ideality of its distinction, it is free necessity" G. W. F. Hegel, *Science of Logic* (New York: Humanities Press, [1812] 1966), 2:365.
4. Pamela Kyle Crossley, *The Wobbling Pivot, China Since 1800: An Interpretive History* (New York: John Wiley & Sons, 2010), 105.
5. See Thomas Nail, *Lucretius I: An Ontology of Motion* (Edinburgh: Edinburgh University Press, 2018), chapter 11, esp. 203.
6. See Thomas Nail, "Theory of the Object" (unpublished manuscript), on the kinetically entrained mind.
7. Rodolphe Gasche, *The Tain of the Mirror: Derrida and the Philosophy of Reflection* (Cambridge, MA: Harvard University Press, 1997).
8. Ancient Greek φάντασμα (phántasma, "ghost") + ἀγορεύειν (agoreúein, "to speak publicly").
9. Thomas Nail, *Being and Motion* (Oxford: Oxford University Press, 2018), chapters 21 and 22.
10. See Eric Schneider and Dorion Sagan, *Into the Cool: Energy Flow, Thermodynamics, and Life* (Chicago: University of Chicago Press, 2006).

CHAPTER 10

1. Adam Smith, *An Inquiry into the Nature and Causes of the Wealth of Nations*, Vols. 1 and 2, ed. R. H. Campbell and A. S. Skinner (Cambridge, UK: Cambridge University Press, 1976), 277.
2. See Walter Johnson, *River of Dark Dreams: Slavery and Empire in the Cotton Kingdom* (Cambridge, MA: Harvard University Press, 2017).
3. Smith, *Inquiry into the Nature and Causes of the Wealth of Nations*, Book I, Chapter III, Section 8.
4. Smith, *Inquiry into the Nature and Causes of the Wealth of Nations*, Book I, Chapter VI, Section 1.
5. Smith, *Inquiry into the Nature and Causes of the Wealth of Nations*, Book I, Chapter VIII, Section 2.
6. Adam Smith, "Lectures on Jurisprudence [1762–1764]," in *The Glasgow Edition of the Works and Correspondence of Adam Smith*, vol. 5, ed. R. L. Meek, D. D. Raphael, and P. G. Stein (Oxford: Oxford University Press, 1978), 27.
7. Adam Smith, *Lectures on Justice, Police, Revenue, and Arms, Delivered in the University of Glasgow, by Adam Smith: Reported by a Student in 1763*, ed. with an

introduction and notes by Edwin Cannan (New York: A.M. Kelley, Bookseller, [1896] 1964), 10.

8. Smith, *Lectures on Justice*, 334.

9. Smith, *Inquiry into the Nature and Causes of the Wealth of Nations,* 4 (emphasis added).

10. Karl Marx, *A Contribution to the Critique of Political Economy* (New York: International Publishers, [1859] 1970), 188.

11. Pierre Proudhon, *What Is Property?*, trans. Bonnie G. Smith and Donald R. Kelley (Cambridge, UK: Cambridge University Press, 1994), 47.

12. Frédéric Bastiat, *Economic Sophisms* (New York: Van Nostrand, ([1845] 1964), 248.

13. Bastiat, *Economic Sophisms*, 244.

14. Henry Carey, *Principles of Political Economy* (New York: Augustus M. Kelley, ([1837–1840] 1965), 7.

15. Robert Torrens, *An Essay on the Production of Wealth* (New York: Augustus M. Kelley, [1821] 1965), 75.

16. For a complete collection of essays on Robinson Crusoe and economics see Ulla Grapard, ed., *Robinson Crusoe's Economic Man: A Construction and Deconstruction* (London: Routledge, 2014).

17. Michael White, "Reading and Rewriting: The Production of an Economic Robinson Crusoe," in *Robinson Crusoe's Economic Man: A Construction and Deconstruction*, ed. Ulla Grapard (London: Routledge, 2014), 37.

18. Marx, *Contribution to the Critique of Political Economy*, 188.

19. "He would not cease to pray for me, yet he would venture to say to me, that if I did take this foolish Step, God would not bless me, and I would have Leisure hereafter to reflect upon having neglected his Counsel when there might be none to assist in my Recovery."
    Daniel Defoe, *Robinson Crusoe*, ed. Tom Keymer and James W. Kelly (Oxford: Oxford University Press, 2007), 7.

20. Defoe, *Robinson Crusoe*, 57–58.

21. Defoe, *Robinson Crusoe*, 60.

22. Although ultimately he ends up attributing this to the Christian god.

23. Defoe, *Robinson Crusoe*, 59.

24. Defoe, *Robinson Crusoe*, 110.

25. Defoe, *Robinson Crusoe*, 50.

26. Although Marx does err in saying that Robinson tames "lamas" when in fact he tamed goats. But perhaps this was a mistranslation in an earlier German edition?

27. Emphasis added.

28. Defoe, *Robinson Crusoe*, 171.

29. Defoe, *Robinson Crusoe*, 172.

30. Defoe, *Robinson Crusoe*, 177.

31. Defoe, *Robinson Crusoe*, 179–180.

32. Ulla Grapard, "Robinson Crusoe: The Quintessential Economic Man?," in *Robinson Crusoe's Economic Man: A Construction and Deconstruction*, ed. Ulla Grapard (London: Routledge, 2014).

33. Defoe, *Robinson Crusoe*, 176.

34. Raj Patel and Jason Moore, *History of the World in Seven Cheap Things* (Berkeley: University of California Press, 2018).

35. Defoe, *Robinson Crusoe*, 195.

36. Defoe, *Robinson Crusoe*, 196.
37. Defoe, *Robinson Crusoe*, 203.
38. Defoe, *Robinson Crusoe*, 208.
39. Defoe, *Robinson Crusoe*, 206.
40. Defoe, *Robinson Crusoe*, 240.
41. Robinson's islanders were not paid wages according to abstract labor time; thus what we see is the essential determinants of value without the direct emergence of value in its waged-labor form.

CHAPTER 11

1. This is the meaning of the final chapter of *Capital* on colonialism: that colonialism exposes the "secret" of primitive accumulation at the heart of capitalism but also exposes the real ability of the colonies to work for themselves and rebel against capitalist colonialism (C, 933).
2. "That man's physical and spiritual life is intra-active [*zusammenhängen*] with nature means simply that nature is intra-active [*zusammenhängen*] with itself, for man is a part of nature" (MECW 3: 276).

CONCLUSION

1. For a full defense of this claim see Thomas Nail, *Being and Motion* (Oxford: Oxford University Press, 2018).
2. For example, Jason Moore, *Capitalism in the Web of Life: Ecology and the Accumulation of Capital* (London: Verso, 2015).
3. For example, Silvia Federici, *Caliban and the Witch: Women, the Body and Primitive Accumulation* (New York: Autonomedia, 2014).
4. For a recent critical assessment of Marxism and postcolonial theory see "Symposium: Marxism and Post-Colonialism," special issue, *Critical Sociology* 43, nos. 4–5 (July 2017).

INDEX

Figures are indicated by *f* following the page number

For the benefit of digital users, indexed terms that span two pages (e.g., 52–53) may, on occasion, appear on only one of those pages.

primitive accumulation and, 179–80,
  186–95, 236n1
production and, 189–90, 192, 194
relation and, 189, 192, 193–94
in *Robinson Crusoe*, 180–97
social appearance and, 184, 186
social structure and, 211
space and, 190, 192, 194–95
time and, 191, 193, 195
transparency and, 185–86
unfolded or expanded form of
  colonialism, 191–93
commodity
  appearance of, 138–39
  body of, 71–72
  Capital (1867) on, 49–51
  desire and, 65–67
  fetishism of, 161–77 (*see also* fetishism
    of commodity)
  language of, 138
  material agency of, 137–39
  material practice of, 139
  objectivity of, 117, 154
  production and consumption
    of, 65–67
  qualities of, 68–70
  quantity of, 68
  recognition by, 137
  thoughts of, 138
  value and, 64–72
communism. *See also* kinetic
    communism
  anthropocentrism and, 200
  colonialism of value and, 200
  historical determinism and, 3
  metabolic, 114–15
  metabolic conditions for, 208–13
  motion theory and, 32
  patriarchy of value and, 200
  racism and, 200
consciousness
  anthropocentrism and, 4–5
  as fetish, 168–69
  ideomotor effect and, 168–69
  material agency of commodity
    and, 137
  metabolic conditions for communism
    and, 208–9, 211, 212
  social structure and, 210–11
consumption

bearers of value and, 72–74
colonialism and, 187–88, 190–91,
  192–93, 195
of commodity, 65–67
communist form of motion and, 201
desire and, 65–67
devalorization and, 78, 89, 94
form of motion and, 166
kinetic theory of value and, 133,
  137, 156
material agency of commodity
  and, 137
metabolism and, 103, 104, 105,
  109–11, 113
motion theory and, 34, 38
production and, 65–67, 69–70
qualities and, 69
theory of the object and, 60, 61–62, 64

Dawn of the Dead (film), 89
declination, 5, 21, 23, 35–36, 50, 63,
  64, 163–64
Defoe, Daniel, 180
DeLanda, Manuel, 10–11, 223n31
Deleuze, Gilles, 10, 13, 224n40, 231n15
Democritus
  atomism and, 41, 62–63
  Bacon on, 39
  Epicurean vs. Democritean
    physics, 20–30
  form of appearance of value
    and, 83–84
  on the individual, 48–49
  kinetic materialism and, 6–7, 14, 41
  kinetic theory of object and, 33
  qualities and, 68
  on time and motion, 92–93
Derrida, Jacques, 10, 221n3
Descartes, René, 39, 40
desire
  body of commodity and, 71–72
  colonialism and, 195
  commodity and, 65–67
  communist form of motion and,
    201–2, 203
  consumption and, 65–67
  devalorization and, 85
  multiplicity of qualities and, 68–69
  production and, 65–67
  qualities and, 68–69

devalorization, 77–99
    abstraction and, 85–89
    appearance and, 86, 87, 89
    appropriation and, 77, 78, 82,
        93, 95, 96
    capitalism and, 77, 78, 79, 94,
        196, 217
    concrete vs. abstract labor and, 86–87
    consumption and, 78, 89, 94
    defined, 75
    desire and, 85
    exchange-value and, 77, 80–81
    form of appearance of value,
        79–84, 81f
    horror of value and, 87–89
    identity and, 82–84
    of labor, 85, 86–87
    metabolic conditions and, 208
    political economy and, 84
    primitive accumulation and, 77, 78,
        79, 84–85, 89
    production and, 78–79, 83, 84–85,
        86–87, 90
    in *Robinson Crusoe*, 182–83, 189–90,
        191, 195–96
    slavery and, 79, 85, 89, 95, 96
    socially necessary primitive
        accumulation, 93–98
    time and motion, 90–93, 91f
    use-values and, 77, 83, 85, 89
    value and, 84–87, 217
dialectical materialism, 21–27, 54–56
domestic labor. *See also* women's labor,
        appropriation of
    colonialism and, 189–90
    metabolism and, 109
    motion theory and, 36, 37
    patriarchy of value and, 117, 118,
        122, 126
domination
    anthropocentrism and, 4–5
    colonialism and, 178, 179–80, 182–83,
        189–90, 191, 192, 194, 195, 196–97
    communist form of motion
        and, 201–2
    feudal form of motion and, 198–99
    form of motion and, 161, 162, 175
    metabolic conditions and, 205, 207,
        208, 209, 212
    optics of, 170–72

    religion and, 172
    in *Robinson Crusoe*, 182–83, 189–90, 191
    social domination, 177, 179–80, 196
    value and, 164, 165, 170, 177, 217

Economic and Philosophical Manuscripts
        (1844), 8, 29–38
Elson, Diane, 228n2
Engels, Friedrich
    Anti-Duhring, 7, 11–12
    Dialectics of Nature, 7–8, 11–12
    on Hegel, 224n38
    materialism and, 6
    theory of motion and, 11–12
Epicurus
    abstraction in, 225–26n14
    commodity and, 68, 71
    conceptual framework for Marx's
        writings on, 216–17
    Democritean vs. Epicurean physics,
        15–16, 20–30
    devalorization and, 87–88
    on form as kinetic folded by motion,
        150–51, 162–63, 166
    form of appearance of value
        and, 83–84
    on freedom of the will, 225n5
    historic materialism and, 13–14
    individualism and, 48–49
    kinetic materialism and, 6–7, 30, 31
    kinetic theory of object and, 33
    materialism and, 17, 47
    materialist philosophy of motion
        and, 203
    on metabolism, 104–5
    motion of matter and, 21–27
    qualities and, 68, 69
    religion critique of, 203–4
    on theory of law, 163–64
    on time and motion, 92–93
    on turbulence, 174
    value and, 59
equality, 81, 143–44, 145–46, 153,
        167–68, 180–81
erscheinen (appearance), 47–48
Establet, Roger, 9–10
exchange-value
    bearers of, 17, 72
    in *Capital* (1867), 53
    devalorization and, 77, 80–81

devalorization and, 87–88
on form as kinetic folded by motion,
    150–51, 162–63
form of appearance of value
    and, 83–84
kinetic materialism and, 13, 17, 30
materialism and, 21, 47
on metabolism, 104–5
motion of matter in, 21–27
on time and motion, 92
on turbulence, 174
value and, 59
Lukács, György, 8
Lyotard, Francois, 10

Macherey, Pierre, 9–10
magnitude of value, 80, 92–93, 139,
    140, 175–76
Marcuse, Herbert, 8, 223n25
Marx, Karl
    anthropocentrism criticism of, 4–5
    decline of Marxism, 2–5
    historical determinism criticism
        of, 2–3
    reductionism criticism of, 3–4
material dialectics, 21–27, 54–56
materialism
    English, 39
    French, 39–40
    German, 40
    historical, 13–14, 54–56
    The Holy Family (1845), 39–40
    kinetic (see kinetic materialism)
    new materialism (see new
        materialism)
    reductionism and, 4
    transcendental, 56–58
Merleau-Ponty, Maurice, 8
metabolism, 100–15
    human metabolism with
        nature, 104–5
    kinetic theory of value and, 132, 133
    metabolic appropriation, 109–11, 116,
        140, 143, 208
    metabolic communism, 114–15
    metabolic drift, 112–14
    metabolic expansion by
        expulsion, 106–12
    metabolic movements, 101–3

metabolic primitive accumulation,
    100–1, 106–8, 109–12, 113
of nature, 104
power and, 113, 114, 115, 209
production and, 103, 104, 105–7,
    109–12, 113–15
social metabolism, 103, 105–6, 115,
    174–75, 205, 206
terminology of, 16–17
threefold theory of, 103–6
methodology, 15–18
    argumentation, 17
    close reading, 15–16
    historical, 18
    translation, 16–17
militarism, 3
motion, theory of, 10–13, 19–45
    Capital (1867) on, 46–58
    dialectics, 21–27
    doctoral dissertation of Marx
        and, 12–13
    Economic and Philosophical Manuscripts
        (1844), 29–38
    Engels and, 11–12
    fetishism of commodity and, 161–77
    The German Ideology (1845), 40–43
    The Holy Family (1845), 39–40
    kinetic theory of the human, 30–33
    kinetic theory of the object, 33–34
    movement of private property, 34–38
    On the Difference Between
        Democritean and Epicurean Physics
        (1841), 22–29
    The Poverty of Philosophy (1847), 43–44
    Soviet Marxism and, 12
    Theses on Feuerbach (1845), 40–43
Murray, Patrick, 228–29n3
mysticism, 42–43, 169

Narcissus, 151
naturalism, 32, 108, 180, 202–3
negation, 7, 23–24, 44, 55
new materialism, 6–7, 10–11, 15, 29, 39,
    217, 222n16
Newton, Isaac, 6–7, 39
Nietzsche, Friedrich, 13, 58, 224n40
nomos, 144–45
nonvalue, 79, 85, 87, 94, 95–96, 111,
    143, 145–46

objectification, 32, 33, 34, 35–36, 111, 202–3
objective aspect, 61–62, 64
objective essential power, 33–34, 61, 110
oikos, 143–46
On the Difference Between Democritean and Epicurean Physics (1841), 22–29

patriarchy of value, 116–28
  appropriation and, 116, 120–21, 126
  communism and, 200
  domestic labor and, 117, 118, 122, 126
  historical determinism and, 3
  home-baked value, 116–17
  kinetic materialism and, 116
  power and, 121–22
  primitive accumulation and, 120–21, 123
  religion and, 121–22
  in Shakespeare's *Henry IV*, 117–28
  use-values and, 117, 122, 124, 126, 127
pedesis
  communist form of motion and, 203, 213
  kinetic dialectics and, 13, 24, 55–56, 162–63, 217
  kinetic folding and, 64
  materialism and, 6–7
  motion theory and, 24, 27–28, 36
  movement of declination as, 24
  pedetic flows, 55
  private property and, 36
  simplex value and, 131
  transcendental materialism and, 56
  value and, 131
Plato, 29
Plutarch, 22
political economy
  atomism and, 49, 51, 174
  colonialism and, 179, 180–82, 184
  devalorization and, 84
  emergence of, 53
  gravity of value and, 176
  kinetic theory of, 43
  kinetic theory of value and, 130–31, 135, 136
  private property and, 34–35
  in *Robinson Crusoe*, 180–82, 184
  transcendental materialism and, 56

post-structuralist Marxism, 9–10, 218–19
The Poverty of Philosophy (1847), 43–44
power. *See also* domination
  anthropocentric nature of, 29
  capitalism's source of, 20
  colonialism and, 178, 179, 185–86, 189, 194–95
  domination and, 172
  form of motion and, 168–69, 177
  metabolism and, 113, 114, 115, 209
  oikos and, 143
  optics of value and, 169–70
  patriarchy and, 121–22
  primitive accumulation and, 179
  production and, 66, 143
  religion and, 203, 204
  value creation and, 109, 110, 152
primitive accumulation
  bearers of value and, 73
  border appropriation, 111–12
  in *Capital* (1867), 53–54
  capitalism and, 228n1
  colonialism and, 178, 179–80, 186–95, 236n1
  degree of skill, 97
  devalorization and, 77, 78, 79, 84–85, 89
  earth appropriation, 111
  extent and effectiveness, 98
  gravity of value and, 176
  horror of value and, 89
  kinetic communism and, 209–10
  kinetic theory of value and, 129–30, 135, 143, 144, 145
  labor appropriation, 111
  metabolic, 100–1, 106–8, 109–12, 113
  oikos and, 143, 145
  patriarchy of value and, 120–21, 123
  post-structuralist Marxism and, 9
  process of, 96–98
  relation to nature, 98
  science and technology, 97
  socially necessary, 93–98
  social organization, 97
  value and, 37–38, 74, 75–76, 216
private property, 27, 34–38, 167–68, 193
production
  of commodity, 65–67, 69–70, 71–72
  desire and, 65–67

devalorization and, 78–79, 83, 84–85,
86–87, 90
form of appearance of value and, 80,
81*f*, 81–82
horror of value and, 88–89
kinetic theory of value and, 156,
157–58, 160
magnetic field of value and, 156
metabolism and, 103, 104, 105–7,
109–12, 113–15
motion theory and, 37–38
performance of value and, 157–58
primitive accumulation and,
93–98, 110–12
Proudhon, Pierre-Joseph, 43, 44, 179–80
Pythagoras, 92

qualities of commodity, 68–70
quantum field theory, 4, 222n12

racism
colonialism and, 177, 178, 184, 187,
189, 193, 195–96
communist form of motion and,
200, 203, 205
devalorization via, 85, 195–96
as pattern of motion, 177
political economy and, 182
primitive accumulation and, 97
in *Robinson Crusoe*, 187, 189, 193, 196
social structure and, 211
Rancière, Jacques, 9–10
reductionism
Marxism and, 3–4
materialism and, 4
religion
accumulation and, 204
colonialism and, 192–93, 195–96
Epicurean critique of, 203–4
feudal form of motion and, 199
fog of, 172–73
form of appearance of value and, 84
horror of value and, 87–88
kinetic communism and, 203–4, 211
kinetic theory of value and, 130–31,
158, 159
Marx's critique of, 20–21,
87–88, 172–73
optics of value and, 169
patriarchy of value and, 121–22

private property and, 38
social structure and, 211
Ricardo, David, 179–81
Robinson Crusoe (Defoe), 180–97
conditions of appearance in, 183–86
consumption in, 190–91, 192–93, 195
general form of colonialism in, 193–95
human appearance in,
183–84, 185–86
natural appearance in, 183, 185
onefold or simplex form of colonialism
in, 188–91
political economy in, 180–82
primitive accumulation in,
179–80, 186–95
production in, 189–90, 192, 194
relation in, 189, 192, 193–94
social appearance in, 184, 186
space in, 190, 192, 194–95
time in, 191, 193, 195
transparency in, 185–86
unfolded or expanded form of
colonialism in, 191–93
Romero, George, 89

Sanctorius, 101–2
Sappho: *Hymn to Aphrodite*, 127
Sartre, Jean-Paul, 1, 8
Schmitt, Alfred, 106
The Concept of Nature in Marx, 13
Schreiner, Jason, 231n13
self-consciousness, 25, 40
sensuous material production, 66, 80,
81–82, 88–89, 93, 132
sensuous objects
appearance and, 47, 50
colonialism and, 187
commodity and, 64–65, 71
desire and, 65, 66, 69
form of appearance of value
and, 82–83
identity and, 82–83
kinetic theory of the object
and, 33–34
motion theory and, 41–43
optics of domination and, 170–71
value and, 62, 63, 64, 74
sexism, 97, 177, 182, 195–96. *See also*
patriarchy of value
Simondon, Gilbert, 232–33n1

wechsel (to continuously change or
fold), 16–17
White, James, 225n8
women's labor, appropriation of, 53, 116,
118, 119, 123, 124, 196, 217. *See also*
patriarchy of value

zusammenhängen (to hang together)
appearance and, 47–48, 48*f*

body of the commodity and, 72
conditioning and, 212
form of motion and, 175
kinetic materialism and, 25–27, 41
metabolism and, 100, 102–3
private property and, 36–37
social forms of motion and, 205, 206
translation of, 16–17
value and, 76

CPSIA information can be obtained
at www.ICGtesting.com
Printed in the USA
BVHW072358040122
624993BV00003B/15